Lecture Notes in Computer Science 4311

Commenced Publication in 1973
Founding and Former Series Editors:
Gerhard Goos, Juris Hartmanis, and Jan van Leeuwe

Kenjiro Cho   Philippe Jacquet (Eds.)

Technologies
for Advanced
Heterogeneous Networks II

Second Asian Internet Engineering Conference, AINTEC 2006
Pathumthani, Thailand, November 28-30, 2006
Proceedings

 Springer

Volume Editors

Kenjiro Cho
Internet Initiative Japan, Inc.
1-105 Kanda Jinbo-cho, Chiyoda-ku, Tokyo 1010051, Japan
E-mail: kjc@iijlab.net

Philippe Jacquet
Institut National de Recherche en Informatique et Automatique
Campus of Rocquencourt, Domaine de Voluceau, BP105, 78153 Le Chesnay, France
E-mail: Philippe.Jacquet@inria.fr

Library of Congress Control Number: 2006936488

CR Subject Classification (1998): C.2.4, C.2, C.3, F.1, F.2.2, K.6

LNCS Sublibrary: SL 5 – Computer Communication Networks and
Telecommunications

ISSN   0302-9743
ISBN-10   3-540-49364-6 Springer Berlin Heidelberg New York
ISBN-13   978-3-540-49364-8 Springer Berlin Heidelberg New York

Springer is a part of Springer Science+Business Media

springer.com

© Springer-Verlag Berlin Heidelberg 2006

Typesetting: Camera-ready by author, data conversion by Scientific Publishing Services, Chennai, India
Printed on acid-free paper   SPIN: 11930181   06/3142   5 4 3 2 1 0

Preface

The Asian Internet Engineering Conference (AINTEC) brings together researchers and engineers interested in practical and theoretical problems in the Internet technologies. The conference aims at addressing issues pertinent to the Asian region with vast diversities of socio-economic and networking conditions while inviting high-quality and recent research results from the global international research community.

After the success of the first AINTEC in 2005, the Organization Committee members agreed to continue AINTEC as annual events, and keep most of the committee members for the second year to foster the community. This year's conference was also jointly organized by the Internet Educational and Research Laboratory of the Asian Institute of Technology (AIT) and the WIDE Project with support from the APAN-TH community.

AINTEC 2006 solicited papers, among other things, on the survival of the Internet in order to provide alternative means of communication in emergency and chaotic situations in response to the recent natural disaster in Asia.

The main topics include: Mobile IP
Mobile Ad Hoc and Emergency Networks
Multimedia or Multi-Services IP-Based Networks
Peer-to-Peer
Measurement and Performance Analysis
Internet over Satellite Communications

These are the same topics as in AINTEC 2005, again to foster the community with focused research agendas. There were 36 submissions to the Technical Program, and we selected the 12 papers presented in these proceedings. In addition, we have five invited papers by leading experts in the field.

Finally, we would like to acknowledge the conference General Chair, Kanchana Kanchanasut of AIT, and the Local Organizers team from AIT, namely, Mohammad Abdul Awal, Withmone Tin Latt and Yasuo Tsuchimoto, for organizing and arranging this conference. We are also grateful to the French Ministry of Foreign Affairs through its French Regional Cooperation and the ICT Asia project (STIC-ASIA) for providing travel support.

November 2006
Kenjiro Cho
Philippe Jacquet
AINTEC 2006 Program Committee Co-chairs

Organization

General Chair

Kanchana Kanchanasut (Asian Institute of Technology, Thailand)

Program Committee Co-chairs

Kenjiro Cho, WIDE Project, Japan
Philippe Jacquet, INRIA, France

Program Committee

Alain Jean-Marie (LIRMM/INRIA, France)
Alexandru Petrescu (Motorola)
Anan Phonphoem (Kasetsart University, Thailand)
Antti Tuominen (Helsinki University of Technology, Finland)
Chalermek Intanagowiwat (Chulalongkorn University, Thailand)
Hyunchul Kim (CAIDA, USA)
Jun Takei (Intel KK, Japan)
Jochen Schiller (Freie Universität, Germany)
Kazunori Sugiura (Keio University, Japan)
Kenjiro Cho (IIJ, Japan)
Noel Crespi (INT, France)
Patcharee Basu (SOI/ASIA, Japan)
Poompat Saengudomlert (Asian Institute of Technology, Thailand)
Ryuji Wakikawa (Keio University, Japan)
Randy Bush (IIJ, USA)
Shigeya Suzuki (USC/ISI, USA)
Tapio Erke (Asian Institute of Technology, Thailand)
T.C. Wan (USM, Malaysia)
Teerapat Sa-nguankotchakorn (Asian Institute of Technology, Thailand)
Thierry Ernst (INRIA, France)
Thomas Clausen (Polytechnique, France)
Thomas Noel (University Louis Pasteur, France)
T.J. Kniveton (NOKIA Research Center, USA)
Yasuo Tsuchimoto (intERLab, AIT, Thailand)
Yoshifumi Nishida (Sony CSL, Japan)
Youki Kadobayashi (NAIST, Japan)
Youngseok Lee (CNU, Korea)

Local Organization

Mohammad Abdul Awal (Asian Institute of Technology, Thailand)
Withmone Tin Latt (Asian Institute of Technology, Thailand)
Yasuo Tsuchimoto (Asian Institute of Technology, Thailand)

Table of Contents

Invited Paper 4

Invited Papers

An End-User-Responsive Sensor Network Architecture for Hazardous Weather Detection, Prediction and Response

Jim Kurose[1,2], Eric Lyons[1], David McLaughlin[1,3], David Pepyne[1], Brenda Philips[1], David Westbrook[1], and Michael Zink[1,2]

[1] Center for Collaborative Adaptive Sensing of the Atmosphere
[2] Department of Computer Science
[3] Department of Electrical and Computer Engineering
University of Massachusetts
Amherst MA 10003 USA
{kurose@cs.umass.edu, elyons19@hotmail.com,
mclaughlin@ecs.umass.edu, pepyne@ecs.umass.edu,
bphilips@ecs.umass.edu, westy@cs.umass.edu, zink@cs.umass.edu}

Abstract. We present an architecture for a class of systems that perform distributed, collaborative, adaptive sensing (DCAS) of the atmosphere. Since the goal of these DCAS systems is to sense the atmosphere when and where the user needs are greatest, end-users naturally play the central role in determining how system resources (sensor targeting, computation, communication) are deployed. We describe the meteorological command and control components that lie at the heart of our testbed DCAS system, and provide timing measurements of component execution times. We then present a utility-based framework that determines how multiple end-user preferences are combined with policy considerations into utility functions that are used to allocate system resources in a manner that dynamically optimizes overall system performance. We also discuss open challenges in the networking and control of such end-user-driven systems.

Keywords: Sensor networks, collaborative adaptive atmospheric sensing, end-user utility.

1 Introduction

Over the past twenty years, the use of networked computing systems has evolved from being primarily general/multi-purpose in nature to often being highly specialized and highly mission-specific. Perhaps nowhere is this trend clearer than in the case of sensor networks [DDAS 2006, Chong 2003, Estrin 2002] – a combined sensing, communication, and computing infrastructure designed to measure, monitor, predict, and (in some cases) control a particular environment or process. Such mission-specific computing naturally implies an increased emphasis on the end-user – the *raison d'etre* for the system in the first place – and on tailoring and optimizing system operation to meet end-user-defined, application-specific goals. Although it is thus

K. Cho and P. Jacquet (Eds.): AINTEC 2006, LNCS 4311, pp. 1–15, 2006.

important to engineer sensor network systems to meet these specific end-user needs and application scenarios, it is also important to avoid a highly-specialized "stovepipe" design that is difficult to evolve for use in new (or changed) application scenarios or end-user/application requirements.

In this paper, we describe the software architecture for a sensor network system consisting of a relatively small number (tens) of low-power X-band radars that detect and predict hazardous weather via distributed, collaborative, adaptive sensing (DCAS) of the lowest few kilometers of the earth's atmosphere. The architecture finds use in a variety of application scenarios including hazardous wind (e.g., tornado) and precipitation sensing, in both resource-rich and resource-challenged environments. *Distributed* refers to the use of a number of small radars, spaced close enough to "see" close to the ground in spite of the Earth's curvature and avoid resolution degradation caused by radar beam spreading. *Collaborative* operation refers to the coordination (when advantageous) of the beams from multiple radars to view the same region in the atmosphere, thus achieving greater sensitivity, precision, and resolution than possible with a single radar. *Adaptive* refers to the ability of these radars and their associated computing and communications infrastructure to dynamically reconfigure in response to changing weather conditions and end-user needs. As part of our activities in the NSF Engineering Research Center for Collaborative Adaptive Sensing of the Atmosphere (CASA) [McLaughlin 2005, CASA 2006a], we have instantiated the DCAS paradigm in an operational testbed for hazardous wind sensing in southwestern Oklahoma, and have several additional DCAS systems under development [Donovan 2005b].

The goal of these DCAS systems is to sense the atmosphere *when and where the user needs are greatest*. Thus, user requirements naturally play *the* central role in determining how system resources (sensor targeting, computation, communication) are deployed at any given point in time. Our DCAS systems adopt a utility-based framework in which multiple end-user preferences are combined with policy considerations into utility functions that are used to allocate system resources in a manner that dynamically optimizes overall system performance. In this paper, we described the software architecture of our DCAS systems, focusing on the driving role of end-user considerations in system design and operation. We also discuss open challenges in the networking and control of such end-user-driven systems.

The remainder of this paper is structured as follows. In section 2, we overview the DCAS software architecture, highlighting the crucial role played by the end users. In section 3, we discuss how end-user preferences and policy considerations are mapped to the utility functions that then determine how system resources are allocated. We discuss our experiences with initial end-user evaluations, and how these experiences have led to changes in our utility functions. In section 4 we discuss several open challenges in the networking area, focusing on those that arise from end-user considerations. Section 5 concludes this paper.

2 Overview of DCAS Software Architecture

Figure 1 shows the overall software architecture of the meteorological command and control (MC&C) components that lie at the heart (or perhaps more appropriately, the

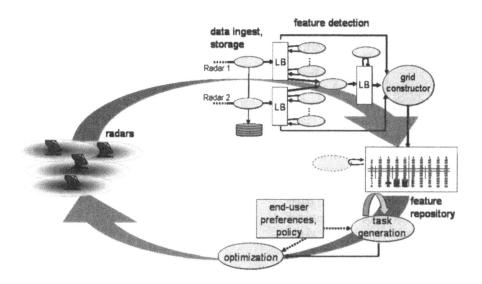

Fig. 1. Software architecture for meteorological command and control (MC&C)

"brains") of our DCAS system. The operational version of the MC&C is currently centralized, but we are currently implementing a distributed version of the MC&C as well. The main system control loop divides into loosely-coupled upper and lower halves. In the upper loop, data is ingested from the remote radars, meteorological features are identified in the data, and higher-level meteorological features (e.g., wind rotation, wind shear and rotational divergence, areas of high precipitation) are posted on a feature repository, from which they (and the underlying radar data) are made available to end users. The shaded ovals in the feature-detection portion of the MC&C are the individual detection algorithms that detect specific features in the data. These modules are connected together by an event-based broadcast publication/subscribe mechanism known as a linear buffer [Hondl 2003] that notifies downstream modules when data or events are available for processing. The feature repository is a blackboard-like module [Jaganathan 1989] that allows data to be asynchronously written (posted) and read. The lower half of the control loop uses the posted features and end-user preferences and policy to identify areas of meteorological interest in the radars' footprints (task generation) and then optimizes the configuration of each radar (i.e., the location and width of the sector within its footprint to be scanned), as discussed in detail in Section 3.

The system operates on a 30-second "heartbeat," with the upper control loop in Figure 1 (data ingest and feature detection) proceeding *asynchronously* from the lower control loop (generation of radar commands for the next 30-second heartbeat). During each heartbeat, data is ingested and processed in streaming mode. Δ seconds before the end of each heartbeat (a value of Δ equal to approximately 4 seconds is currently used in our testbed), command generation components begin their computation to determine how to best target the radars for the next 30-second heartbeat based on data currently posted in the feature repository. This temporal decoupling of the upper and lower halves of the control loop avoids stalling the lower half of the control loop in the presence of late-arriving data (e.g., due to unanticipated network and processing delays elsewhere in the system). Thus, while late-arriving data may affect the quality of the computed control (since the targeting decision is based on older data), it will not delay the generation of radar targeting commands. A heartbeat of 30 seconds was chosen given the coverage of each radar (a radius of approximately 30km), the timescale at which meteorological features evolve, and the operating characteristics

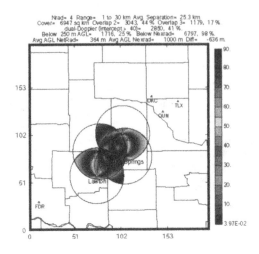

Fig. 2. Radar siting in southwestern OK, showing dual-Doppler regions

of the mechanically-scanned radars currently in our testbed. The value of Δ will clearly play an important role in how well the radar network is able to sense the environment. The smaller the value of Δ, the more recent the data that will be used to re-target the radars. We report on the measured runtimes of various system components below that indicate that a value of Δ of approximately 4 seconds is appropriate in our operational system.

We have completed an initial four-radar testbed that covers a 7,000 square km region in southwestern Oklahoma, a region that receives an average of four tornado warnings and 53 thunderstorm warnings per year. Figure 2 shows the radar locations, including their dual Doppler (overlap) regions. Data is streamed from each of the four radars at up to 1 Mbps, over a pre-provisioned network with adequate capacity to handle this peak rate, to a central site where the MC&C operates. (Thus, in this resource-rich initial testbed, network concerns such as routing and congestion control are not of significant concern; we discuss networking challenges in resource-poor DCAS system in Section 4). The MC&C itself executes on a 3-node (3.2 GHz Intel CPU, 1 GB RAM) cluster with 4 TB of storage; the cluster can be easily scaled by adding additional processors if additional computing or storage resources are needed. The end-users of this testbed are the National Weather Service (NWS) Forecast Office in Norman, OK, a group of emergency managers who have jurisdictional authority within and upstream of the testbed area, several private sector entities, and CASA's science researchers themselves.

Given the soft-real-time nature of this system, it is crucial that the execution times of the various software components shown in Figure 1 fit well into the fundamental 30-second heartbeat. Figure 3 shows the execution times of selected MC&C components: per-elevation execution times for data ingest, a peak echo detection algorithm, and task generation and optimization. These execution times were measured in our 4-node testbed during a period of time when several storm cells were moving through the testbed's coverage area. The data ingest algorithm receives data in an elevation scan from a radar (there may be several sequential elevation scans within one 30-second heartbeat), performs simple cleanup (thresholding) of the data, sequentially stores the reflectivity, wind-velocity and other data in separate files in a common format, and notifies the downstream detection modules of the availability of data via the broadcast pub/sub mechanism. The peak echo algorithm identifies the region of peak reflectivity within a radar's footprint. Since the data ingest algorithm operates in a streaming manner, and since peak echo detection, task generation, and optimization components all execute in subsecond times, these execution times are relatively small with respect to the 30-second heartbeat interval. Execution times from other MC&C components (using emulated radar input data) have been report in [Zink 2005].

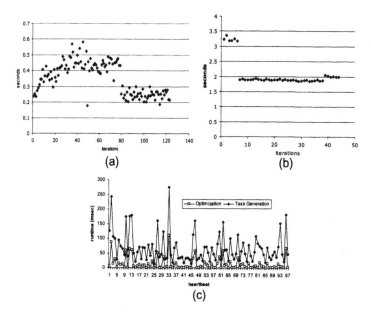

Fig. 3. Execution runtimes for (a) data ingest, (b) peak echo detection, and (c) task generation/optimization

3   Responsiveness to End User Requirements

Our discussion above has focussed on the overall DCAS software system architecture and software component runtimes within the 30-second heartbeat. We now turn our attention to *the* central aspect of DCAS control – determining *where* and *how* the radars should target their scans during a 30-second interval. This is the role of the task generation and optimization components of the MC&C and it is here that end-user considerations are of central concern.

3.1   The MC&C Equation

In order to simplify our discussion below, we consider the "simpler" problem of determining only *where* the radars should focus their scanning, ignoring additional considerations such as the most appropriate radar waveform to be employed, the pulse repetition frequency (PRF), and more. This simple setting will nonetheless allow us to illustrate the key end-user-related aspects of the MC&C.

We define a *radar configuration* to be the set of sectors to be scanned by the radars during a 30-second interval. The MC&C takes a *utility-based approach* towards determining the optimal radar configuration for a particular interval, where (as we will see) utility is directly defined in terms of end-user requirements. Two sets of factors contribute to the utility of a particular radar configuration. The first set of factors is concerned with *how well* a particular portion of the atmosphere is sensed by a given radar configuration. The second set of factors is concerned with *how important* the scanned sectors are to the end users. The overall utility of a particular configuration combines these two considerations of "how well" and "how important."

Before specifying how utility is computed, let us first qualitatively discuss the factors that will come into consideration. The first set of factors is related to the quality of the data from the scanned sectors ("how well"):

- **Scan sector size.** Each radar can be tasked to scan a sector with an arbitrary starting point and at any width from 60 degrees to 360 degrees during the 30-second heartbeat. Scanning a smaller sector allows more sensing energy to be focussed into that sector, either by dwelling on each radial position for a longer period of time (than in the case of a wider scan) and hence obtaining more accurate estimates of sensed values [Donovan 2005a], or by scanning a larger number of elevations. The increased "quality" of sensed data within a narrowly-scanned sector must then be weighed against obtaining no data from those portions of the radar's coverage that were not scanned during the heartbeat.
- **Coordination among radars.** It is often advantageous to have two or more radars focus their scans on overlapping regions in the atmosphere, a so-called dual-Doppler region. One radar may be able to "see" that portion of the atmosphere better (e.g., due to less signal attenuation), and data from multiple radars allows for more accurate estimation of wind velocity vectors. Another benefit of radar coordination arises even when each meteorological feature is scanned by a single radar – when a particularly high utility feature can be scanned by more than one radar, the system can scan that feature with the radar that allows remaining radars to scan other meteorological features of next highest utility.

The second set of factors is concerned with *how important* the scanned portions of the atmosphere are to the end-users:

- **Expressing the preferences of multiple end users.** The initial end users in our Oklahoma testbed are *(i)* the National Weather Service (NWS) forecasters, both in the Norman, Oklahoma Forecast Office and in the NWS Warning Decision Training Branch which trains forecasters nationally, *(ii)* a group of emergency managers who have jurisdictional authority within and upstream of the test bed area, and *(iii)* CASA's science researchers themselves. Different end users will derive different utility from a particular radar configuration. For example, an NWS forecast office may use 360 degree sweeps of DCAS radar data close to the ground to monitor the evolution of a storm to determine whether to issue a tornado warning, while at the same time an emergency manager may require two collaborating radars to locate precisely the most intense part of a storm for public notification or for deploying weather spotters. A researcher initializing a numerical prediction model needs 360 degree scans at all elevations. Each of the end user groups must be able to express their relative preferences among different radar configurations, and these preferences must then be incorporated into system operation.

- **Policy: mediating among the conflicting scanning requests of different end users.** The differing information requirements of different end users means that it may not be possible to satisfy the needs of all end users at the same time. If a given radar configuration is of particularly high utility to one group of users but of lower utility to another group of users, while a second configuration is of low utility to the first group of users but of high utility to the second group of users, the system must decide which of these two alternatives is preferable. That is, a *policy* mechanism must be defined for mediating among the conflicting scanning demands of different end-users.

The above considerations give rise to the following optimization problem (which we refer to as the MC&C equation) that must be solved by the MC&C:

$$J = \max_{\substack{configurations, C}} \sum_{tasks, t} U(t, k) Q(t, C) \tag{1}$$

where:

- t is the set of so-called *tasks* – meteorological features that are within the radars' coverage areas and thus can potentially be scanned at time interval k. Examples of tasks include areas of wind rotation, areas of high reflectivity, and areas of wind shear. These tasks are created by the task-generation module shown in Figure 1, based on detected features posted in the feature repository. As we saw in Figure 3, the set of tasks in our testbed can be generated in less than a second by the task-generation module.

- $U(t,k)$ is the *aggregate end-user utility* of task t to the set of end users, and captures the "how important" aspect of utility. $U(t,k)$ in turn is defined as:

$$U(t, k) = \sum_{groups, g} w_g U_g(t, k)$$

where g is the set of user groups, $U_g(t,k)$ is the utility of task t at time interval k to user group g, and w_g is the weight associated with user group g. In section 3.2 below, we discuss how $U_g(t,k)$ is computed. w_g is a value between 0 and 1, reflecting the relative priority of user group g with respect to other user groups. The values of w_g are set by policy. Note that the architecture itself is policy-neutral in that it does not prescribe values for w_g but instead provides a *mechanism* for weighting the relative importance of different user groups.

- $Q(t,C)$ is the *quality* of the scanning of task t under radar configuration C, capturing the "how well" aspect of utility. $Q(t,C)$ is a value between 0 and 1, with a value of 1 representing the highest quality possible. The details of the computation of $Q(t,C)$ can be found in [Pepyne 2006]. We note here that for a particular task, t, the value of $Q(t,C)$ *(i)* increases as the physical location (center) of the task becomes closer to a radar *(ii)* increases as increasingly more of the physical extent of the task is covered by a radar in configuration C, and *(iii)* increases as function of the number of radars whose scans cover the task.

Several comments are in order regarding the MC&C equation. First, note that the form of the MC&C equation involves a sum over all tasks, where the utility of each task has a quality component, $Q(t,C)$ (reflecting "how well" the task is sensed by the radars in a particular configuration) and an end-user utility component, $U(t,k)$ (reflecting how important that task is to the end users). The overall utility of a given task is the product of these two components. Rather than taking the product of these two components, an alternate approach would be to allow end-user utility itself to depend on the quality component, i.e., to define task utility under configuration C in the form $U(t,k,Q(t,C))$, rather than $U(t,k)Q(t,C)$ as in Equation 1. This alternative formulation would have resulted in a significantly more complex optimization problem, since end-user utility would be a function of the scan quality of the configuration. Our separation of "how well" and "how important" into two independent considerations represents an architectural decision to separate lower-level, radar-specific, sensing considerations from higher-level end-user considerations. This also illustrates one way in which we have avoided building a stovepipe system. If a new set of radars, with new operating characteristics were to be used, we need only change $Q(t,C)$. On the other hand, with a task utility of the form $U(t,k,Q(t,C))$, we would have to redefine end-user utility as well – a difficult and time-consuming task that requires numerous interactions with the end users, as we will see in Section 3.2. We emphasize, however, that both task quality *and* task importance are taken into account in the end-user utility calculation (through their product).

Second, we note that while it appears that the optimization is considering each 30-second heartbeat as an independent optimization problem, this is actually not the case. As we will see in section 3.2, users have specified not only *what* tasks they want scanned, but also how *often* different types of tasks need to be scanned. As we will see, a typical end-user rule has the form: *"If a meteorological phenomena of type X is detected, then scan it with Y radars (when possible) at least once every Z heartbeats."* To implement this capability we keep track of the *time-since-last-scanned* for each task. If the *time-since-last-scanned* is less than the user-defined interval between scans (Z heartbeats in the previous sentence), then the task has a base utility value. If the *time-since-last-scanned* is greater than the user-defined interval, we scale (increase) the utility value $U_g(t,k)$ of task t at each heartbeat until the task is eventually scanned. At this point, the task's utility value is set to its base value, and the scaling process begins again. With this simple scheme, we implicitly solve what is otherwise a complex multistage optimization problem. [Manfredi 2006] examines a non-myopic multistage optimization formulation of the MC&C optimization problem.

3.2 End-User Utility

Given the importance of end-users in our DCAS systems, a crucial challenge is to define the end-user utility functions, $U_g(t,k)$, in a manner that is consistent with the preferences and the decision making process of each user group *g*. In order to do so, we conducted in-depth interviews, discussions, and table-top experiments (using simulated DCAS data) with our end-user groups. Eliciting and understanding user preferences, and then defining user utility functions is an iterative process. We illustrate this below by discussing not only the current set of rules that define how utility is computed, but also an earlier set of rules that were ultimately judged inadequate by our end users.

We elicited preferences for DCAS data from three groups of users: NWS forecasters, emergency managers in Oklahoma, and CASA researchers. We were faced with the challenge of asking users for their preferences for data from a system that has only recently become operational, and that presents a very new way of visualizing radar data with sector scanning, rapid data updates, and high resolution. Because of this challenge, our focus has been on obtaining qualitative information from a smaller group of experts who provided input based on their use of current radar data and their best determination of how DCAS data would provide additional benefits.

Let us consider a specific user group, NWS forecasters (including the forecast Office in Norman, Oklahoma and the NWS Warning Decision Training Branch which trains NWS forecasters across the US), to demonstrate how preferences were elicited and how these preferences impacted the evolution of our system design. As background, a primary task of NWS forecasters is to issue severe weather warnings for thunderstorms, tornados, and high winds for counties under their jurisdictional authority with the goal of saving lives and property. Among other tasks, NWS forecasters interact with emergency managers leading up to and during a severe weather event to communicate their weather expertise. In order to make a warning decision, forecasters create a conceptual model of developing weather events based on multiple sources of information: WSR-88D radar data [NOAA 2006], ground truth reports from storm spotters and the media, potential location/impact of the weather, on-going mesoscale (regional) analysis of weather, staffing and intuition. By looking for specific signatures and trends in base wind velocity and reflectivity data, forecasters use radar data to increase or reduce their confidence in an existing or potential warning decision. They analyze radar data by creating a "mental movie" of an evolving event using the closest radar to the phenomena of interest.

End User Policy, V0 and V1. The initial set of rules we developed to define user-based utility, End User Policy V0, focused on the relative importance of specific detected weather features, such as tornados, mesocyclones, storm cells, and hail cores. Each user group, such as NWS forecasters, was asked to rank the relative importance of these weather features. Each weather feature was then assigned a utility ("how important") value $U_g(t,k)$ that depended only on the type of task being scanned (but not on the *time-since-last-scanned*). We then conducted a table-top experiment, a case study using a numerical storm simulation sampled at 3-kilometer spatial resolution, and showed it to the NWS-FO Norman to obtain feedback on End User Policy V0. We learned that the NWS warning decision process focused more on analyzing areas of uncertainty at regular intervals than on evaluating specific weather features, such as a mesocyclone. Based on this feedback, the following modifications were made to create End User Policy V1:

- **Incorporation of interval-based scanning.** User preferences for adaptive scanning are now expressed in terms of timed intervals (e.g., scan a severe storm at all elevations every 2.5 minutes) as well as the detection of weather features. At this stage, the NWS is more interested in scanning areas of interest at regular intervals, rather than in looking at specific weather features such as a mesocyclone.
- **Expansion of the definition of a storm cell.** The definition of a storm's extent by our weather-feature detection algorithms was judged to be too narrow for use by forecasters. In End User Policy V0, a storm cell was identified as an area of high reflectivity and therefore storm cell scans did not include the boundaries of the storm. We learned, however, that NWS forecasters are interested in looking at these boundaries (reflectivity gradients), in areas of lower reflectivity, to look for cues of how a storm may evolve or where new storms may develop. The storm-cell detection algorithm in End User Policy V1, now includes areas of low reflectivity.
- **Introducing contiguous scans.** Visualization and scanning strategies must address continuity of data so forecasters can create a "mental movie" of an evolving event. Version 0 produced sector scans that were too "jumpy" from one scan to the next and interrupted this mental movie.

A second table-top experiment was conducted, again using a numerical storm simulation to obtain feedback on Version 1 of the policy. This version was acceptable to the expert group NWS forecasters. The next crucial step will be to obtain user feedback on the rules when actual data is generated from the Oklahoma Test bed.

The End User Policy V1 rules are shown below in Table 1. There are rules for three user groups (NWS, researchers, and emergency response managers) and one default user group that requests that the lowest two elevation scans be performed at least once every 5 minutes. Of particular note in Table 1 are the columns labeled "Rule trigger" and "Sampling interval." Some tasks are instantiated (triggered) only

Table 1. End User Policy Rules, V1

Rules	Rule trigger	Sector Selection	Elevations	# radars	Contig.	Sampling interval
NWS						
N1	time	360	lowest	1	Yes	1 / min
N2	storm	task size	full volume	1	Yes	1 / 2.5 min
Researcher						
R1	rotation	task size	full volume	2+	Yes	1 / 30 sec
R2	reflectivity	task size	lowest two	1	Yes	1 / min
R2	velocity	task size	lowest two	2+	Yes	1/ min
R3	time	360	all 7 every 15 min	1	No	1/ 5 min
EMs						
E1	time	360	lowest	1	Yes	1 / min
E2	reflectivity over AOI	task size	lowest	1	Yes	1 / min
E3	velocity over AOI	task size	lowest	2+	Yes	1/ 2.5 min
OS						
O1	time	360	lowest two	1	No	1 / 5 min

when a particular feature (storm, rotation, reflectivity, velocity) is detected in the coverage area, while other tasks (360 degree surveillance scans at one or more elevations) are triggered periodically. The sampling interval indicates the *time-since-last-scanned* value discussed above.

3.3 Quantifying the Benefits of DCAS Versus Sit-and-Spin

Given the utility function in Equation 1, we can quantitatively evaluate the benefit of DCAS operation of radars, using overall system utility as our performance metric of interest. Our baseline for comparison is the traditional "sit-and-spin" (or surveillance) mode of operation in which each radar continuously performs 360 degree scans, independent of the meteorological features present in the coverage area.

Because we can not operate DCAS and sit-and-spin meteorological sensing networks side-by-side over the same weather scenario, we have used an emulation environment (referred to as an observing system simulation experiment, OSSE, in the radar meteorological community [Lord 1997]) to quantify the utility gain realized by a DCAS system. The OSSE system consists of a simulation of the evolution of weather within a volume of the atmosphere over time, coupled with a radar emulator that computes the data produced by a simulated radar pointing its beam along a particular radial in the simulated atmosphere at a particular point in time. In this OSSE experiment, the 130km by 130km domain covered by our Oklahoma testbed was emulated at a grid resolution of 100m. A movie showing emulated storms passing through this coverage area during the OSSE emulation can be found at [CASA 2006b].

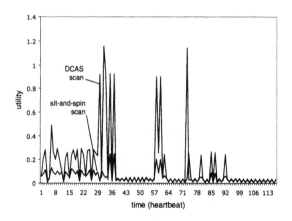

Fig. 4. Utility of DCAS scanning versus sit-and spin for an emulated OSSE experiment

Figure 4 shows the higher utility achieved under the optimal DCAS scan strategy versus the utility achieved under a sit-and-spin mode of operation for this OSSE scenario. While the initial results of Figure 4 are indeed encouraging, a fundamental question still remains – to what extent does the increased utility, as computed using the quantitative formulation in Section 3.2, result in an increased ability of the system's end users to better detect, predict, understand, and respond to severe whether events. The answer to this crucial question can only be answered once end users have the opportunity to view and use actual data from the test bed in their decision making. CASA is also planning to investigate alternate methods of eliciting and aggregating multiple user utilities, the value of DCAS data to users, and incorporation of socioeconomic variables into the End User Policy formulation using decision sciences methodologies.

4 Networking Challenges Ahead

In previous sections, we have focussed on the overall DCAS software architecture and the crucial role played by end users. In this section we identify a number of networking challenges in resource-constrained DCAS systems. In most cases, the challenges we identify again arise as a result of the central role of end user. We note that our discussion below is selective rather than exhaustive, reflecting our own views on promising areas for research.

To make our discussion concrete, we will consider an experimental "off the grid" DCAS testbed currently being developed for the western portion of Puerto Rico [Donovan 2005b]. The system consists of modified low-power 24-inch, 4kW marine magnetron radars (with a power consumption of 34W) connected via an 802.11 mesh network with (non-steerable) directional antennas. The system is resource-constrained in that *(i)* all energy consumed must be harvested via solar panels and stored in batteries [Kansal 2004], *(ii)* communication link bandwidth may vary with changing meteorological conditions.

In such a system, scarce resources – now including not only sensing resources (as in Section 3.1) but also power and network bandwidth – should be allocated to optimize an overall end-user defined utility function, in a manner similar to Equation 1. The principal challenge here is to develop *distributed* utility-maximizing routing, congestion control, and packet scheduling mechanisms that achieve a balance of energy expenditure among sensing (operating the radars), communication, and computation. This balance needs to be achieved not just locally at an individual node, but *systematically,* since sensor network nodes must interact and collaborate with each other to perform the sensor network's task.

We have recently developed a distributed algorithm for optimal joint allocation of energy between sensing and communication at each node to maximize the overall aggregate amount of information received at a central site for an off-the-grid meteorological sensing network [Zhang 2006]. A distributed gradient-based algorithm iteratively adjusts the per-node amount of energy allocated between sensing (gathering meteorological data) and communication (rate control, and routing) to reach the system-wide optimum. While we believe this work is an important first step, it must be extended in several directions. First, as noted in section 3 above, the ultimate goal should not be to deliver a maximum amount of data to a central site, but rather to deliver data that results in maximal system utility, in the sense of Equation 1. This is a subtle, but important difference. Also, with limited communication capabilities, it will likely be important to distribute the detection, task generation, and optimization capabilities of the MC&C.

We have argued above that application-specific, end-user concerns must play a crucial role in system optimization. This view naturally encompasses the notion of application-specific congestion control, including both packet-discard policies at intermediate nodes and source rate control. [Banka 2006a, Banka 2006b] presents a packet marking/deletion scheme for meteorological sensing networks. [Zhang 2006] addresses the problem of jointly optimizing source sensing and rate control (subject to power constraints), but with the goal of maximizing throughput rather than maximizing utility.

Finally, we believe that techniques for networked distributed control that can deal with the delay, loss and other impairments attendant with networked control is an important area for research.   [Liberatore 2006] has recently investigated the importance of predictable timing in networked control of sensors, developing buffering/playout mechanisms similar to those used for packetized audio or video to provide predictable sampling and application of control. In [Malouch 2006], we have studied the effects of different packet-scheduling mechanisms (aggregate FCFS of both radar data and control commands versus priority for control traffic) within the network. Our aim was to understand when it is (and when it is not) advantageous to separate the forwarding of control and data traffic in a meteorological sensing application. Our results show that while the separate handling of control and data results in a decrease in the round-trip control-loop delay, and a consequent increase in the number of reflectivity samples examined during each pass through the control loop in Figure 1, the gain in reflectivity estimate accuracy is relatively small, except at very high loads; we find a similar result for the performance of a meteorological tracking application as well. We show, however, that because sensing accuracy both improves *and* degrades slowly in the number of sensed values obtained, the system is robust in that it can still perform well in the case of severe overload, but *only* in the case that control messages receive priority and remain unaffected by data overload.

5 Conclusion

In this paper, we have presented an architecture for a class of systems that perform distributed, collaborative, adaptive sensing (DCAS) of the atmosphere. Since the goal of these DCAS systems is to sense the atmosphere *when and where the user needs are greatest*, user requirements naturally play *the* central role in determining how system resources (sensor targeting, computation, communication) are deployed within such systems. We described the software components of the meteorological command and control (MC&C) software that lie at the heart of our testbed DCAS system, and provided timing measurements of component execution times. We then presented a utility-based framework that determines how multiple end-user preferences are combined with policy considerations into utility functions that are used to allocate system resources in a manner that dynamically optimizes overall system performance. We also discussed open challenges in the networking and control of such end-user-driven systems.

We believe that emerging DCAS systems represent a step forward in the evolution of computing systems from being primarily general/multi-purpose in nature to often being highly specialized and highly mission-specific. Such mission-specific computing naturally implies an increased emphasis on the end-user, and on tailoring and optimizing system operation to meet end-user, application-specific goals. It is our hope that the lessons learned in our development of DCAS systems – particularly with respect to our emphasis on end users - will provide a foundation for the understanding and further development of future user-centric sense-and-response systems.

Acknowledgments. This work was supported in part by the National Science Foundation under grant EEC-0313747.

References

[Banka 2006a] P. Lee, T. Banka, A.P. Jayasumana, and V. Chandrasekar, "Content-based Packet Marking for Application-Aware Processing in Overlay Networks,", *2006 IEEE Intl. Conf. on Local Computer Networks*, Tampa, FL, Nov. 2006

[Banka 2006b] T. Banka, P. Lee, A.P. Jayasumana, J. Kurose, "An Architecture and a Programming Interface for Application-Aware Data Dissemination Using Overlay Networks," submitted.

[CASA 2006a] http://www.casa.umass.edu

[CASA 2006b] Corner OSEE, http://gaia.cs.umass.edu/casa/cornerOSSE.mpg

[Chong 2003] C. Chong; S. Kumar, "Sensor networks: Evolution, opportunities, and challenges," *Proc. IEEE*, August 2003.

[DDAS 2006] Dynamic Data Driven Application Systems Workshop 2006, http://www.nsf.gov/cise/cns/dddas/2006_Workshop/

[Donovan 2005a] B. Donovan and D. J. McLaughlin, "Improved radar sensitivity through limited sector scanning: The DCAS approach," *Proc. of AMS Radar Meteorology*, 2005.

[Donovan 2005b] B. Donovan, D. J. McLaughlin, J. Kurose, V. Chandrasekar, "Principles and Design Considerations for Short-Range Energy Balanced Radar Networks", *Proc. IGARSS05*, Seoul, Republic of Korea.

[Estrin 2002] D. Estrin, D. Culler, and K. Pister, "Connecting the Physical World with Pervasive Networks," *IEEE Pervasive Computing*, 1,1 (Jan.-March 2002).

[Hondl 2003] K. Hondl, "Capabilities and Components of the Warning Decision and Support System – Integrated Information (WDSS-II), *Proc. American Meteorological Society Annual Meeting, Jan. 2003, (Long Beach).*

[Jaganathan 1989] V. Jaganathan, R. Dodhiawala, L. Baum, *Blackboard Architectures, Applications.* Academic Press, 1989.

[Kansal 2004] A. Kansal, D. Potter, and M. B. Srivastava, "Performance aware tasking for environmentally powered sensor networks," *Proc. ACM SIGMETRICS*, 2004.

[Liberatore 2006] V. Liberatore, "Integrated Play-Back, Sensing, and Networked Control, *Proc. 2006 IEEE Infocom.*

[Lord 1997] Lord, S. J., E. Kalnay, R. Daley, G. D. Emmitt, and R. Atlas, 1997: Using OSSEs in the design of the future generation of integrated observing systems. Preprints, *First Symp. Integrated Observation Systems*, Amer. Meteor. Soc., 45–47.

[Manfredi 2006] V. Manfredi *et al.*, "A Comparison of Myopic and Non-Myopic Scanning Strategies in a DCAS Meteorological Sensing Network, in preparation.

[Malouch 2006] N. Malouch, V. Manfredi, J. Kurose, C. Zhang, "On the Value of Separation of Control and Data in a Distributed Meteorological Sensing Network," submitted.

[McLaughlin 2005] D. McLaughlin, V. Chandrasekar, K. Droegemeier, S. Frasier, J. Kurose, F. Junyent, B. Philips, S. Cruz-Pol, and J. Colom, "Distributed Collaborative Adaptive Sensing (DCAS) for Improved Detection, Understanding, and Prediction of Atmospheric Hazards," *9th Symp. on Integrated Observing and Assimilation Systems for the Atmosphere, Oceans, and Land Surface*, , 2005, San Diego, CA, American Meteorological Society.

[NOAA 2006] National Oceanic and Atmospheric Administration, "Radar Resources," http://www.ncdc.noaa.gov/oa/radar/radarresources.html

[Pepyne 2006] D. Pepyne *et al.,* "Defining and Optimizing Utility in NetRad, a Collaborative Adaptive Sensor Network for Hazardous Weather Detection," CASA Technical Report.

[Zhang 2006] C. Zhang, J. Kurose, Y. Liu, D. Towsley, M. Zink, "A Distributed Algorithm for Joint Sensing and Routing in Wireless Networks with Non-Steerable Directional Antennas," *IEEE Int. Conference on Network Protocols,* Oct. 2006.

[Zink 2005] M. Zink, D. Westbrook, S. Abdallah, B. Horling, V. Lakamraju, E. Lyons, V. Manfredi, J. Kurose, and K. Hondl, "Meteorological command and control: An end-to-end architecture for a hazardous weather detection sensor network," *ACM Mobisys Workshop on End-end Sense-and-Response Systems,* 2005.

On Scalability of
DHT-DNS Hybrid Naming System

Yusuke Doi, Shirou Wakayama, Masahiro Ishiyama, Satoshi Ozaki,
and Atsushi Inoue

Corporate R&D Center, TOSHIBA Corp.

Abstract. In this paper, we describe our evaluation work of a DHT-DNS hybrid naming system together with our prototype design and implementation of the DHT-DNS mounter. For the evaluation we conducted a series of experiments in a large-scale emulation testbed. We found a bottleneck limiting scalability of the proposed hybrid naming system at the mounter.

1 Background

RFID tags and object traceability systems are among promising solutions in ubiquitous computing and networking. The standards from EPCglobal Inc. define how tags and readers communicate, how a reader transfers a set of IDs and related data to appropriate servers, and how a user retrieves related data.

In a traceability system, a naming system is essential to bind IDs and other information. In the architecture proposed by EPCglobal, Object Name Service (ONS[1]) is the naming system to define bindings between ID carried by a tag and its corresponding data. The first version of ONS depends on DNS (Domain Name System)[2] to resolve ID to a database address, using NAPTR DNS resource records (RR)[3].

Looking beyond a traceability system, naming systems such as ONS may become fundamental technologies in common ubiquitous networking applications. Ubiquitous networking applications such as the scenarios described below need such a naming system. Objects in real space are tagged by any kind of ID, and each space (streets, buildings, floors, rooms, desks, and cabinets) has its corresponding database to maintain the current state of the space.

Because relations between objects and spaces are dynamic and have no apparent restrictions, traces of an object may appear in any databases worldwide. In addition, to focus on the object, the user must locate the set of databases out of a huge number of databases in the world.

Thus, product traceability systems including ONS are a significant step toward the ubiquitous computing and networking scenarios described above. A naming system is required to glue tagged real space objects and logical objects in computers to make an object traceability system.

K. Cho and P. Jacquet (Eds.): AINTEC 2006, LNCS 4311, pp. 16–30, 2006.
© Springer-Verlag Berlin Heidelberg 2006

1.1   The Problem with Monolithic Naming Systems

ONS, and more generically naming systems for traceability, requires the following characteristics. Well-known solutions for naming systems cannot satisfy all of the characteristics simultaneously. The solutions include DNS and some DHT (Distributed Hash Table) such as Chord[4], Pastry[5], Tapestry[6], and many other variants.

Firstly, naming systems for traceability must have superior **scalability** to support lookup of billions of items in the world.

Secondly, naming systems for traceability must have enough **flexibility** in resource allocation for demand fluctuation. This is because needs for some kinds of products, such as holiday gifts, change seasonally. In addition, works for adding computing resources to the system must be easy enough to avoid service failure if the overall resources were insufficient and it must not cause the system maintenance downtime.

Thirdly, naming systems for traceability must be very **easy to maintain**. Ideally, the system should be as autonomic as possible. Broken parts of the system must be replaced without human intervention.

Fourthly, naming systems for traceability must have **heterogeneity**. Because each kind of product may have its own requirements for naming systems, the whole system must be able to allocate different classes of resources. In addition, heterogeneity of the system is required if companies using the system need to define the boundary of responsibilities between them.

Finally, a wide range of clients should be able to use the naming systems directly or indirectly. In other words, a naming system must be **legacy friendly**. Consumers will not own dedicated clients for product traceability systems. Clients expected to be held in common are web browser and DNS.

Table 1 indicates how the known naming systems match those requirements. In the table, DHT and DNS are compared against each requirement for naming systems for traceability. The letter x indicates the system with better conformity for the requirement.

DHT has better scalability for flat name space, flexibility, and easiness of maintenance. DNS also has a good level of scalability on tree-structured name

Table 1. Systems that have better conformity with requirements for naming systems for traceability

requirement	DNS	DHT
Scalability		
on tree-structured name space	x	
on flat name space		x
Flexibility		x
Easy to maintain		x
Heterogeneity	x	
Legacy friendly	x	

space. Because DNS name space structure defines distribution of name servers, it has less flexibility for server replacement. In DHT, no single server is assigned for predefined partition in the DHT name space. Relations between each server define the partition and authority of the space automatically. Thus, DHT is easier to maintain than DNS.

On the other hand, DNS is better in terms of heterogeneity and legacy friendliness. In DHT there is no clear binding between DHT servers and name space partitions. Thus, a DHT name space is homogeneous. In DNS, careful design can make heterogeneous requirements for zones match name servers.

Considering the object traceability scenario, product codes are the names in queries. A product code has a semi-structured style such as EPCglobal GID-96 format[7] shown in figure 1. The general manager field corresponds to companies, the object class field corresponds to products, and serial numbers are assigned for product instances. The general manager and the object class fields have two-level tree structure and are relatively static. On the other hand, new IDs are dynamically used day by day in the serial number field. In addition, serial numbers in GID-96 are huge, requiring 36-bit space without any structure.

DNS is suitable for the general manager and the object class resolution, because DNS also has a tree structure and name delegation in DNS matches authority delegation in such a tree-like name space. However, the product serial number part has no structure inside and is dynamic. Thus, the part does not fit to the DNS.

Header	General Manager	Object Class	Serial Number
8bits	28bits	24bits	36bits

Fig. 1. The Structure of GID-96

1.2   Related Works

This section describes Distributed Hash Table (DHT), a new scheme of naming system, and introduces former researches that evaluates DHT against DNS.

The load distribution mechanism of DNS depends on design of zones. A zone is a unit of name space hierarchy, and NS RR (Name Server Resource Record) defines name servers authoritative for the zone. A zone delegates a name (subdomain) in the zone by a set of NS RR. The servers manage the name space tree in divided zones.

DHT is the name of a set of algorithms that provide *key* → *value* relationships as conventional hash tables do. Some characteristics of DHT are suitable for naming systems for traceability. First, DHT has good scalability against number of keys. Second, DHT has good flexibility for service node replacement because service nodes automatically coordinate name space partitions (like DNS zone, but not hierarchical) in the whole name space.

Cox[8] et al. implemented and evaluated DDNS. DDNS is a name service that has a DNS equivalent interface and is implemented using Chord algorithm. According to their evaluation, DDNS has the following characteristics.

Compared with regular DNS, DDNS has good load balancing and distribution characteristics. On the other hand, DDNS is too homogeneous to support the variety of services in DNS. A DNS name server can handle some names differently. DNS-based load balancing is an example of such special handling. On the other hand, it is difficult to handle some names differently from other names on DHT-based systems because of its homogeneity.

In previous work[9], we have proposed a hybrid naming system using DHT-DNS Mounter. Compared with our proposed hybrid naming system, DDNS has an advantage in terms of simple administration. DDNS decouples name administration and hardware administration completely. In DDNS, failed nodes are purged in autonomously by an underlying mechanism. However, this may have some side effects such as the incentive problem and the homogeneity problem.

With the hybrid naming system, users must invest their resource under their own DNS subtree. Motivation and investment are loosely coupled (users may contribute its resource for shared DHT) and there is no incentive problem. In addition, for users who require different service quality, the hybrid naming system can provide suitable DHT implementations for each name subtree. For example, users requiring greater update frequency may use DHT implementation with lower cache lifetime.

2   The Objective of the Research

In this paper, we describe a series of our scalability evaluations of a previously proposed hybrid naming system using DHT-DNS mounter and Chord-like DHT. Along with the evaluation, we also describe implementations used in the naming system and the evaluation testbed.

Our evaluation is still in a preliminary state. We also discuss some bottlenecks and our estimations based on some stand-alone experiments.

We describe our design and implementation of components in the proposed hybrid naming system in section 3. In section 4, we describe the testbed we used because our design of evaluation depends on its structure. The design of the evaluation and its results are described in section 5 and discussed in section 6. We conclude this paper in section 7.

3   Design and Implementation of DHT-DNS Mounter

3.1   Hybrid Naming System with DHT-DNS Mounter

To satisfy the requirements described in section 1.1, we have proposed DHT-DNS Mounter in our previous work[9]. Figure 2 shows the structure of DHT-DNS hybrid naming system using the DHT-DNS Mounter.

In figure 2, a DHT key x is mapped under the DNS domain k.mnt.dhtdns.net. The upper part of the figure is in DNS and the lower part is in DHT. From left to right, three ideas depicted. A name space is a logical definition space of names. Name servers are physical servers to manage the name spaces. In many cases, the

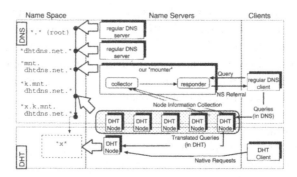

Fig. 2. The Structure of DHT-DNS Hybrid Naming System

whole name space is divided into subspaces (e.g. subdomains in DNS) and each subspace is bound to one or more servers. In the figure, white bold arrows indicates bindings between namespaces and name servers. On the right, there are some clients.

The DHT namespace is mounted under the DNS domain tree, namely under dhtdns.net. Two levels of name delegation makes the DHT namespace accessible from regular DNS clients with least bottleneck. First, our "mounter" works as an authoritative name server on a gateway zone with the intermediate DNS domain name mnt.dhtdns.net. This mounter collects IP addresses of DHT nodes that serve as DNS authoritative name servers of a corresponding translator zone. In the example, the translator zone is k.mnt.dhtdns.net and the zone represents the DHT mounted.

A query from a client is processed in the following order. At the first query, the client side DNS resolver has no cache of related name servers. The resolver finds NS resource records of dhtdns.net. The domain is the gateway zone and a set of mounters is the authoritative DNS name servers. The resolver proceeds to a mounter to find authoritative name servers on mnt.dhtdns.net, the translator zone. The mounter replies NS resource records with one or a set of DHT nodes collected by a background node collector thread.

Finally, the resolver sends the query to a DHT node. The node also serves as an authoritative server of the translator zone. As it receives the query, it try to lookup a DHT entry using the top label x in the DNS query. It also constructs a set of RR using the DHT query results, and sends back to the original DNS resolver.

The records returned from the mounter are created dynamically using different DHT node per query. Hence, each DHT nodes should serve as a translator to a small number of DNS resolvers. Using cached data, the resolves can directly access to the DHT nodes for successive query until the cached record expires.

3.2   Domain Name Translation

In this section we describe how to map a DNS domain name into a DHT key.

The proposed method mounts a DHT key namespace under a DNS subdomain. The label assigned for translator zone (k in the example) decides how the name label under translator zone (x in the example) translated into names in DHT. A zone k in the example is the zone for direct key-label mapping from a DNS label into a DHT key. In the example, a domain name x.k.dhtdns.net is translated into a DHT key x.

To fit this structure in GID-96[10], a label for a gateway zone corresponds to a General Manager ID and a label for a translator zone corresponds to an Object Class ID.

Actually, we need to take some care in direct key-label mapping zone. Because characters allowed in DNS label strings are a limited set, some keys cannot have a corresponding DNS labels. Apparently, long keys cannot be represented in DNS labels because an excessively long DNS label is not allowed.

Our scheme of key-label mapping has two parts. Direct key-label mapping is for keys only consisting of ASCII characters allowed in DNS label. The keys have their labels without modification. A longer key may split into several labels. In such a case, labels are concatenated in preserved order. For example, the label 1.4a.2x.3 is for key 14a2x3.

3.3   Resource Record Translation

We defined a resource record translation rule. Zone master file notation is defined in RFC1035[11]. Our DHT-DNS translator implementation uses altered format of a line in master files.

The following string is an example of a resource record we used in practice.

```
#!dns_rr NAPTR 101 100 "u" "EPC+html"
  "!^.*!http://rfid.isl.rdc.toshiba.co.jp/PIServer/index.php!" .
```

This string is stored as an entry corresponding to an ID. Because entries in DHT correspond to zero or one domain name with high probability, the domain name is omitted in the line. Instead, a constant string #!dns_rr appears. The string indicates this entry can be translated in a DNS resource record (RR), and the actual domain name will be in the place at the time of conversion. The rest is a NAPTR[3] resource record used in our RFID experiment. This is converted into DNS RR data just the same as regular DNS software does with master files.

3.4   Implementation of Translators

In our system, all DHT nodes start with a common configuration of translator. The configuration specifies a translator zone for direct key-label mapping.

As shown in figure 2, any DHT node is an authoritative node of translator zone and regular DNS clients send their queries under translator zone.

There are three tasks in translator. When a DNS query is received, it converts the given label into a hash value in DHT. With the hash value, a translator sends a query to retrieve data entries under the hash value. At last, it sends a DNS answer with corresponding resource records by comparing the retrieved data entries and the initial DNS query. The TTL value of the answer RR set is statically configured.

In our implementation, the default value is 5 seconds. Actually, we do not expect successive queries on a name in object traceability scenarios. If client wants to do so, the object must be a kind of dynamic object. Hence, we select a large enough value to avoid unnecessary loads from defective resolvers[12].

In response, the translator declares itself to be the authoritative name server. An NS RR and a corresponding A and/or AAAA are required in order to declare it.

However, A/AAAA RR is not always available for DHT nodes. Hence, we introduce the other zone (address zone) for name-to-address mapping. For example, a translator with IP address 10.1.2.3 can declare a mapped domain name 3.2.1.10.a.dhtdns.net as A RR of itself. In queries of a mapped domain, labels are parsed and a dynamically generated A/AAAA RR is returned. Using this mapping, anyone can declare authority on a zone using NS and A/AAAA pair. Note that address zone is implemented in mounter.

3.5   Implementation of Mounter

A mounter consists of two threads: a Collector and a Responder. A FIFO queue of DHT node endpoint information connects the modules. Using the collector, a mounter distributes name query loads among the DHT nodes efficiently. Figure 2 illustrates the structure of a mounter.

The Collector collects endpoint information of DHT nodes. It tries to start from a random DHT node by finding the successor of a random hash value. Until the queue length reaches a threshold (MAXLEN), the collector tries to find the successor node of current target node, and it puts the endpoint information of the new node into the queue. As the queue length reaches the MAXLEN, the collector tries to keep freshness of the queue contents. If no one pops the queue during a period (NODE_EXPIRE_INTERVAL), it drops the oldest entry out and fills a new one at the tail of the queue.

The responder is the authoritative name server of a gateway zone and an address zone under the gateway zone. It also knows a translator zone and generates name delegation responses for queries to the translator zone. The TTL value of the RRs in the response is statically defined in the configuration (DEFAULT_TTL).

Upon a request under the translator zone, the responder pops IP address of a node from the queue. Using the IP address, it creates a response with an NS RR and corresponding A or AAAA address under address zone. A responder may reuse an IP address several times (defined by MAXUSECOUNT) to avoid excessively fast consumption of queue contents.

For the address zone, a responder parses labels of queries under the zone to dynamically generate an A or AAAA RR. The responder prepares a zone to generate both IPv4 and IPv6 addresses. For A queries, it parses labels under address zone in reversed dotted-decimal format to generate corresponding IPv4 address. For IPv6 address, we avoid using popular format used in reverse lookup zones because it becomes too long. Instead, our implementation uses reversed dotted-16bit-hexadecimal format to indicate an IPv6 address, replacing :: by x. For example, a AAAA query for 53.x.1b1.200.2001.a.mnt.dhtdns.net. returns AAAA RR with 2001:200:1b1::53.

Table 2 describes default parameters of the mounter. These values are selected without strong reasoning (i.e. heuristic values).

Table 2. Default Values of Mounter Parameters

MAXLEN	8
MAXUSECOUNT	2
NODE_EXPIRE_INTERVAL	60
DEFAULT_TTL	3600

4   The StarBED Emulation Testbed

We used the StarBED emulation testbed in NICT Hokuriku IT Open Laboratory [1]. StarBED is a testbed to emulate real network and software environments. It has more than 500 PC nodes interconnected with a few high-end Ethernet switches. With the switches, users can make network segments for emulation experiments using port VLANs. Users can also make complex network topology. In addition, all nodes have at least two network interfaces and experiment designers can use one Ethernet segment for management and others for experiments. Hence, management traffic has very limited impact on the experiment.

There are five groups of cluster nodes. We have used group A with 208 NEC Express5800 110Rc-1 hardware (Pentium 3/1GHz with 512MB memory) and an Ethernet switch.

Boot process of the cluster nodes can be controlled from a management node using DHCP and PXEBoot. Hence, it is an ideal evaluation environment for launching as many DHT nodes using PXEBoot without per-node configuration troubles.

4.1   Emulation Scenario Execution

There is a toolkit[13] [2] to support emulation scenario executions under StarBED. It has some components to execute each experiment automatically using given *scenarios*. Among the components, three representative components are described below.

The first component is ERM (Experiment Resource Manager). It dynamically assigns hardware nodes to each experiment. Ideally, an ERM manages a whole cluster and VLAN IDs. In practice, a group of nodes and VLAN IDs are assigned to each user in advance. Hence, our ERM manages the assigned resources among our concurrent experiments.

A "kuroyuri master" is the second component of the execution toolkit. Each kuroyuri master has a scenario and it controls an experiment. It gets information of a set of nodes from ERM, boots the nodes, and starts scenario execution and message exchange between kuroyuri master and "kuroyuri slave" in each node.

---

[1] It became Hokuriku Research Center in April 2006.
[2] See also: http://www.starbed.org/

A kuroyuri slave works within each emulation node. It controls the node. It launches processes that perform actual communication of the experiments. Slaves also have their own execution scenario per node class definition.

A definition of the experiment consists of two parts: an experiment environment definition and a scenario. The experiment environment definition is the static part of the experiment. Within the definition, a user can define a class of nodes, number of nodes in each class, network segment, and binding between node network interfaces and nodes.

On the other hand, the master scenario defines execution of the experiment scenario. Most of the execution is performed through message exchange between kuroyuri master and kuroyuri slaves. Kuroyuri slaves also have slave scenarios (defined in node class definition). Each kuroyuri slave launches processes (like queryperf or DHT node process) to perform an actual experiment as it receives the corresponding message.

5   Evaluations and Results

In this section we describe our design of the evaluation experiments and their results. The first objective of the evaluations is to confirm our system scales well. The second goal is to find bottlenecks if the system does not scale well.

First, we describe the design of our evaluations on StarBED. Then , the results and analysis are presented.

5.1   Evaluation Design on StarBED

In the experiment design on StarBED, we focus on two issues: traffic balance between the DHT nodes and performance bottlenecks. In the experiment, we did not consider comparison with other equivalent solutions. So far, DNS server implementations are far more mature than DHT implementations, including ours and direct comparison of performance is almost meaningless.

In our evaluation, we assume the system is static and steady instead of adopting a realistic dynamic scenario. To find traffic balance and bottlenecks of the system, we don't need to emulate realistic traffic including query traffic pattern and dynamic configuration of DHT nodes. In addition, models of query traffic dynamics in this system are not yet well analyzed.

Our experiment consists of the following classes of nodes. With the exception of the kuroyuri master node, a kuroyuri slave process runs on each node.

- A **DHT seed node:**
  All other DHT nodes start bootstrap process using a well known seed node. The seed node helps other DHT nodes to construct a DHT network.
- $N \times$ **DHT nodes:**
  DHT nodes to make services. A DHT seed node and the other DHT nodes form a distributed hash table service. In addition, all DHT nodes including the seed node are able to translate between DNS and DHT. Each of them serves as a primary DNS name server of a domain name.

- **Root Name Server:**
  Dedicated DNS root name server for the experiments. We use BIND 9 series (9.2.4rc5).
- **Mounter:**
  The mounter process. Using name delegation, it distributes load from each load client among known DHT nodes.
- $M \times$**Load Client:**
  They create DNS queries on a name domain. Each load client has a dedicated cache name server (BIND 9.2.4rc5). It also has a python interpreter (version 2.3.4) to run a DHT node.
- **A Master Node:**
  On the master node, a kuroyuri master process and an ERM process run to control the experiment. It also provides NFS service to all classes of experiment nodes to feed configuration and to collect result log files. We use Debian Sarge on VMware(TM) virtual machine to implement the master node.

Figure 3 presents an overview of the configuration of our experiment setup. As described in the figure, all the nodes participating in the experiments have two network interfaces. This is another advantage of the StarBED configuration. Because of the configuration, management traffic such as kuroyuri master-slave communication and NFS access has little impact on the experiment. Management traffic is exchanged between the kuroyuri master and kuroyuri slaves on the management network. DNS and DHT traffic are on the experiment network.

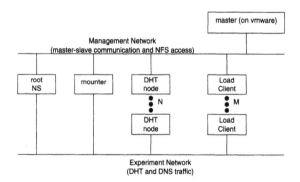

Fig. 3. Experiment Setup Overview in StarBED

As we want to measure traffic balance and performance bottlenecks in the naming system with DHT-DNS mounter, we measure the number of messages exchanged in each physical node in the experiment. We also measure response time distribution measured on each load client to find out if the system scales well or not.

5.2 Implementation of the Evaluation Environment

To implement our evaluation environment, we need to consider the following things: scenario design, the master node, implementation of node classes, physical node boot method, and log collection.

In the experiment, we use `queryperf` command that comes together with BIND9 software distribution as the load generator. To set up all the nodes properly before the load test, we take the following steps per experiment.

1. Verification of network configuration
2. Dynamic configuration files for BIND
3. NFS mount of shared files / logs
4. NTP time synchronization
5. Starting log collection to local memory file system
6. BIND named (on root name server and load clients) startup
7. DHT seed node startup
8. DHT nodes startup
9. Verification of the DHT overlay network
10. queryperf startup →stop
11. DHT nodes stop (including the seed)
12. BIND named stop
13. Dumping log files to NFS storage

In order to avoid any impact on the experiment body (step 10), there is no access to NFS during the step. Before step 10, all the processes are loaded on the physical memory (no swapfile is used), and all logs are written to memory file system (`/tmp`) by the time that the test body finishes.

Besides the above scenario, we need to boot each physical node with an appropriate operating system. On StarBED, all nodes boot from PXE.

We have three ways to create nodes for the experiments. First, pre-installed FreeBSD, Linux, and Windows 2000 can be modified to execute experiments. Second, each physical node has an empty hard disk partition and one may install one's selected OS to execute experiments. Third, without touching the hard disks, one may launch diskless nodes using PXEBoot.

Because the first approach requires a vast amount of configuration tasks and the second approach takes much time to copy images among hundreds of physical nodes, we took the third approach. We use PXELinux [3] to boot Linux kernels (version 2.4.27) in this experiment.

However, diskless nodes usually have a small storage space to keep many programs in boot image. In addition, we need to collect log files to see what happened in the experiments. Hence, the master node serves as an NFS server to give some configurations and object files, and to receive log files from emulation nodes.

Because IP addresses assigned to each experiment node differ in each experiment, we need to configure programs dynamically. We need to recreate zone files per experiment for named configurations, including IP address of the root and mounter nodes (step 2).

---

[3] http://syslinux.zytor.com/pxe.php

5.3   Results of StarBED Experiments

In the experiments we have tried many combinations of N (number of DHT nodes [4]) and M (number of load clients). Figure 4 depicts the parameter set. To summarize, we tried three series of experiments: $(N = 10, M = vary)$, $(N = 20, M = vary)$, and $(M = 40, N = vary)$. We also tried $(N = 40, M = 60)$.

Figure 5 shows the average number of messages per DHT node against M. $N = 10, 20$ are shown. It shows that adding DHT nodes can decrease load per DHT node.

Figure 6 shows the total number of messages received in the all DHT nodes against the number of load clients. According to the figure, even if the number of DHT nodes doubles, there are only minor differences in DHT traffic.

Figure 7 shows the average number of received messages per DHT node at constant load. It shows loads are distributed and the number of received messages per DHT node decreases as the number of DHT nodes increase.

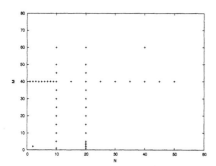

Fig. 4. Parameter Sets (N: Number of DHT Nodes, M: Number of Load Clients)

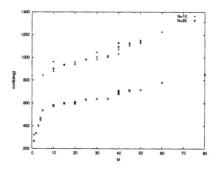

Fig. 5. Average Number of Received Messages per DHT Node against M

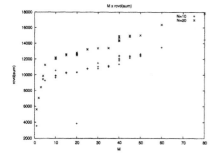

Fig. 6. Number of Total Messages in DHT against M

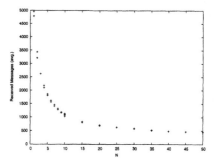

Fig. 7. Average Number of Received Messages at Constant Load

---

[4] N does not include the seed node in this paper.

6   Discussions

6.1   Evaluation of Results in StarBED

As shown in figure 5 and 6, the number of received message is not proportional to the number of load clients. This indicates the existence of a bottleneck.

Figure 8 shows the relation between the number of queries per second (qps total) and the number of messages received (message total). This tells that the number of queries per second does not exceed around $72 \sim 74$ in most of experiments. This clearly indicates a bottleneck. On the other hand, the number of messages at $N = 10$ and $N = 20$ is not proportional to N.

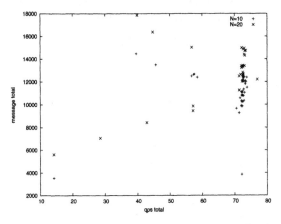

Fig. 8. Relation between Queries Amount and Traffic Amount

On the contrary, there are some cases with lower qps total. We suppose the following two causes for such cases: (1) smaller M in the experiment (lower message totals) and (2) an excessive number of queries causes messages to be dropped (higher message totals).

Comparing $N = 10$ and $N = 20$ cases in figure 8, message total for $N = 10$ is around $9000 \sim 12000$ around qps total$= 72$. On the other hand, message total is around $12000 \sim 15000$ when $N = 20$. This indicates cases on $N = 20$ consumes $1.25 \sim 1.33$ times more messages than $N = 10$. It is far less than double.

We cannot assume our DHT scales logarithmically with only two sets of N. However, this indicates our DHT based naming system does *not* scale badly. We are now planning another session of experiments to clarify the scalability of our system.

6.2   Bottleneck Analysis

Because we found the bottleneck after the experiments, we have tried to determine the performance of each component. We found our DHT-DNS mounter has far less performance than we expect because protocol translation work involves copying of too many bytes.

Based on the assumption that the bottleneck is in our components, we made a series of performance analysis for the DHT nodes and the mounter.

For the DHT nodes, we set up the following minimalistic environment to estimate query/response throughput and found it can process over 600 put/get pairs per seconds. Two DHT nodes are on a physical Linux machine and 5 parallel load testers (on the same machine) make pairs of put/get request with random short values.

For the mounter, we inserted a dummy collector that just gives a constant value to evaluate query/response performance of responder alone. With experiments with queryperf, we found the responder alone can handle about 35 queries per second. Apparently, this is the bottleneck.

We also tried profiling to find the hotspot of the mounter implementation and found DNS message processing is the source of the bottleneck. At about 5 seconds of total processing time against a dummy query load, at least 2.19 seconds are consumed in parse and validation of incoming DNS messages.

7 Conclusions and Future Work

In this paper, we described our evaluation work and preliminary results. Together with the evaluation work, we described our detailed model of hybrid name space and the implementation of DHT-DNS mounter.

At this stage of the research, we have found scalability of the implementation is limited. However, we have identified a bottleneck and intend to eliminate it in future work. We intend to update the DNS processing part of the mounter to improve the performance. We also have an alternative (less mature) implementation of the mounter in C. In the next series of experiments, we expect we can use the C version.

We also note that the prototype of the hybrid naming system is used in our experimental distributed traceability system[14]. In the experimental system, we bind some kinds of identifiers including cattle IDs with distributed traceability databases. Combination of the hybrid naming system and distributed traceability databases makes a flexible yet scalable traceability system.

Acknowledgements. Prof. Shinoda, Dr. Chinen, and Mr. Miyachi of Japan Advanced Institute of Technology helped us greatly with on StarBED. We gratefully acknowledge their technical advice and consideration. For hardware configuration support, we are indebted to the staffs of NICT Hokuriku IT Open Laboratory.

This research is supported/funded by the Ministry of Internal Affairs and Communications of Japan.

References

1. EPCglobal: Auto-id Object Name Service (ONS) 1.0. Auto-ID Center Working Draft (2003)
2. Mockapetris, P.: Domain names - concepts and facilities. IETF RFC 1034 (1987)
3. Mealling, M., Daniel, R.: The naming authority pointer (NAPTR) DNS resource record. IETF RFC 2915 (2000)
4. Stoica, I., Morris, R., Karger, D., Kaashoek, M.F., Balakrishnan, H.: Chord: A scalable peer-to-peer lookup service for internet applications. In: Proceedings of ACM SIGCOMM. (2001)
5. Rowstron, A., Druschel, P.: Pastry: Scalable, decentralized object location and routing for large-scale peer-to-peer systems. In: Proceedings of the 18th IFIP/ACM International Conference on Distributed Systems Platforms (Middleware 2001). (2001)
6. Zhao, B.Y., Kubiatowicz, J.D., Joseph, A.D.: Tapestry: An infrastructure for fault-tolerant wide-area location and routing. Technical Report UCB//CSD-01-1141, U.C.Berkeley (2000)
7. EPCglobal: EPC tag data standards version 1.3. EPCglobal Ratified Specification (2006)
8. Cox, R., Muthitacharoen, A., Morris, R.: Serving DNS using a peer-to-peer lookup service. In: Proceedings of the 1st International Workshop on Peer-to-Peer Systems (IPTPS), Cambridge, MA (2002)
9. DOI, Y.: DNS meets DHT: Treating massive ID resolution using DNS over DHT. In: Proceedings of SAINT 2005. (2005) pp. 9–15
10. EPCglobal: Object naming service (ONS) version 1.0. EPCglobal Ratified Specification (2005)
11. Mockapetris, P.: Domain names - implementation and specification. IETF RFC 1035 (1987)
12. Jung, J., Sit, E., Balakrishnan, H., Morris, R.: DNS performance and the effectiveness of caching. In: Proceedings of the ACM SIGCOMM Internet Measurement Workshop '01, San Francisco, California (2001)
13. Miyachi, T., Chinen, K., Shinoda, Y.: Automatic configuration and execution of internet experiments on an actual node-based testbed. In: Proceedings of Tridentcom 2005. (2005) pp.274–282
14. Wakayama, S., Doi, Y., Ozaki, S., Inoue, A.: Extendable product traceability system from small start. In: Proceedings of SAINT 2006 RFID and Extended Network Workshop. (2006)

A Topology-Aware Overlay Multicast Approach for Mobile Ad-Hoc Networks

Mohamed Ali Kaafar, Cyrine Mrabet, and Thierry Turletti

INRIA Sophia Antipolis
2004 route des lucioles, 06902 Sophia Antipolis, France
{mkaafar, cmrabet, turletti}@sophia.inria.fr

Abstract. AOMP (Ad-hoc Overlay Multicast Protocol) is a novel approach for application-layer multicast in ad-hoc networks. We introduce in this paper a new algorithm that exploits a few properties of IP-routing to extract underlying topology information. The basic idea is to match nodes' path to the source in order to detect near neighbors in the physical topology. Then, in a dynamic and decentralized way, we construct a minimum cost mobility-aware delivery tree, connecting nodes that are close to each other. We design a tree improvement algorithm in order to enhance the global performance of AOMP during data distribution. Our simulations results show that, compared to previously proposed application-layer multicast structures, AOMP yields trees with lower cost and traffic redundancy. In addition, it performs well in terms of packet losses, especially in case of node mobility.

1 Introduction

Using mobile and wireless devices is becoming ubiquitous. In recent years, the study and developments of wireless networks have been very popular, leading to flexible and efficient wireless devices. In particular, *Mobile Ad-hoc NETworks* (MANETs) are dynamically reconfigurable wireless networks with no fixed infrastructure, where nodes act as hosts as well as routers. MANETs are deployed in applications such as disaster recovery, distributed collaborative computing, vehicular communication, data and information sharing in difficult terrain, extension of the infrastructure-based networks and video-conferences.

Multicasting provides a mean for group communication by enabling applications to seemingly communicate with a set of nodes. Traditionally a well suited tool for collaborative applications, multicasting is especially useful in ad-hoc networks where tasks may be carried out by groups of nodes. Due to scarcity of bandwidth, varying network connectivity and frequent topology changes caused by node mobility and transient availability, routing algorithms tailored for wired networks will not operate well if directly transposed to MANET. All the more so with multicasting, which adds to the difficulties of unicast routing the complexity of maintaining and handling dynamic multicast group membership changes. Multicast routing protocols have been proposed for MANET. These protocols assume however, that even non member nodes actively participate in maintaining multicast state information and replicating multicast packets. If some non member nodes are fast moving or refusing multicast cooperation, they affect all the involved multicast sessions.

K. Cho and P. Jacquet (Eds.): AINTEC 2006, LNCS 4311, pp. 31–47, 2006.

Application Layer Multicasting has been proposed as the possible solution for this scenario. In this case, multicast group members organize themselves to form an overlay topology; multicast communication between end systems is implemented by forwarding messages through the overlay links over unicast IP. By moving the multicast functionality to the end systems, we solve the problems associated with fast moving intermediate nodes in maintaining multicast state information. But we pay the penalty of increase in end-to-end latency due to duplication of packets flowing over underlying network, and significant bandwidth consumption by proximity measurements overhead or application-level topology adaptation, etc.

Existing studies focus then on the differentiation between application layer multicast protocols and routing (network layer) protocols. This differentiation stands in the traditional Internet, because overlays are built to circumvent the fact that router-assisted approaches are not feasible, and thus message routing is done at the application layer. In contrast, because nodes in MANETs are end hosts as well as routers, all nodes in MANETs are effectively involved in supporting P2P overlay abstractions, and thus P2P overlay abstractions in MANETs have the option of being implemented either at the network layer or above, that is, at the application layer. However, built separately, these two options would cumulate each other disadvantages and would induce overhead, due to inefficient communication between both layers. What is implemented in network layer would be designed and run in a redundant way, by application layer, and vice versa.

In this paper, we propose a new scheme, named AOMP(Ad-hoc Overlay Multicast Protocol), to construct an efficient topology-aware overlay multicast without inducing measurements overhead. In our proposal, while building an overlay multicast structure, we rely first on information provided by the network layer to construct a virtual topology closer to the actual underlying network topology. Adaptation to nodes' mobility is also detected and triggered by the network layer. Routing information needed by AOMP, means "shortest" IP paths that mobile nodes maintain. Actually, "shortest" depends on the particular routing protocol employed, but typically denotes shortest in terms of delay or number of hops. AOMP relies thus on reactive routing protocols, that maintain route paths from a source to a destination.

In a first stage (section 4), we introduce a novel algorithm that connects newcomers to the underlying topology-aware overlay, namely the path matching algorithm. The algorithm is similar to the concept of car pooling. Suppose that your friend is, more or less, on your way home, so giving him/her a ride will not excessively delay you, and you can reduce overall traffic by car pooling. If he/she is out of your way, however, you decide to drive separately. The major strengths of the path matching algorithm are that it exploits path information provided by already-run reactive routing protocols, to construct a topology-aware overlay. It ensures that no specific (costly) route discovery mechanism is deployed, and no end-to-end measurements are exchanged, and thus avoids channel overhead and improves scalability. Moreover, the constructed overlay network has a low delay penalty and avoids "useless" duplication of packets sent on the same link.

In a second stage (section 5), we construct the multicast spanning tree. We propose runtime adaptation mechanisms that allows to enhance efficiency during data distribution. These are non-greedy link adjustments designed to optimize the overall overlay performance, and not a few particular nodes. Moreover, AOMP adapts to nodes mobility (section 5.4). AOMP does not track nodes mobility at the application level, since this issue is totally handled by the underlying unicast protocol. A mobility adaptation procedure is then triggered by a link status change raised by the routing protocol. This procedure connects nodes to the "next" closest overlay member within a local predefined search scope. It allows to adapt smoothly to frequent and continuous topology changes in ad-hoc networks. The main advantages of our procedure are to maintain virtual-physical topology mapping, while avoiding much overhead resultant from classical 'leave/join' operations used by most of application layer multicast protocols.

Taken into consideration overlay messages control overhead, mobility management and difference that may exist between reactive routing protocols, we evaluated our proposed scheme using extensive simulations, comparing it to previously proposed overlay and network-based multicast protocols. Our findings can be summarized in the following points:

- AOMP outperforms the previous best-performing application layer multicast in terms of delay, packets duplication and reliability.
- AOMP performs favorably even when compared with network layer multicast protocols, more specifically ODMRP [LEE 02]. For ad-hoc groups where 20% to 40% of nodes are part of the multicast group, AOMP exhibits better results in terms of packet delivery ratio.
- AOMP achieves promising delivery ratio in different mobility scenarios, outperforming other proposed protocols.

In the following section, we outline the related literature. We describe the general architecture of AOMP in section 3. The path matching algorithm used in the initial connection of nodes to the AOMP overlay is described in section 4. The second phase of AOMP is presented in section 5. We introduce mechanisms to construct and manage the delivery tree, then we discuss how AOMP adapts to nodes mobility. In section 6, we demonstrate and study the performance of AOMP, through extensive simulations, by providing comparison with several previous approaches. Section 7 concludes the paper.

2   Multicasting in MANETs

In this section, we mention existing ad-hoc multicast protocols and summarize their basic operations. Research efforts can be classified whether they adopt multicasting techniques on the networking layer with multicast routing protocols or on the application layer with overlay multicast schemes.

2.1   Multicast Routing Protocols

As with unicast routing, multicast routing comes in *proactive*, *reactive*, or a combination of the two flavors (*hybrid*). Reactive algorithms represented by MAODV [ROG 99], ADMR [JET 01], OLAM [BAS 00] and ODMRP [LEE 02] present reduced maintenance overhead by maintaining state information only when a multicast session is active. The drawback is decreased responsiveness. Proactive algorithms such as CAMP

[GAR 99] and FGMP [CHI 98] react faster since multicast routing information is readily available, but at the price of introducing high overhead for maintaining multicast group structure even when no multicast session is active. The hybrid approach represented by MZR [DEV 01] aims at obtaining a satisfactory balance among the characteristics of both methods by limiting the scope of the proactive procedures to the local neighborhood of nodes and implementing reactive procedures for longer distances.

State management is one of the most important issues of these multicast protocols. State management involves timely updating of the multicast routing tables at all the nodes (including nodes that are not involved in the multicast session) to maintain the correctness of the multicast routing structure, tree or mesh, according to the current network topology. Even under moderate node mobility and multicast member size, state management incurs considerable amount of control traffic. To address the scalability issues, we need to reduce the protocol states and constrain their distribution, or even use methods that do not need to have protocol state. A number of research efforts have adopted this method, which leads to overlay multicasting.

2.2 Overlay Multicast Protocols

A recent shift towards stateless multicasting is represented by DDM [JI 01], LGT [CHE 02] and RDG [PAT 03]. In overlay multicast, a virtual infrastructure is built to form an overlay network on top of the physical network. Each link in the virtual infrastructure is a unicast tunnel in the physical network. IP layer implements a best-effort unicast datagram service, while the overlay network implements multicast functionalities such as dynamic membership maintenance, packet duplication and multicast routing. All these protocols do not require maintenance of any routing structure at the forwarding nodes. These protocols use different techniques to achieve stateless multicasting. LGT builds an overlay packet delivery tree on top of the underlying unicast routing protocol, using geometric distances between member nodes. Multicast packets are encapsulated in a unicast envelop and unicasted between the group members. When an overlay node receives a data packet from its parent node, it gets the identities of its children from the information included in the header of the packet. For RDG, a probabilistically controlled flooding technique, termed as gossiping, is used to deliver packets to all the group members. In DDM, a source encapsulates a list of destination addresses in the header of each data packet it sends out. When an intermediate node receives the packet, its DDM agent queries the unicast routing protocol about which next-hop node to forward the packet towards each destination in the packet header. DDM is intended for small groups. When group size is large, placing the addresses of all members into the packet headers will not be efficient. The protocol has a caching mode, so that only the difference from the previous states is actually placed in the headers. However, as the forwarding set at the on-route nodes inevitably grow large, each intermediate node needs to keep routes for a large set of destinations. This poses a heavy burden on the supporting unicast protocol even under moderate mobility.

PAST-DM (Progressively Adapted Sub-Tree in Dynamic Mesh) [GUI 03] and ALMA (Application Layer Multicast Algorithm) [GE 04], are two recent overlay multicast approaches. With PAST-DM, each node implements an expanded ring search algorithm [PER 99] to become aware of neighboring member nodes. Nodes periodically exchange the link-state table with their neighbors in a non flooding manner such that, after several exchanges, a given nodes link state reaches distant nodes. Thus, by looking at each nodes link state, a node can view the entire network. PAST-DM suffers from scalability issues, considering the important overhead caused by control and measurement messages during neighbors discovery and the exchange of link state tables.

ALMA constructs a multicast tree in a decentralized and incremental way. This approach is based on RTT (Round Trip Time) measurements in order to detect and manage nodes' mobility. When periodic RTT measurements towards its parent exceed a threshold, a node has to perform a reconfiguration procedure of its delivery tree. ALMA is also based on an 'expanded ring search' technique limited by a maximum hop count, to detect neighbors. This makes ALMA running over costly positioning systems, that incur considerable amount of control traffic, and thus is more likely to contribute to the overall congestion in the network.

3   AOMP: General Description

In the following, we describe the basic model of AOMP. We have designed a topology-aware overlay multicast architecture to provide a scalable and efficient multicast distribution service to mobile ad-hoc end users. Basically, the AOMP overlay construction is divided into two processes: (1) initial connection to a *backbone Tree*, and (2) delivery tree construction and management.

The initial connection process consists in finding the closest neighbor of each newcomer. It constructs gradually the backbone tree, which is a low cost spanning tree rooted at the source node, and connecting nodes that are topologically close together. The process is based on a *path matching* algorithm that consists in matching the overlay path of a newcomer to the source, with those of other existing overlay members. Each new member of a multicast session first extracts the path (route) from the root (source as a primary sender) of the session to itself. The overlap among this path and other paths from the root is used to partially traverse the overlay data delivery tree, and determine the best parent and children for the new member. We denote the newcomer's parent in the backbone tree, the principal parent. The heuristic used in the path matching algorithm is subject to both capacity or node's fan-out (referring back to the car pooling example, space in your car) and delay (e.g., car pooling will not make the journey excessively long) constraints.

As a spanning tree uses the minimal number of links, additional links can be included in the overlay to improve the delay properties of the low cost backbone tree. The resultant mesh is degree-bounded based on each individual nodes capacity constraint (fan-out). The second process aims thus, in a first step, to derive the delivery tree from the mesh, while respecting the degree constraints of each overlay node. Figure 1 shows a sample AOMP overlay. In the figure, s is the data source and the rest of the nodes are receivers. The dashed lines define the mesh links, and the backbone and delivery tree links are shown as respectively arc and solid lines connecting a parent node to its child.

In a second step, the delivery tree management process aims to periodically refine the delivery tree links. Basically, this is done by adding/deleting links to/from the overlay using a set of local rules running at each node. The rules prioritize the minimization of

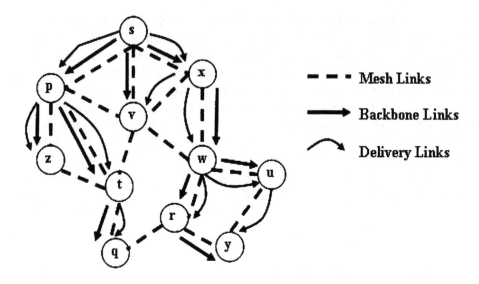

Fig. 1. Example of an overlay tree

each node subtree delay, weighted by the number of its descendants, over a greedy delay minimization of a unique node. Each add/delete link operation involves only the endpoints of the link, and requires no global coordination with other nodes in the overlay.

4   AOMP: Connection Process

The AOMP connection protocol is based on the path matching algorithm. Typically, it uses the following heuristic: a newcomer selects, as a parent in the backbone tree, the node whose shortest path from the source has maximal overlap with its own path from the source. This minimizes the increase in number of hops (and hence delay [SIK 04]) over the unicast path, and interestingly decreases the number of duplicated packets on the same physical link.

The path matching algorithm is initiated by every newcomer joining the overlay. The algorithm traverses the overlay data delivery tree to determine the best parent for a new node. The main goal is to build a tree connecting the neighboring nodes (proximity in the physical topology), i.e. the *backbone Tree* (see figure 1). In the following, we present terminology and notation to be used throughout this paper. We then describe the path matching algorithm process.

We denote the path between two nodes x and y by $P(x, y)$. It is the sequence of nodes comprising the shortest path from node x to node y according to the reactive underlying routing protocol. $|P(x, y)|$ is the number of hops in $P(x, y)$. A path $P(x, y)$ is a **prefix** of $P(x, y')$ if and only if $P(x, y)$ is included in $P(x, y')$. This property is denoted as: $P(x, y) \hookrightarrow P(x', y')$. In figure 1, $P(s, t)$ is a prefix of $P(s, q)$.

The path matching algorithm is a decentralized process that determines the overlay node, y that shares the longest path prefix (from the source) with the newcomer, x. In other words, the algorithm has to search for y satisfying:

$$(P(s,y) \hookrightarrow P(s,x)) \; and \; \nexists \, z \, , P(s,z) \hookrightarrow P(s,x), such that \, |P(s,z)| > |P(s,y)| \tag{1}$$

Let n be a new member wishing to join a multicast session. n sends then a "Joining_Request" to s. Upon being requested, the source node s extracts its path to the newcomer, and executes the path algorithm. If s estimates itself as the principal parent of n, then the process is terminated and s answers the newcomer accordingly. Otherwise, the request, is forwarded to the child of s of which the path satisfies equation 1. The path of the newcomer to the source is piggybacked in the forwarded request. The algorithm is then processed by the overlay node that has been transmitted the (propagated) "Joining_Request", say y. The algorithm considers three mutually exclusive conditions, as depicted in figure 2.

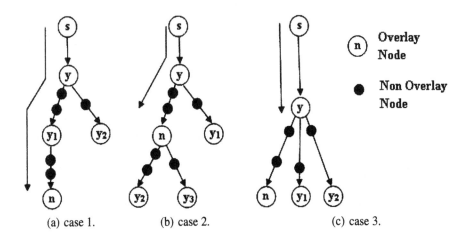

(a) case 1.   (b) case 2.   (c) case 3.

Fig. 2. The three cases for the path matching

If possible, node y selects, one of its children y_i, such as $P(y, y_i)$ is the longest prefix of $P(y, n)$. If such a child exists, the algorithm proceeds to traverse the sub-tree rooted by y_i (Case 1 in figure 2(a)). Otherwise, if there are children y_i of y such that the path of n is a prefix of those of y_i for some i, n becomes a child of y with y_i as its children (Case 2 in figure 2(b)). In case no child of y satisfying the first or second conditions exists, n becomes a child of y (Case 3 in figure 2(c)). It is important to note that no more than one child of y satisfying the first condition can exist, since the algorithm searches for the node corresponding for the longest path matching. The "Joining_Request" is then propagated on a unique subtree rooted by a unique child.

Next, we describe the multicast delivery tree management protocol. We specifically discuss the following issues with regards to AOMP:

– Creating and maintaining the multicast tree, i.e. member joins and data distribution.
– Improving efficiency by run-time refinements in mobile scenarios or when members experienced poor performances.
– Ensuring packet level reliability during reconfigurations and mobility.

5 AOMP: Tree Management Process

After the connection process terminates, a newcomer connects to its principal parent in the backbone tree. It is important to notice that at this stage, connection to the backbone tree does not consider any capacity constraints. This allows to define for each newcomer its closest node in the backbone tree, and delay fan-out constraints to its process of connection to the delivery tree. This process starts by constructing a mesh structure from which the delivery tree would be derived.

Maintaining a mesh has several advantages over maintaining only the delivery tree structure. First, a mesh topology consists of multiple paths to the data source, and hence is more robust than a tree structure which can be partitioned even with a single node failure. The multiple paths property is also useful for the overlay optimization. The routing protocol also automatically handles the potential looping problem in distributed tree maintenance[1]. Next, we provide a description of the AOMP mesh structure, and how the newcomer joins the mesh.

5.1 The Mesh Structure

The backbone tree, constructed during the connection process, constitutes the main skeleton of the mesh. This structure is ever since added with additional links to evolute towards a mesh connecting each newcomer to not only its principal parent (or one of its descendants as described in section 5.2), but also to a few specific nodes that may improve the delay properties of the delivery tree. Adding such links is established as follows: as soon as a newcomer connects to its principal parent, it is informed of the addresses of its grand parent as well as those of its uncles. The newcomer then establishes connections with theses considered nodes, constituting the mesh links. Specifically, two nodes are said to have a neighboring (or peering) relationship when the overlay link between them exists in the constructed mesh. The link may appear in one or both or none of the backbone and delivery trees.

5.2 Joining the Mesh

The connection process terminates when the path matching algorithm is executed by the principal parent of a newcomer. The principal parent sends then a response message to the "Joining_Request" of the newcomer. The response includes position of the newcomer according to the three path matching cases described above. It also contains the principal parent acceptance or not in the delivery tree, as a child. If it is not accepted, the list of the parent's children in the delivery tree is transmitted to the newcomer, "Join_DeliveryTree" messages will be transmitted to each descendant recursively until it can be attached to the delivery tree. Thus, despite the path matching-based connection process that allows the newcomer to detect the closest node in the underlying topology, that one can yield its position in case its principal parent has not the capacity to connect it to the delivery tree (fan-out constraints). Indeed, all the children of a unique principal parent are worth in terms of the metric number of hops. A newcomer will then concede

---

[1] In [FRA 00], Francis et al. provide a detailed discussion on the looping problem in an overlay tree.

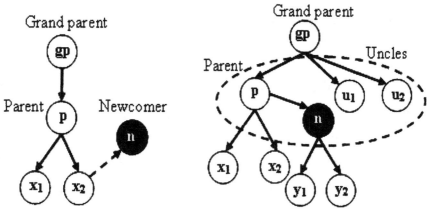

(a) Fan-out constraints prevent full adaptabil-
ity to underlying topology: non adapted delivery tree.

(b) Local search scope for node n.

Fig. 3. Run-time refinements example

its position in the delivery tree to other overlay nodes that already exist. Figure 3(a)
illustrates the case where the newcomer does not connect in the delivery tree to its principal parent, but to the child x_2. The refinement procedure will allow it thereafter to go
up in the tree, if ever it acquires a superior weight in the delivery tree, as and when few
nodes connect to it or if its performance impose that, as described in the next paragraph.

5.3 Delivery Tree Refinement

We described above how refinements are necessary for nodes that conceded their positions in the delivery tree, due to capacity constraints. The refinement procedure is
also important to reorganize the overlay due to the changes in the overlay memberships
(when members join, leave or fail) and in the underlying network conditions.

State at an AOMP node. During data transmission, each node is able to maintain its
current latency, denoted L_i induced by the overlay routing from the delivery tree source,
s. It is computed as the difference between transmission and reception time stamps of
data packets. Based on the latency time, each node i estimates its weight w_i in the
delivery tree. Typically, a node weight is the sum of latencies of all its descendants to
their parents. We notice that a high value of a node's weight implies that the subtree
rooted by this node is poorly served in the delivery tree. In other words, this indicates
that the subtree members suffer from a significant increase of transmission delay. The
weight is computed as:

$$w_i = L_i + \sum_{j \in Children(i)} w_j \qquad (2)$$

where w_l, denoting the weight of a leaf node l is equal to its latency L_f. Equation 2
implies that the computation of node's weight is decentralized and recursively transmitted from the children to their respective parents. Moreover, the weight information

is shared between each parent and their children, through "Keep Alive" messages used for the overlay maintenance. In this paper, we will not focus on the mechanisms of maintenance well studied in previous works.

Which node is concerned by the refinement, and when? Refinement procedures are periodically executed by all overlay nodes, except the source. However, the setting of the refinement interval represents a trade-off between the overhead and the accuracy of the delivery tree. To be conservative, by default a node executes a refinement procedure only once every 1200 received data packets (approximately every 5 minutes). However, we use a more aggressive strategy for nodes that concede their position, returned by the connection process, in the delivery tree. Actually, this type of nodes execute the refinement procedure once per 60 seconds, during the 5 first minutes. The refinement procedure is triggered for further reasons, such as drastic change in the network topology, nodes failures, etc. Each node that is concerned by the refinement, estimates its performance while substituting itself to one randomly selected node in its search scope. The latter is composed of the node's parent and uncles, as depicted by figure 3(b).

Refinement decisions. Once a node i selects a node in its local search scope, say j, it computes what would be its potential weight, it connects directly to its grand parent, gp. The potential weight is computed as follows:

$$w_i^{potential} = w_i + (N_i + 1) \cdot [d(gp, i) - d(i, j) - d(j, gp)] \qquad (3)$$

where N_i is the number of nodes in the subtree rooted by i. Node i sends then this information to node j, as a "Refinement_Request" message. Upon receiving such request, node j considers henceforth its weight while eliminating the subtree rooted by i, $w'_j = w_j - w_i$. Requested node j computes then its potential weight if ever it yields its position in the delivery tree to the requesting node i:

$$w_j^{potential} = w'_j + (N_j - N_i) \cdot [d(gp, i) + d(i, j) - d(gp, j)] \qquad (4)$$

The substitution is processed (and accepted by node j) only if the potential weight of the requesting node i is greater than to the potential weight computed by the requested node j: $w_i^{potential} > w_j^{potential}$.

5.4   Adaptation to Mobility of Nodes

In an ad-hoc environment, it is necessary that the delivery tree adapts to mobility of nodes. A basic adaptation in the AOMP overlay, would result in periodic operations to check if paths to the source have changed or not. An initial connection process would be imposed to the concerned nodes. Nevertheless, such a mechanism may incur high overhead, as well as eventual overload of the source.

We propose a mechanism that allows intermediary overlay nodes (in the path of each node to the source), to take part in the detection of mobility and reconnection to the backbone tree and thus to the delivery tree. First, this would induce less overhead and less sollicitation of the source. Second, the adaptation process would be faster, while relying on the first overlay node that is aware of the topology change due to mobility.

Our mechanism exploits yet another time path information provided by the underlying reactive routing protocol. In fact, we use the route maintenance, automatically (and continuously) processed by the routing protocol, that detects any route changes, caused by nodes mobility. The route to the source change in the routing layer triggers a procedure of adaptation to mobility at the application level. The basic idea is to proceed locally with a connection to the backbone tree in a first step, then reconfigure links of the delivery tree. Let us take the example of the figure 1, and suppose that node w moves towards node v in a way that $P(s, w)$ changes. This change will be noticed at the level of not only the routing layer of w, but also of its parent x, since the latter maintains IP addresses as well as routes to its children, during data transmission. First, x verifies the impact of such movement. Typically, it checks in the new path generated by its child movement, whether it contains at least an overlay node in its neighborhood or not. If no such nodes exist, x reconfigures only its IP path to its child w without imposing any change in overlay structure. Otherwise, connections to the backbone tree are carried out by both w and its children. The request to reconnect to the backbone tree is imposed by x to w, which forwards the request to its children. Reconnection to the backbone differs from the initial connection, in the fact that it is local and is initiated at the first overlay node met in the new path (v in our example for a reconnection of w). Like the initial connection, the reconnection to the backbone applies the path matching algorithm, with v as a source, rather than s. It is finally important to note that the delivery tree is modified only when all connections of w and its children are established in the backbone tree.

6 Performance Evaluation of AOMP

We evaluate the performance of AOMP by carrying out various simulation studies. AOMP is based on both DSR [JOH 03] and AODV [PER 99], as underlying routing protocols, and is denoted respectively AOMP-DSR and AOMP-AODV. For AODV, we extract from the routing tables, the source route accumulation (feature of DSR) to run the path matching algorithm.

We performed simulations to provide quantitative performance analysis according to group members in terms of packet delivery ratio, control overhead as well as average end-to-end delay. We also observe the behavior of AOMP in case of mobility of nodes.

We compared AOMP to both ALMA [GE 04] and PAST-DM [GUI 03] as overlay multicast approaches. For reference purpose, we also compare it to an IP-layer multicast protocol: the On-Demand Multicast Routing Protocol, namely ODMRP [LEE 02]. The detailed parameters on each protocol are described in Table 1.

6.1 Simulation Model and Performance Metrics

The simulation model was built around the NS-2.28 [CAN 04] simulator. Our simulation models a network of 140 mobile nodes placed randomly within a 1000×1000 meters square area. By varying the group size, we vary the percentage of mobile nodes that are involved in the multicast session. The simulation duration is 900 seconds. Each node has a transmission range of 200 meters and channel capacity is 2Mbit/sec. The mobility model follows random waypoint model which has 50 seconds as pause time.

Table 1. Simulation parameters over each protocol

Protocol	Parameter	value
PAST-DM	The period of virtual link exchange	15s
ALMA	Tree reconfiguration period	20s
ODMRP	Interval between join query floods	3s
	Duration of group forwarding state	10s

The minimum speed is 0 m/s and the maximum speed is set to 20 m/s. For the experiments for which no group size is specified a default size of 50 group members is used. A default node's speed of 2 m/s is set as a default mobility parameter. Traffic is generated as constant bit rate (4 packets/second) and packet size is set to 512 kbytes. Nodes fan-out is uniformly distributed in [2..20]. Finally, we use IEEE 802.11 DCF as MAC protocol. The following metrics are studied for comparing protocol performances:

1. **Delivery Tree cost:** The total number of the physical links that make up the logical links in the multicast delivery tree. This metric represents the "goodness" of the structure created by the overlay multicast.
2. **Stress:** The stress of a physical link is the number of identical copies of a multicast packet that needs to traverse the link. This metric quantifies the efficiency of the overlay multicast scheme.
3. **Average Relative Delay Penalty (ARDP):** The relative delay penalty is the relative increase in delay between the source and an overlay member against unicast delay between the source and the same member. ARDP is then the average ratio between the overlay delay (d') and the shortest path delay in the underlying network (d) from s to all other nodes: $\frac{1}{N-1}\sum_{i=1}^{N-1}\frac{d'(s,i)}{d(s,i)}$, where N is the number of nodes in the overlay. This metric is used to quantify the relative cost of routing on the overlay.
4. **Control Overhead:** The number of control packets for delivering per data packet. It includes in AOMP the number of all control packets generated by path matching during the connection to the backbone tree, establishing connections in the delivery tree and refinements. This metric evaluates the cost of the overlay structure according to the overlay goodput.
5. **Data Delivery Ratio:** The ratio of the number of packets actually delivered to the receivers versus the number of data packets that were expected. This metric is used to quantify the reliability of the multicast protocol.

6.2 Performance Analysis

In the following, we detail our simulation results and provide explanations of the observed behavior.

AOMP creates a less expensive delivery tree than PAST-DM and ALMA. Our proposed protocol constructs a multicast delivery tree with a lower cost in terms of physical

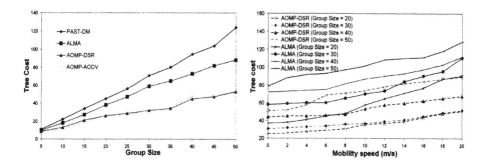

Fig. 4. Tree Cost versus the Group Size   **Fig. 5.** Tree cost var according to mobility

hop counts than PAST-DM and ALMA. In figure 4 , we plot the tree cost versus the size of the group. We observe that AOMP (AOMP-DSR and AOMP-AODV) achieves delivery trees with an average cost of 42.8 for a group size of 50, i.e. 1.5 to 2.5 less than PAST-DM and ALMA. First, we attribute the difference between PAST-DM and both ALMA and AOMP to the "locally-adaptive" nature of these two protocols. Indeed, PAST-DM creates a logical tree in somewhat centralized way; the decisions of any node transmitting data (considered as a source) affect the creation of the tree globally. In both ALMA and AOMP, the reconfigurations are handled by the receivers, and these local decisions turn out to respond more efficiently to the effects of mobility, and topology changes in case of group membership variation. Second, we observe that AOMP scales better than ALMA. In fact, the ALMA tree cost increases drastically to more than 80 physical links making up the overlay links. This demonstrates that ALMA does not scale to tens of overlay members. AOMP has almost a constant tree cost with a maximum of 51 for AOMP supported by the AODV protocol. Topology information is of paramount importance in this observation, as data packets in AOMP are sent through the shortest path defined by the underlying routing protocol. This fact makes the AOMP overlay structure maps the routing (physical) structure that packets would be guided through anyway. Exploiting this information allow then to build the delivery tree at a minimum cost. In figure 5, we observe the tree cost as a function of mobility speed, for both AOMP-DSR and ALMA. While tree cost is expected to increase with mobility speed, this simulation shows how far a protocol could adapt to mobility. For AOMP, we observe that the tree cost increases "smoothly" while this value drastically reaches high values for ALMA. The ALMA tree cost is 91 for a group size of 20 nodes, under high mobility, which oversteps the tree cost of a 50 nodes group in AOMP. The latter is less affected by mobility and continues to construct less expensive trees, as and when nodes are moving due to its reliance on the routing protocol to detect and extract the new path of the mobile node.

The path matching algorithm of AOMP avoids "useless" packet duplications. Figure 6 shows average physical network stress for each of the overlays, namely PAST-DM, ALMA and AOMP supported by DSR and AODV. The average stress in this simulation is tracked 2 minutes after the last node joined the overlay. The average stress observed in a delivery tree constructed by AOMP is much smaller than those with ALMA and

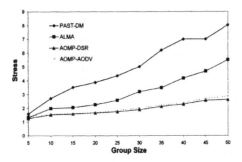

Fig. 6. Average Stress versus the Group Size

PAST-DM. This value stabilizes for AOMP between 2.62 and 2.88 for a group size of 50 members, while it exceeds 5 and 8 for other overlays. Besides the difference that may exist between AOMP-DSR and AOMP-AODV, the results show the efficiency of the path matching algorithm that avoids redundant packets over the same physical links, by binding overlay nodes according to their proximity. Consequently, the possibility of bottlenecks are much lower in AOMP, than in PAST-DM or ALMA. We attribute the slight difference between AOMP-DSR and AOMP-AODV to the fact that while both routing protocols share the on-demand behavior in that they initiate routing activities only in the presence of data packets in need of a route, many of their routing mechanics are very different. In particular, DSR uses source routing, whereas AODV uses a table-driven routing framework and destination sequence numbers. The shortest path extracted by AOMP to be exploited in the path matching algorithm is then different from DSR to AODV. However, the simulation prove that for both cases, AOMP is able to reduce considerably the amount of redundant flows traversing the ad-hoc network, demonstrating the efficiency of the path matching algorithm heuristic.

AOMP achieves a much better $ARDP$ as compared to PAST-DM and ALMA. We characterize the average incurred delay observed by the receivers in a large populated overlay by observing the $ARDP$ variation according to the overlay size in figure 7. In PAST-DM, the $ARDP$ value increases drastically to more than 6 demonstrating that this protocol does not scale to a few number of nodes. We note also that ALMA has lower $ARDP$ than the PAST-DM delivery tree, but suffers relatively poor performance with $ARDP \geq 5.5$ in a 50-nodes overlay. AOMP, for both DSR and AODV as underlying routing protocol, maintains a stable $ARDP$ value while the overlay size is increasing. Thanks to the topology awareness of this protocol, $ARDP$ values are roughly maintained between 1.2 and 2.8.

AOMP incurs low control overhead. We ran simulations to evaluate the control overhead in the overlay and analyse the protocol behavior under dynamic ad-hoc overlay. We assumed a basic header size of 40 bytes per IP-packet and we measured the overall control message traffic sent and received by each node throughout a session. Figure 8 shows the average overhead per node when varying the speed of nodes. Additional messages cost increases with mobility of nodes, particulary with PAST-DM. Recall that

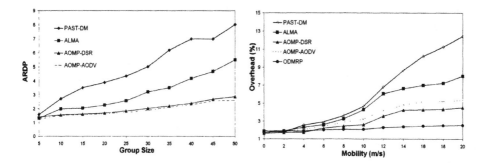

Fig. 7. Average Relative Delay Penalty property **Fig. 8.** Control overhead as function of mobility versus the Group Size

PAST-DM creates a logical Steiner tree in a somewhat centralized way; the decisions at the source affect the creation of the tree globally and generate an important cost of control messages. ALMA has a less important additional cost that PAST-DM but more important than AOMP when mobility increases (twice more control overhead messages). The periodic measurements processed by ALMA nodes to know their RTT towards their parent and neighbors make ALMA less efficient than AOMP in terms of control overhead. By relying on the path matching mechanism, AOMP generates lower control trafic. In fact, exploiting path information provided by either DSR or AODV ensures that no costly end-to-end measurements are exchanged and thus alleviates nodes overhead. AOMP-DSR and AOMP-AODV have almost identically shaped curves. However, the absolute overhead required by AOMP-AODV is more important than AOMP-DSR because each of its route discoveries typically propagates to every node in the ad-hoc network. AOMP-DSR sends less overhead, but bigger control packets. In ODMRP, the control overhead remains relatively constant because no updates are triggered by mobility. JOIN QUERY refresh interval was set constant to three seconds and hence no additional overhead is required as mobility increases.

AOMP is reliable. Figure 9 illustrates the packet delivery ratio for different protocols as a function of varying movement speed with static group members. Since ODMRP provides redundant routes with a mesh topology, it shows good performance event in high dynamic situations. On the other hand, AOMP shows similar packets delivery ratio to ODMRP. AOMP is even more reliable in high speed scenarios (> 10m/s), with a ratio slightly decreasing from 0.8% to 0.73%. ALMA and AOMP are very close to each other when nodes are static (lower than 4m/s), but ALMA is much less reliable than AOMP when the speed exceeds 10m/s. ALMA uses the RTT metric to define closeness and to detect topology changes. This may be sufficient when nodes are static, but could lead to many losses in case of high dynamic network. AOMP detects topology changes by exploiting information provided by the routing protocol. It then reacts better. Moreover, if a mobile node moved away from its parent in the delivery tree, and cannot connect anymore to its principal parent, the delivery tree is not modified until a new principal parent has been found.

We vary the number of overlay nodes in figure 10 and observe the data delivery ratio. ODMRP is not affected by the number of multicast members. The data delivery ratio shows slightly better performance (less than 30 overlay nodes) than the case with small group members. As the number of group members increases, more redundant routes may be established, and thus many alternative paths remain available even though the primary path is broken. Similar to ODMRP, the data delivery ratio in AOMP is improved as the number of overlay nodes increases. In particular for groups were 20% to 40% of nodes are part of the multicast session, AOMP exhibits better delivery ratios. In fact, the larger the group size, the greater the probability to detect an overlay node in the path to the source is.

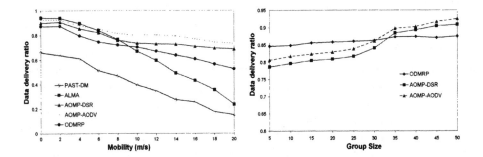

Fig. 9. Packet Delivery Ratio as function of mobility

Fig. 10. Packet Delivery Ratio as function of group size

7   Conclusion

In this paper, we proposed a new multicast overlay construction for mobile ad-hoc networks, named AOMP. Based on a path matching algorithm that is underlying routing-aware, the protocol consists in a first step to connect the closest nodes in a backbone tree. An efficient delivery tree is then generated. Run-time refinements are processed during data distribution to adapt to both underlying network and membership changes, and to optimize the overlay performance. The overlay construction process includes also mechanisms to adapt to ad-hoc nodes mobility in a smooth and reliable manner. We carry out simulations to quantify our protocol performance and demonstrate that AOMP outperforms previously proposed overlay schemes. Our main findings prove that exploiting path information at the connection process, allows AOMP to be highly efficient by creating low cost delivery trees and avoiding useless packet duplication without inducing high overhead. Furthermore, AOMP is reliable, achieving promising delivery ratios in case of high mobility scenarios. Our future works consist first in adapting our connection process to different routing protocols, in particular to proactive protocols. The idea is to extract recursively routing information from overlay members tables, exploit it to gradually get a local view of the newcomer and locate it. In a second step, we will focus on designing mechanisms to pro-actively manage nodes mobility in the overlay, using mobility prediction models.

References

[BAS 00]   BASAGNI S., ET AL., *On-Demand Location Aware Multicast (OLAM) for Ad Hoc Networks*, Proceedings of IEEE Wireless Communications and Networking Conference (WCNC), Chicago, 2000.

[CAN 04]   MCCANNE S., ET AL., *NS network simulator*, http://www.isi.edu/nsnam/ns/, 2004.

[CHE 02]   CHEN K., NAHRSTEDT K., *Effective Location - Guided Tree Construction Algorithm for Small Group Multicast in MANET*, Proceedings of IEEE Infocom'02, 2002.

[CHI 98]   CHIANG C., GERLA M., ZHANG L., *Forwarding group multicast protocol (FGMP) for multihop mobile wireless networks*, Proceedings of Cluster Computing, 1998.

[DEV 01]   DEVARAPALLI V., SIDHU D., *MZR: A multicast protocol for mobile ad hoc networks*, Proceedings of IEEE International Conference on Communications, 2001.

[FRA 00]   FRANCIS P., *Yoid Tree Management Protocol (YTMP) Specification*, Technical report, AT&T Center for Internet Research at ICSI (ACIRI), 2000.

[GAR 99]   GARCIA-LUNA-ACEVES J.J., ET AL., *The Core-Assisted Mesh Protocol*, Proceedings of IEEE Journal on Selected Areas in Communications, 1999.

[GE 04]   GE M., ET AL., *Overlay multicasting for ad hoc networks*, Proceedings of Third Annual Mediterranean Ad Hoc Networking Workshop, 2004.

[GUI 03]   GUI C., MOHAPATRA P., *Efficient Overlay Multicast for Mobile ad-hoc Networks*, Proceedings of IEEE WCNC, 2003.

[JET 01]   JETCHEVA J., JOHNSON D. B., *Adaptive Demand-Driven Multicast Routing in Multi-Hop Wireless Ad Hoc Networks*, Proceedings of the Second Symposium on Mobile Ad Hoc Networking and Computing, 2001.

[JI 01]   JI L., CORSON S., *Differential Destination Multicast–A MANET Multicast Routing Protocol for Small Groups*, Proceedings of IEEE INFOCOM, 2001.

[JOH 03]   JOHNSON D.B., ET AL., *The Dynamic Source Routing Protocol for Mobile ad-hoc Networks (DSR)*, draft IETF MQNET 2003.

[LEE99]   LEE S.J., GERLA M., CHIANG C.-C., *On Demand Multicast Routing Protocol*, Proceedings of IEEE WCNC99, pp. 1298-1302, September 1999.

[LEE 02]   LEE S.J., ET AL., *On-Demand Multicast Routing Protocol in Multihop Wireless Mobile Networks*, ACM/Baltzer Mobile Networks and Applications, Proceedings of Communications in Wireless Mobile Networks, 2002.

[PAT 03]   PATRICK J.L., EUGSTER T., *Route driven gossip: Probabilistic reliable multicast in ad hoc networks*, Proceedings of IEEEINFOCOM, 2003.

[PER 99]   PERKINS E. AND ROYER E.M., *Ad hoc on-demand distance vector routing*, In Proceedings of the 2nd IEEE Workshop on Mobile Computing Systems and Applications, pages 90100, Feb 1999.

[ROG 99]   ROYER E., PERKINS C.E., *Multicast Operations of the Ad-hoc On-Demand Distance Vector Routing Protocol*, Proceedings of ACM/IEEE MOBICOM'99, 1999.

[SIK 04]   SIKORA M., ET AL., *On the Optimum Number of Hops in Linear Wireless Networks*, Proceedings of IEEE Information Theory Workshop, San Antonio, 2004.

Next Generation Network Service Architecture in the IP Multimedia Subsystem

Anahita Gouya, Noël Crespi, and Lina Oueslati

Institut National des Télécommunications (GET-INT)
9 rue Charles Fourier, 91011 Evry, France
{anahita.gouya, noel.crespi, lina.oueslati}@int-evry.fr

Abstract. The objective of this research work is to provide the IP Multimedia Subsystem of UMTS with a SIP-based mechanism for managing the interaction, composition and reuse of a limited number of standardized Service Capabilities in order to develop the Next Generation Network (NGN) services. The service invocation mechanism that we propose in this paper is extensible to deal with the interaction and composition management of a wide range of NGN services.

Keywords: Service Capability Interaction Management, Service Architecture, SIP, IMS, NGN.

1 Introduction

NGN supports a wide range of services varying from real time and interactive multimedia services (audio & video telephony, conferencing, Instant Messaging, Presence and Location based services) to non-interactive (multimedia streaming and Push services) and web (e-commerce, e-learning, and e-medicine) services.

The convergence of the "*vertically integrated networks*" (where for each kind of services (data, audio and video) a specific network is considered) to a "*horizontally integrated network*" that offers a unique network infrastructure is one of the foremost advantages brought by NGN [9]. The principles, characteristics and issues of NGN are studied in [12, 13 and 14].

The 3GPP (3rd Generation Partnership Project) open IP-based infrastructure, IP Multimedia Subsystem (IMS) [1], that uses Session Initiation Protocol (SIP) [6] as signalling protocol, is an emerging but recognized standardization effort for supporting the service convergence over the heterogeneous networks.

Realizing the service convergence paradigm by IMS enables service providers to offer enhanced NGN services to their users.

As presented in figure 1, IMS contains a horizontally integrated service architecture where the service and control layers are separated.

Besides, one of the goals of IMS is to design its service layer in a way of enabling the creation of innovative services by integrating existing service building blocks. In other words, IMS offers the elementary and standardized service building blocks that

K. Cho and P. Jacquet (Eds.): AINTEC 2006, LNCS 4311, pp. 48 – 60, 2006.

can be reused by different application servers to enrich their services. Sharing these service building blocks reduces the time-to-market of services.

However enabling this reuse and share of the service building blocks by application servers and managing the integration and composition of these service building blocks necessitates the introduction of a service composition and interaction manager mechanism.

In this paper we propose a service invocation mechanism that ensures the development of NGN services in IMS by enabling the integration of different service building blocks. Furthermore, we present in detail the functional and architectural aspects of this proposition and we discuss about the requirements and the technical approaches proposed for developing the NGN services.

The rest of this paper is structured as follows:

In the next section, after outlining standardized service invocation mechanism in IMS, we present our proposed IMS service invocation mechanism that is based on the introduction of a service controller between the session control and the service layer of IMS.

The introduction of this service controller necessitates precise functional and architectural considerations. We highlight the functional aspects of our proposal in this section.

Section 3 gives an overview of the architectural aspects including the mechanisms to be defined for the service controller in order to control the access to the service building blocks and to manage the integration of the services.

A use case, of our proposition is presented in section 4. Finally we conclude this paper by presenting the advantages of the proposed service invocation mechanism and discussing about the reaming development issues of the NGN services in IMS.

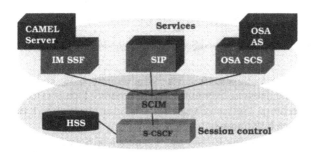

Fig. 1. The Horizontally Integrated Architecture of IMS

2 Service Invocation in IMS

In this section after explaining the already specified service invocation mechanism in IMS, we introduce our proposed service invocation mechanism and we present the functional aspects of this proposal.

2.1 3GPP Service Invocation Mechanism

In IMS, as presented in figure 1, services are invoked through a SIP server in the session control layer called: Serving Call Session Control Function (S-CSCF). S-CSCF is the functional entity of IMS that performs the session control and service triggering.

IMS services may be hosted by SIP Application Servers (AS), Open Service Access (OSA) AS (through OSA-Service Capability Server (OSA-SCS)) and CAMEL servers (Customized Application for the Mobile network Enhanced Logic) (through IP Multimedia Service Switching Function (IM-SSF)).

All of the three types of the AS hosted in the service layer of IMS (SIP AS, OSA SCS and IM-SSF) behave as SIP AS over the SIP-based interface ISC (IP Multimedia Service Control) and S-CSCF invokes them without disposing any functional description of these ASs: S-CSCF knows ASs only by their names/addresses.

2.2 Proposed Service Invocation Mechanism

Figure 2 illustrates the functional vision of our proposition, where we define a boundary between the Network Operator (NO) domain and the third party Service Provider(s) (SP) domain(s).

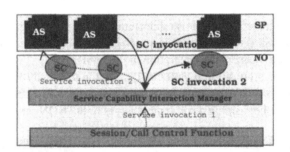

Fig. 2. Proposed Service Invocation Mechanism

Based on this proposition different service providers share and reuse the service building blocks of the network operator in order to enrich their services.

3GPP uses the term of "Service Capability" (SC) for referring to these modular and self contained service building blocks.

Presence [4] and Messaging [5] are two examples of Service Capabilities that can be reused in the creation of integrated service such as voicemail.

On the one hand, reusing Service Capabilities enables network operators to offer a multitude of unique services with rich personalisation possibilities to their users (depending on the schedule, preferences, terminal capabilities, location and presence information of the user) and on the other hand it offers service providers the possibility of implementing rich services.

However even if Service Capabilities are relatively stable and that their implementation obey the standard specifications, providing the possibility of reusing Service Capabilities of IMS for offering enriched services to users reclaims precise service interaction management.

Although Open Service Access (OSA) [3] provides the glue between services by means of open standardized Application Programming Interfaces, it can not be regarded as an optimal answer to the service interaction management needs in IMS, while, OSA has not been developed specifically for IMS and therefore "adapting" OSA to IMS will lead to complex and costly solutions that can be simplified out of OSA scope.

Hence, In order to deal with this issue, we propose a service composition management mechanism that is an alternative to the already existing IT based mechanisms. This management consists of controlling the access of different Application Server(s) to the Service Capabilities and preventing the violation of the confidentiality of the user information. Contrary to the existing mechanisms, our proposition is SIP based and adaptable for IMS.

In this proposition we enable IMS with a SIP-based service composition manager by using the SIP AS Service Capability Interaction Manager (SCIM) of IMS (illustrated in figure 1).

SCIM is initially introduced by 3GPP for managing the interactions between application servers. But the service interaction management functionalities of SCIM are not specified.

We propose to use the SIP AS SCIM for managing the interaction between services in order to ensure the coherency of our proposed SIP-based service composition management with the SIP-based service invocation mechanism of IMS.

As presented in figure 1, we consider SCIM as an entity between the session control layer and the service layer of IMS that provides among other functionalities [10,11] a uniform Service Capability access mechanism for AS(s).

3 Architectural and Technical Aspects of the Proposed Service Invocation Mechanism

The introduction of SCIM between the session control layer and the service layer requires the definition of a relation model between SCIM and its surrounding entities. In this section we will first discuss about the constraints for defining this relation model and then we present the technical approaches of this relation model by indicating the exact proposed mechanisms.

3.1 Architectural Aspects

Defining a model that presents the relation of SCIM with its surrounding entities i.e. S-CSCF, AS/SC and HSS is faced to the following two constraints:

Constraints for defining the relation model of SCIM
I. S-CSCF needs the address of SCIM:
When S-CSCF receives an initial request, it checks iFCs (presented in figure 4) in the order given by their priorities. If the Trigger Point of an iFC is met, the corresponding AS will be invoked.

According to the specifications, S-CSCF should forward the request to the AS and waits for an answer. But as in this proposition we add SCIM in the service invocation path, the request must be first forwarded to SCIM. Hence, the address of SCIM must be available for S-CSCF.

II. SCIM needs the service composition information for controlling SC access:
Using a SC by a service must be based on the agreement performed between the network operator and the service provider. This agreement indicates the necessary information that SCIM needs for managing the service composition. Hence, SCIM as an intermediate between Application Server and Service Capability must be provided with this service composition information.

Solution for Defining the Relation Model of SCIM
One possible solution to the first issue is to associate one SCIM to one S-CSCF. Therefore, once S-CSCF needs to invoke an AS according to the service profile of the user, it forwards the incoming request to AS by passing it through the known SCIM.

According to this solution, the service composition information related to each AS to be invoked from one S-CSCF, will be saved over the SCIM associated to the S-CSCF. Therefore the service composition information of *one* AS may be available over *many* SCIMs (each SCIM that invokes the AS will contain this information) resulting redundancy of the service composition information over multiple SCIMs.

In order to prevent the dispersion of service composition information all over the network, we propose to associate one SCIM to one (or more) AS(s). Based on this proposition, each AS has one unique SCIM that could "serve it". Therefore all the requests destined to this AS from any S-CSCF passes through this unique SCIM. This association is presented in the diagram of figure 3:

Fig. 3. Proposed AS-SCIM Association

However, this association doesn't solve the problem of SCIM address availability to S-CSCF. This issue can be resolved by providing HSS with a dynamic AS-SCIM association. Although this proposition ensures the service availability; but enabling such a dynamic SCIM discovery procedure is very complex, costly and heavy to manage. Moreover introducing a supplementary transaction (SCIM/HSS interface) for SCIM address discovery at each AS invocation request; increases the service invocation process time.

Therefore faced to the compromises regarding in the one hand the *service availability* and on the other hand the *service invocation time-span*, we have more preferences to focus on the time constraints rather than ensuring the dynamic service availability.

Based on this preference we propose the following modifications to the current service invocation mechanism of IMS in order to provide the address of SCIM to S-CSCF:

1. Modifying the content of iFC (illustrated in figure 4):
The Application Server class of iFC contains zero or one instance of the Service Information class that is initially defined to enable the transparent information transferring to AS. We propose to use the "Service Information" class to indicate the

AS to be invoked and the "Application Service" class to indicate the SCIM associated to this AS.

Therefore the address of SCIM is given to S-CSCF at the same time as the name/address of AS (i.e. at the user profile retrieving phase).

2. Introducing the supplementary routing functionalities over S-CSCF in order to route the message first to SCIM and then to AS.

Following to the proposed SCIM-AS association, the second constraint (i.e. defining the service composition information format and providing SCIM with this information) can be resolved by introducing an "**Application Server – User**" analogy.

In other words, as in the case of user subscription procedure to IMS a *user profile* is created and saved in HSS [2], we propose that the Application Server subscription to the use of one or more Service Capabilities be represented by a template called: *Service Capability Profile (SCP)*.

This analogy is interpreted as following:

- *User subscribes for using an **Application Server**, <u>as</u> **Application Server** subscribes for using a **Service Capability**.*
- *User services are invoked based on the initial Filter Criteria (**iFC**) defined in the service profile of the user, <u>as</u> Service Capabilities are invoked based on the Service Capability Criteria (**SCC**) defined in the Service Capability Profile of an Application Server.*
- *User access to an Application Server is controlled in **iFC**, <u>as</u> Application Server access to a Service Capability is controlled in **SCC**.*
- *One **S-CSCF** is associated to one **user** and contains the service profile of the user, <u>as</u> one **SCIM** is associated to one **Application Server** and contains the Service Capability Profile of the Application Server.*
- ***S-CSCF** enables the access of the user to Application Server, <u>as</u> **SCIM** that enables the access of Application Server to Service Capability.*

This analogy is illustrated in thML diagrams of the figures 4 and 5:

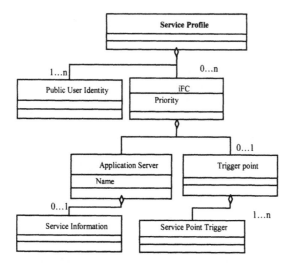

Fig. 4. IMS user Service Profile defined by 3GPP

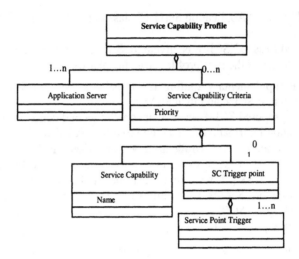

Fig. 5. Proposed Service Capability Profile of AS

At the service provisioning time, the network operator may whether store the service capability profile of an AS over the SCIM associated to this AS, or it may use the central data base of IMS, i.e. HSS, for storing this information.

Alongside with the proposed analogy between the service profile of an IMS subscriber (stored in HSS and retrieved by S-CSCF at the user registration time), and the service capability profile of an AS, we propose to store the service capability profile in HSS.

Then, once an AS is to be invoked, the SCIM associated to AS, retrieves the service capability profile of AS from HSS and stores it. This information will be used not only for service composition management of AS during the current session; but also subsequent sessions; as long as SCP related to this AS remains in the SCIM.

This solution brings the following modification to the actual IMS service invocation platform:

1) Defining SCP in HSS (at service definition time)
2) Defining the SCIM/HSS interface for SCP retrieving at the "first" AS invocation request (Sh interface can be applied)
3) Modifying the iFC as explained in 3.1 in order to include SCIM in the route from S-CSCF to AS
4) Modifying the S-CSCF service invocation mechanism by adding SCIM on the service path and introducing the supplementary routing functionalities over S-CSCF for routing the message first to SCIM and then to AS
5) Creating SCIM as a SIP AS performing the controls detailed in the next section.

3.2 Technical Aspects

In Figure 6 we present step by step the control procedures that must be performed in order to enable the management of the use of SC1 by AS1.

1. iFC Matching
On the reception of an initial SIP request, S-CSCF checks the iFCs one by one (based on their priorities) and once an iFC is matched (and that an AS must be invoked), S-CSCF forwards the SIP request to the SCIM associated to the AS to be invoked mentioned in the Application Server element of the iFC.

2. AS Activation Memorizing
By the "first" AS invocation request, SCIM retrieves the SCP related to the AS from HSS. (This information may already be available over SCIM, if the AS has been previously invoked by SCIM). Afterwards, SCIM memorizes that the AS is being activated to the Public User Identity (mentioned in the incoming SIP request). Then SCIM forwards the SIP request to the related AS.

3. Service Logic Execution
AS executes its service logic and recognizes that for continuing the execution it needs to contact a SC. From a SIP point of view AS may contact an SC in one of the two following ways:
    I. AS constructs a new SIP request that either creates a new SIP dialog with SC (e.g. SIP SUBSCRIBE request [7]), or a request being part of an existing dialog or finally of a standalone transaction (e.g. SIP MESSAGE request [8]).
    II. AS simply forwards the initial received SIP request to the SC.

4. Service Composition Control while Service Capability Criteria (SCC) Evaluation
When SCIM receives the request from AS, based on the information memorized in step 2, it checks if the AS has already been activated for the concerned public user identity or not. If not, the access to the service will be denied and SCIM sends an error message.

If this check is passed, SCIM evaluates the SCC related to the AS in order to find out based on the received request which SC should be invoked. Then, SCIM forwards the request to the SC indicated in the SCC.

As multiple AS(s) may share one SC, SC should be aware by which AS the SC invocation is asked, while in some cases we need different information to be delivered depending on the AS. In other words, without indicating the address of AS to SC, SC behaviour will be the same for any AS.

In our platform we consider that SC will be aware of the address of AS based on the address of AS that is indicated in the "From" header field of the SIP message sent from AS to SCIM.

5. Service Capability Execution
The SC executes its service and based on its behaviour answers to the SIP message:

If SC acts as Proxy server, it sends the same message back to SCIM.

If SC acts as Terminating User Agent, it finishes the incoming request by a final response.

If SC acts as Back to Back User Agent, it finishes the incoming request by a final response and creates a new request.

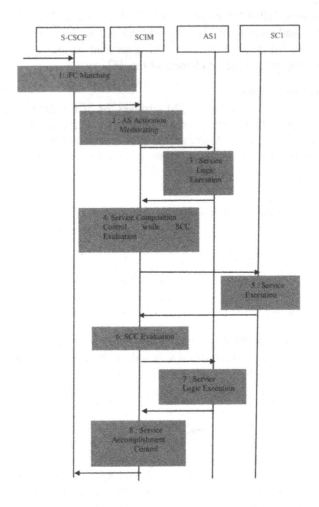

Fig. 6. Controlling the Service Capability Composition

6. Service Capability Criteria (SCC) Evaluation
Respecting the proposed SCC–iFC analogy, SCIM continues the SCC evaluation (on the reception of the SIP message from SC) in order to invoke other SCs if needed. Once all the SCCs are evaluated, the request is sent back to the AS. As SCIM and SC are in the same operator's domain (i.e. SC is a trusted entity and is supposed to behave correctly) SCIM will not control the interactions from SC to AS.

7. Service Logic Execution
Based on the service logic in AS, whether it requests the invocation of another SC (repeating from step 4) or terminates its service execution.

8. Service Accomplishment Control
Based on the received message from AS, SCIM verifies the SCC and recognizes that SC invocation is terminated and therefore it sends the message back to S-CSCF.

4 Use Case

In this section we present an example in which a Presence (PS) service capability is reused by a Chatting (Chat) and a Conferencing (Conf) application server.
In figure 7, we suppose that: User B is in chat list and conference list of user A; A invites B to a conference, but B is not available for the conference; therefore A invites B to a chat. The description of each step is as follows:

1. A invites B to a conference.

2. S-CSCF receives an initial request (Invite) and after iFC evaluation it recognizes that the Conference Server (Conf) must be invoked. S-CSCF forwards the request to the SCIM associated to Conf indicated in the Application Server class of iFC.

3. SCIM memorizes that Conf is being activated for the public user identity of A. Then SCIM retrieves the SCP related to Conf from HSS (if not already locally available), and forwards the request to Conf.

4. Conf performs its service logic and recognizes that for continuing the execution it needs to contact PS. Conf constructs a Subscribe request in order to get the presence information of B, sends the request to SCIM and waits for the answer.

5. When SCIM receives the request, it controls if Conf has already been activated for A or not. If the check is passed, SCIM evaluates the SCC and recognizes that it has to forward the request to PS.

6,7. PS executes its service logic and terminates the Subscribe request by a 200 OK response that will follow the request path i.e. SCIM and Conf.

8. Also PS creates a Notify request that contains the presence information of B in the body part. This information is related to the Conf address that SCIM had supplied in the incoming Subscribe request to PS.

9. On the reception of the answer (Notify) from PS, SCIM continues the SCC evaluation in order to invoke other SCs if needed. In this example we suppose that no other SCs are to be invoked, therefore SCIM sends back the Notify to Conf.

10. Based on the service logic and the presence information of B, Conf recognizes that the service execution is accomplished. Hence it creates an appropriate answer (that terminates the Invite request received at step 3) and forwards it to SCIM. In this example, according to the presence information of B indicating "Don't disturb" in the note element of the body part, Conf decides to abort the session and sends back an error final response (Busy).

11. SCIM receives SIP answer related to the first SIP Dialog (created by the initial Invite request) and forwards it to S-CSCF according to the Via header.

12. S-CSCF sends the request to A.

13. Now, A invites B to a chat.

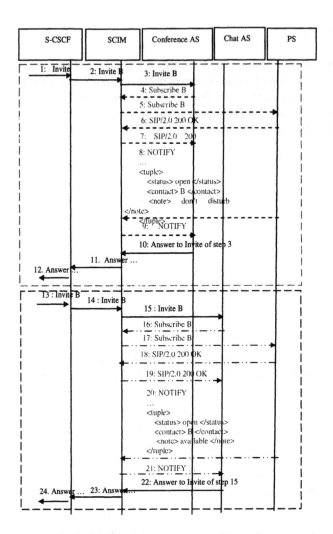

Fig. 7. Presence Service Capability (PS) shared in Chatting and Conferencing Application Servers (AS)

14. S-CSCF evaluates the iFC and it recognizes that the Chat AS must be invoked. S-CSCF retrieves the address of the SCIM associated to Chat from HSS and forwards the request to the discovered SCIM. (We suppose that same SCIM is serving Conf and Chat servers).

15. SCIM memorizes that Chat is being activated for the public user identity of A. Then it retrieves the SCP related to Chat from HSS (if not already locally available) and forwards the request to Chat.

16. Chat performs its service logic and recognizes that for continuing the execution it needs to contact PS. The Chat server constructs a Subscribe request in order to get the presence information of B. Then it sends the request to SCIM and waits for the answer.

17. When SCIM receives the request, it controls if Chat has already been activated for A or not. If the check is passed, SCIM evaluates the SCC and recognizes that it has to forward the request to PS.

18-19. PS executes its service logic and terminates the Subscribe request by a 200 OK response that will follow the request path i.e. SCIM and Chat available in the Via header.

20. Also PS creates a Notify request that contains the presence information of B in the body part indicating that B is "available" for Chat.

21. On the reception of the answer (Notify) from PS, SCIM continues the SCC evaluation in order to invoke other SCs if needed. In this example we suppose that no other SCs are to be invoked, therefore it sends back the answer to Chat.

22. Based on the presence information of B, Chat accomplishes the service execution and hence it creates an appropriate answer (that terminates the Invite request received at step 15) and forwards it to SCIM. In this example that B is "available" for chat, this later sends back the Invite request to the SCIM.

23. SCIM evaluated the SCC and recognizes that the request doesn't require any SC invocation and that it must therefore be forwarded to S-CSCF.

24. S-CSCF sends the request to A.

5 Conclusion

In this paper we have proposed improvements to the actual service invocation mechanism of IMS. This proposition brings new insights to the NGN service capability integration mechanisms in IMS:

- The Service Capability Profile that we defined for each application server resolves the foremost service composition issues that are:
  o How to bind multiple Service Capabilities to an AS
  o How to provide a Service Capability for an AS
- Moreover as presented in the use case, this proposed service invocation mechanism enables the invocation orchestration of a wide range of NGN services.
- Finally the proposed mechanism can be considered as a pioneer step towards the realization of NGN service convergence using SIP based solutions instead of IT based ones. However, these two approaches will need to be analysed and compared in further studies.

By taking the advantage of the proposed service invocation mechanism and based on the architectural and technical issues discussed in this paper, in the next step of our work, we will focus on the implementation and development of this service invocation mechanism over IMS.

Moreover we will extend our mechanism to enable a dynamic service capability discovery by concentrating on a more extended range of service capabilities including mobility manager, terminal capability manager, and location manager.

References

1. 3GPP, "IP Multimedia Subsystem (IMS)", TS 23.228
2. 3GPP, "IP Multimedia (IM) Subsystem Cx and Dx interfaces; Signalling flows and message contents", TS 29.228
3. 3GPP, "Service requirement for the Open Services Access (OSA)", TS 22.127
4. 3GPP, "Presence service using the IP Multimedia (IM) Core Network (CN) subsystem"; TS 24.141
5. 3GPP, "Messaging using the IP Multimedia (IM) Core Network (CN) subsystem; TS 24.247
6. IETF RFC 3261, "SIP: Session Initiation Protocol"
7. IETF RFC 3265, "Session Initiation Protocol - Specific Event Notification"
8. IETF RFC 3428, "Session Initiation Protocol for Instant Messaging"
9. ITU-T Recommendation Y.2001, "General overview of NGN"
10. Gouya A., Crespi N., Bertin E. and Oueslati L. "Managing Service Capability and Service Feature Interactions in the IMS of UMTS", International Conference on Networking and Services, ICNS'06.
11. Gouya A., Crespi N., Bertin E. "SCIM Implementation Issues in IMS Service Architecture", ICC 2006.
12. Lee C., Knight D. "Realization of the Next-Generation Network", IEEE Communications Magazine, October 2005.
13. Carugi M., Hirschman B., Narita A. "Introduction to the ITU-T NGN Focus Group Release 1: Target Environment, Services and Capabilities", IEEE Communications Magazine, October 2005.
14. Knightson K., Morita N., Towle T. "NGN Architecture: Generic Principles, Functional Architecture and Implementation", IEEE Communications Magazine, October 2005.

Live E! Project: Sensing the Earth

Masaya Nakayama[1], Satoshi Matsuura[2],
Hiroshi Esaki[1], and Hideki Sunahara[2]

[1] The University of Tokyo,
7-3-1 Hongo, Bunkyo-ku, Tokyo, 113-8656, Japan
[2] Nara Institute of Science and Technology,
8916-5 Takayama-cho, Ikoma-shi, Nara, 630-0192, Japan
nakayama@nc.u-tokyo.ac.jp, sato-mat@is.naist.jp,
{hiroshi, suna}@wide.ad.jp
http://www.live-e.org

Abstract. The Live E! project is an open research consortium among industry and academia to explore the platform to share the digital information related with the earth and our living environment. We have getting a lot of low cost sensor nodes with Internet connectivity. The deployment of broadband and ubiquitous networks will enable autonomous and global digital information sharing over the globe. In this paper, we describe the technical and operational overview of Live E! project, while discussing the objective, such as education, disaster protection/reduction/recovery or business cases, and goal of this project activity.

Keywords: Live E!, sensor network, environmental information.

1 Introduction

Recent natural disaster, e.g., hurricane or global warming, or heat island effect in the metropolitan let increase the attention and interesting on grasping the detailed status of space. This is because, due to these disasters, our social life and business activity could be seriously degraded or sometimes be damaged. When we could realize the relationship of cause and effect, it would be expected to reduce and protect the damage by these disasters. The structure change of metropolitans in the developed countries and rapid inflation of cities in Asian countries make complex and difficult to realize the real status and tendency of global weather system. As symbolized by Kyoto Protocol proposed by United Nation in February of 2005, so called COP3, it is realized as the urgent and serious global agenda to reduce or to stop the global warming effect.

We have getting a lot of low cost sensor nodes with Internet connectivity. The deployment of broadband and ubiquitous networks will enable autonomous and global digital information sharing over the globe, using these sensor nodes. When these wide variety of sensor nodes are autonomously connected and the sensor information let available to all the node on the Internet space, different types of sensor information, e.g., video or still image captured by Web camera, temperature, location, IR-image or chemical, can be integrated for data analysis. Then,

K. Cho and P. Jacquet (Eds.): AINTEC 2006, LNCS 4311, pp. 61–74, 2006.

we will be able to create so wide variety of applications and possibilities. When these sensor nodes are connected with broadband Internet, these information can be available even in real-time fashion. We have realized and proposed the activity, called Live E! Project (http://www.live-e.org), that is a sensor networks sharing all the digital information related with the at large status of the Earth for any purpose and for anyone. We expect that these digital information will be used for various purposes, e.g., educational material, public service, business cases, by the deployment of effective and safe physical space for all the human being.

Internet has been originally invented and developed to use and to share the expensive high performance computers, remotely. In these days, the jobs executed at the computer were numerical calculation for particular work to provide more effective working environment for researchers. Digital information has the following five primitives; generation, collection, circulation, processing, sharing. Through these five primitives, the computer system can improve and innovate the life-style of human being or the professional/commercial activities. Also, we have realized that the ICT can contribute to improve and innovate the human life and industrial activities more effective and safer.

In this paper, we describes the technical and operational overview of Live E! project, while discussing it's objective, such as education, disaster protection/reduction/recovery or business cases, and goal of this project activity.

2   Internet for Facility Networks

2.1   Challenges of Internet

"Internet", not "The Internet", is a logical architecture, that enable autonomous circulation and sharing of digital information. The Internet should provide a transparent platform with the following characteristics.

(1) can use any data-link
(2) can use any data distribution channel
(3) can be used by anyone

This chrematistics (or could be said requirement) are truly critical for ubiquitous networks. In the ubiquitous networks, there is huge number of device nodes (such as sensor nodes), and it is desired all the digital information generated by these device nodes should be available from any node on the Internet space and be able to be shared among all the nodes on the Internet space.

The Internet is the system where the computers are interconnected via any type of data-link, so that the digital data is autonomously transferred from any node to any other node on the Internet space, transparently. Any node on the Internet space should be able to use and process these data, autonomously. In other words, the Internet is;

(a) independent from application
(b) independent from user
(c) independent from data transmission infrastructure

This means that the Internet satisfy the requirements of "Commons" discussed in [1]. The Internet should not have any exclusiveness related with the information exchange.

Internet has experienced major three innovations in the past, and is now exploring the fourth. Past innovations are open global network with TCP/IP, easier use with WWW and professional application with Web Service. The fourth innovation is broadband and ubiquitous. Broadband includes always-on environment, and the ubiquitous means the Internet accommodates embedded devices, such as sensor nodes or actuator nodes.

The facility networks is a kind of embedded network for some particular purpose or for some particular application, while having a strong interaction with the real and physical objects. Since the facility network has a lot of interaction with physical objects, it is said that the network must be dependable. People starts to realize that, in order to build dependable facility network, the network should be operated autonomously and with multi-vendor environment (i.e., open system). Open and autonomous system can provide the alternatives for users. Providing the alternatives to the users leads a competition among vendors for technology improvement and cost reduction, and leads the service continuation capability as a result.

Some of the challenges of the Internet discussed in this paper is (1) how to accommodate wide variety of and large number of sensor/actuator nodes into the Internet space, and (2) identify new applications using the weather sensor nodes deployed in the Live E! project.

2.2   Facility Networking with TCP/IP

Facility networking includes factory automation, building automation or home automation, which is the integration of different type of networks, such as sensor network, control network or security network. Especially the role of sensor networking and actuator networking has the important role for the near future facility networking architecture. The facility networking would be toward the integration of real-space and cyber-space using common IP technology.

We have worked with the industry so that the TCP/IP technology, especially the IPv6, is applied to the basic protocol to be shared by various systems in facility networking. Since they have used proprietary technologies for each company and for each sub-systems, they are interested in the IP-Centric system, to achieve highly cost-effective system operation. We had the world first interoperability testing among building automation components with IPv6 transport, using the BACnet [2] and LonWorks [3], in 2004, as shown in figure 1. And, in 2006, we have achieved the world first interoperability of management and control of system components across these different systems using the Web service over IPv6 infrastructure.

With applying the open technology such as TCP/IP, the system components can be easily replaceable, while achieving the remote monitoring and controlling. For the business operation of "facility", the cost of human labor due to maintenance and the cost of component replacement, modification, improvement and

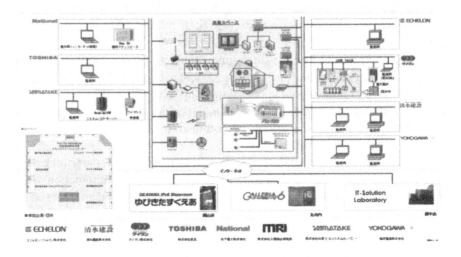

Fig. 1. Interoperability Test in 2004

upgrade occupy a large portion in their financial portfolio. The remote monitoring and control capability by the TCP/IP contributes to the reduction of required human labors, and the multi-vendor environment due to the open networking with the TCP/IP technology contributes to the total cost reduction of system components management by the availability of alternative products. Based on these observation, we have realized that the facility networking industry will be able to enjoy the technical and economical benefits by the adoption of TCP/IP technology.

When we consider the application of and role of sensor networking in the facility networking, there are a lot of potential roles for their effective operation and management. Let consider the application of energy saving in the building automation. In general, the energy cost in the operation of building system (and in the at large facility networks) is extremely large. Especially in Japan, the energy cost is about 1/3, regarding all the life-time cost of building system, that includes the initial designing building system, construction and daily maintenance cost. As well as the benefit of energy saving activity from the view point of economical portfolio for the land-lords, we have another reason why we must perform the energy saving in the facility networking. In 1997, the United Nation has adopted the international energy saving program, so called Kyoto Protocol in COP3 [4]. This is global agenda to preserve the healthy earth by the improvement of global worming effect. One of the important agenda of this program is to reduce the energy consumption by every single office or factory. For example, in Japan, the energy saving program has been applied to all the large scale facility, that has more than 2,000 square-meters footprint. These facilities must reduce the energy consumption 10%-20%, as a government regulation.

We have got some private reports from some private companies. They try to energy saving at their computer room, using the temperature sensors, to success

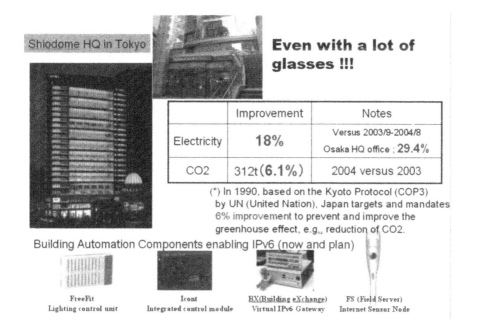

Fig. 2. Energy saving at HQ of Matsushita Works

reducing about 40% electricity. Also, at the 24th floor high recent building system with a lot of glasses, it is reported that 18% reduction of electricity and 6.1% reduction of CO2 consumption has been achieved, using sensors and actuators, which are interconnected with open networking protocol, such as TCP/IP. This is shown in figure 2.

As discussed above, the sensor and actuator networks are not separated or isolated network, anymore. They are interconnected to each other, and they are going to be networked with the usual information network and with the Internet, in order to achieve more cost effective and functional rich system operation, as well as to generate new function or services. The larger sharing of sensor information among various facility networks leads to better and more cost effective and attractive system operation.

3   Live E! Project

3.1   Overview of Live E! Project

Live E! Project [5] is a R&D consortium founded by WIDE project and IPv6 Promotion Council, Japan. This project is aiming to establish the platform to share all digital information, generated by sensor devices all over the world. Now, these devices are installed and operated individually by each organization. The information should be related with the live environmental information of the Earth. By sharing this digital information, we will be able to create new

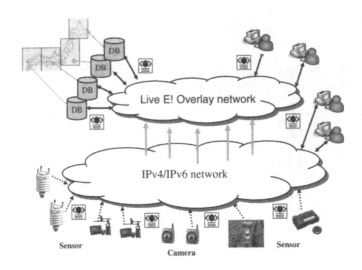

Fig. 3. Overview architecture of Live E! project

applications, which can contribute to safety and effective space (environment). Some applications, such as basic information for the protection of environment (e.g., a heat-island phenomena in metropolitan), educational material, public service, public safety or business applications, could use the common digital information for different purposes. Figure 3 shows the overview architecture of Live E! project. The followings are the working agenda of Live E! project.

(1) By the installation of larger number of digital sensor nodes, the environmental information can be richer and finer, i.e, connectivity is own rewards.

(2) Every individual and every organization should recognize all has the responsibility on the preservation and improvement of global environment and should think all must contribute.

(3) We could give away the ownership on the digital (raw) data for the public, and let them available for all the people on the Internet or on the globe.

(4) Educate and encourage the interesting on the science and technology through the participation on the program and using the data for educational program.

3.2   Live E! Deployment with Digital Weather Stations

The related original work would be back in 2001, when the WIDE project with Yokogawa Electric Corp.(http://www.yokogawa.com/) had developed a temperature node with IPv6 protocol stack, called i-node (http://www.i-node.co.jp/).

We have realized that the weather station with Internet connectivity has the following three application areas with single device.

(1) For Educational Material
    Weather information data is useful data for education and for research on geophysics. There are wide variety of educational program on geophysics,

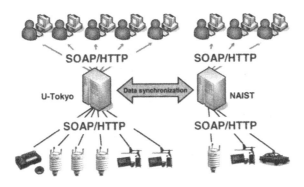

Fig. 4. integrate interface by SOAP

related with the weather system, from the elementary school to the college. Actually, in Live E! project, we have worked on the educational program in the elementary school in Minato-ku in Metropolitan Tokyo, and on the engineering program in some high schools collaborating with university in Hiroshima.

(2) For Public Service, e.g., disaster reduction/recovery

Weather information is very important and critical information for the case of disaster. In these days, we have a lot of natural disasters, such as flooding or earth-quake. Grasping the detailed information for the disaster case is useful for proactive and reactive program. These are disaster protection, reduction, and recovery. For example, the detailed weather information on the road or at the evacuation sites, the people could take appropriate evacuation path. Also, none knows the exact and detailed data on the heat-island effect at metropolitan. We must grasp the real status of town with large number of weather sensors.

In the fiscal year of 2006, Live E! project will deploy the Internet weather sensors for public service at Minato-ku in metropolitan Tokyo [6] and at Kurashiki-city in Okayama. Kurashiki-city [7] is focusing on the disaster protection and reduction, against the flooding due to heavy rain. Minato-ku is focusing on the disaster protection and reduction against some natural disasters (e.g., flooding or earth-quake), and focusing on the understanding the detail of heat-island effect of metropolitan Tokyo.

(3) For Business case

There are a lot of potential business applications, by the use of weather information. One of example would be effective taxi dispatching using the rainfall information. Dispatching the taxi cabs around the area, getting the rain, leads to higher income by the increase of customer. The other example would be electricity power company. Once they can operate total energy control and management system, they could reduce the amount of investments on the power generator or power supplying system, which is very expensive facility for them. Seriously, they may start to think about total portfolio for business investments.

Table 1. Normalized name & unit

name	unit
Temperature	℃
Humidity	%
Pressure	hPa
RainFall	mm/h
WindSpeed	m/s
WindDir	°

Table 2. Examples of profile data

name	explanation
address	address of sensor
location	name of installation location
ipAddr	IPv4 address
ip6Addr	IPv6 address
latitude	latitude of sensor
longitude	longitude of sensor
altitude	altitude of sensor

Table 3. examples of SOAP web-services

getCurrentDataAll()
- get current data from all sensors
getCurrentDataByAreaRect(x1, y1, x2, y2)
- get data generated in paticular region
getDataByTimespan(sensorID, startTime, endTime)
- get data by time-span
getCurrentDataByType(sensorType)
- get current data of specific sensor type
getProfileAll()
- get all profile data
getProfileByType(sensorType)
- get profile data of specific sensor type
putData(xmlDocument)
- put sensing data
setProfile(xmlDocument)
- set profile data

3.3   Data Normalization and Access Method

In last section, we show the effectiveness of facility networking with TCP/IP. The reason why the facility network can improve energy conservation is that we access to all building information seamlessly on this network. In order to expand this success into the sensor network, first we need to normalize a data format and access method. In this sub-section we introduce our data format with some examples.

The weather information is expressed by XML and transferred among the servers and clients using the SOAP. The sensor is not defined by node, but is defined by each sensor function. A typical internet weather station has multiple sensors in a single station in it, which sensors are temperature, humidity, pressure, rainfall, wind-speed and wind-direction. This typical weather station has 5 objectives defined by XML. Each objective has their own profile information, such as location, sensor type, IP address or name.

As shown in Table 1, we basically adopt MKS-system on our platform. If a new kind of sensor is installed, project member will define its name and the unit (recently, we installed $CO2$ sensors, illumination sensors, acceleration sensors and other sensors). By SOAP web-services, we create a user interface (Figure 4). When user program provides the name of sensor function to web-service, it can access all of sensing data without any conversion. As whole databases are synchronized between two locaitons, users can select web services which they want to use.

As the table 2 shows, we also provide attribute information of sensors called "profile data". We normalize and provide sensing data and profile data as XML document. Application creators freely combine sensing data with profile data to meet each requirement.

Example web service we prepared are shown in Table 3. Here, we introduce an example way to retrieve sensor data. The most popular web-service is "getCurrentDataAll()". By this function, user gets current data generated by all sensors. Following Perl script is an example code to do it.Of course, any language and operating system can access to sensor data by using SOAP.

```perl
#!/usr/local/bin/perl -w
use encoding 'UTF-8', STDOUT => 'shiftjis';
use SOAP::Lite;

$service = SOAP::Lite -> service('http://example.com/axis/
                                 DataProvider?wsdl');
$currentData = $service->GetCurrentDataAll();
print $currentData;
```

Figure 5 shows the result XML documnets when above example Perl script executed. We standardized XML format. Using other SOAP web-services, user always receives data as same XML format. Defining the name of web-services and XML format contributes to create application easily. In addition, as the above XML documents shows, we define a sensor-group. Sensor-group organizes individual sensors. In above XML document, class of sensor-group is "combinedSensor". This sensor-group organizes a multiple sensor as one of sensors. We define a new class of sensor-group for several purposes. For example, class of "zipCode" is to manage a particular area, and class of "highAccuracy" is to pick up high performance sensors. Of course, we create new web-services by combining several classes. Sensor-group improves a creativeness of raw sensing data.

Here, we introduce some of our applications created by SOAP web-services. Figure 6 shows the example of data displaying. On the web site, user can search each place for detailed data, which are graph of sensors, XML (or CVS) data and pictures of web cameras.

We also provide educational materials. We made a weather information viewer called weather checker (Figure 7). This viewer displays real time data of each place. Students of elementary school constantly check and record the data of this viewer. Students will plot a graph with these data and discuss the difference of daily weather and local climate, and compare climate of home town with other place. Students will take interest in science with such actual experiences.

```
<sensorGroup address="東京都文京区弥生2-11-16 " class="combinedSensor" id="live-
e.org/WXT510/03000005c3a2/" latitude="35.712194" location="東大情報基盤センター"
longitude="139.76775" sensorModel="WXT510" sensorVendor="vaisala">
<sensor id="live-e.org/WXT510/03000005c3a2/Temperature" sensorType="Temperature">
<value time="2006-07-25T19:37:33.0000000+09:00">25.8</value>
</sensor>
<sensor id="live-e.org/WXT510/03000005c3a2/Humidity" sensorType="Humidity">
<value time="2006-07-25T19:37:33.0000000+09:00">73.3</value>
</sensor>
<sensor id="live-e.org/WXT510/03000005c3a2/Pressure" sensorType="Pressure">
<value time="2006-07-25T19:37:33.0000000+09:00">1009.4</value>
</sensor>
<sensor id="live-e.org/WXT510/03000005c3a2/RainFall" sensorType="RainFall">
<value time="2006-07-25T19:37:33.0000000+09:00">0</value>
</sensor>
<sensor id="live-e.org/WXT510/03000005c3a2/DayRainFall" sensorType="DayRainFall">
<value time="2006-07-25T19:37:33.0000000+09:00">0.64</value>
</sensor>
<sensor id="live-e.org/WXT510/03000005c3a2/WindDir" sensorType="WindDir">
<value time="2006-07-25T19:37:33.0000000+09:00">174</value>
</sensor>
<sensor id="live-e.org/WXT510/03000005c3a2/WindSpeed" sensorType="WindSpeed">
<value time="2006-07-25T19:37:33.0000000+09:00">0.9</value>
</sensor>
</sensorGroup>
```

Fig. 5. Example of reply as XML document

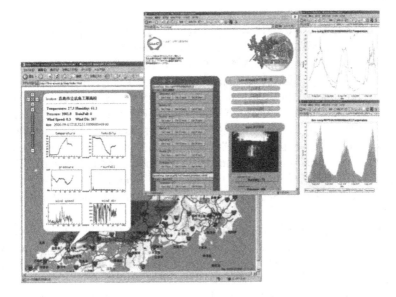

Fig. 6. web page providing weather information at each place

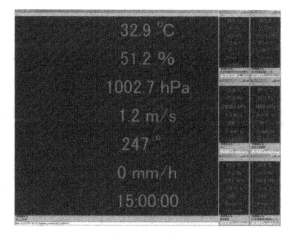

Fig. 7. weather information viewer

Figure 8 shows another application which displays weather information. This application shows the status of clouds and path information of a typhoon with sensor data. Live E! Project doesn't observe cloud and typhoon. Collaborating with other organizations, our project provides these data. Just one organization never collects all kinds of information. We enhance the collaboration with others.

As shown in figure 3, the sensors are connected to the IPv4 and IPv6 dual-stack network with multicasting capability. The sensor information can be simultaneously deliver to multiple nodes, that want to get the sensor information, without requesting the copying data at the sensor node. Topping on the IPv4/IPv6 multicast-capable IP network, the Live E! overlay network is defined. The live E! overlay network has the distributed database system across the nation-wide Japan. This is for load balancing and for robust data management against some system failure. Also, as shown in the figure, this system has already included Web camera for obtaining the live video information and the sound information from the network.

We have installed more than 100 stations and let them on-line. Some of stations have installed in Philippine by the collaboration with ASTI [8], or have installed in Thailand by the collaboration with PSU [9].

For dense installation of weather sensors, we collaborate with Minato-ku in metropolitan Tokyo. Several sensors are installed at some elementary schools at Minato-ku. We will install about 30 stations in this fiscal year of 2006. By this installation, Minato-ku can have about 2 km mesh weather station network.

3.4   Future Enhancement of Internet Weather Station System

– XML based Publish/Subscribe system
  The more sensor devices and users increase, the more data and queries should be processed. The most popular web-service is "getCurrentDataAll()". Users are very interested in real time data. In order to provide this web-service

Fig. 8. data displaying on google earth

stable, we create XML based Publish-Subscribe system (Figure 9). This system don't store archived data but only provide current data. If users register for subscribing data, they constantly receive current data of all sensors.

- Integration with InternetCAR system
  WIDE project has long time worked on the R&D activity, where automobiles connect to the Internet. Automobiles can be realized as the mobile sensor node, running on the surface of the earth. We are now integrating the "InternetCAR" into our platform [10]. In addition, we are trying to use ad-hoc network for sensors not having the connectivity to the internet. Patrol nodes (ex. Post office cars, garbage trucks or buses) gather the sensing data via ad-hoc network [11].
- Support small nodes
  There are lots of microcomputers not having the ability to translate XML document. In order to integrate lots of data created by microcomputers generate, we study about XML translational machinery [12].
- Scalable and autonomous data collection and distribution system
  The current system is a kind of client-server system. This is just fine for small scale system. However, the system must come up with the increase of sensors and the increase of type of sensors. Distributed and autonomous management and operation is mandatory. We are studying about geographical location based peer-to-peer network [13].

We are evaluating the requirements of future sensor network, and integrate several kinds of researches.

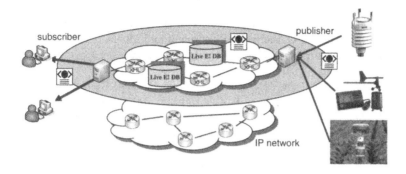

Fig. 9. XML based publish/subscribe system

4 Conclusion

The Live E! project is an open research consortium among industry and academia to explore the platform to share the digital information related with the earth and our living environment. Using the low cost weather sensor nodes with Internet connectivity, we deployed the nation-wide sensor network. The network has accommodate more than 100 station, and has two of dense installation. The application of this weather station network is for disaster protection/reduction/recovery and for educational material for various level of students.

Acknowledgment

The authors thanks to all the organization and peoples contributing to the Live E! project. These are; WIDE project sponsor organizations, NiCT/JGN, Netone Systems Co.Ltd, Echelon Japan KK, WeatherNews Inc., NTT Neo-mate, Wilcom Japan Ltd., IRI Ubiteq Inc., NTT East Corp., Matsushita Electric Works Ltd., Cisco Systems Japan K.K., Dai-Dan Co.Ltd., Uchida Yoko Co.Ltd., INTEC Inc., Shimizu Corp., Yamatake Corp., OBIS Corp., and Mitubishi Research Institute Inc.

References

1. Lawrence Lessig, "The future of Ideas; The Fate of the Commons in a Connected World" Random House Inc., ISBN 0375505784, November 2002.
2. Home Page of BACnet, http://www.bacnet.org/
3. Home Page of Lon Mark, http://www.lonmark.org/
4. Kyoto Protocol by United nation, http://www.cop3.org/
5. Home Page of Live E! Project, http://www.live-e.org/
6. Minato-ku, Tokyo, http://www.city.minato.tokyo.jp/
7. Kurashiki-City, http://www.city.kurashiki.okayama.jp/
8. ASTI (Advanced Science and Technology Institute), http://www.asti.dost.gov.ph/

9. PSU (Prince of Songkla University), http://www.psu.ac.th/

10. Shinichi Doui, Satoshi Matsuura, Hideki Sunahara: An Infrastructure for Environmental Information Gathered by Fixed-point and Mobile Sensors, Multimedia, Distributed, Cooperative and Mobile Symposium(2006), IPSJ Symposium Series Vol.2006, No.6, 801 – 804.

11. Hiroki Ishizuka, Kenji Sasaki, Satoshi Matsuura, Makoto Kamiya, Hideki Sunahara, Hiroshi Esaki: Collecting Adaptive Data for Isolated Wireless Sensors with Patrol Nodes in Live E!, International Workshop on Future Mobile and Ubiquitous Information Technologies, Proceeding of FMUIT2006, 249 – 253.

12. Hideya Ochiai, Hiroshi Esaki: The Application of XML Translator for a Large-Scale Sensor Node Network, IEICE 2006, A-21-5.

13. MATSUURA Satoshi and FUJIKAWA Kazutoshi and SUNAHARA Hideki: Mill: Scalable Area Management for P2P Network based on Geographical Location, Proceedings Euromedia 2006, 46 – 52.

Performance Analysis and Comparison Between Multicast and Unicast over Infrastructure Wireless LAN

Anan Phonphoem and Suchaisri Li-On

Department of Computer Engineering, Faculty of Engineering
Kasetsart University, Thailand
{anan.p, g4685039}@ku.ac.th

Abstract. Although multicast communication has been widely deployed and extensively studied for several years, it is still difficult to quantitatively compare the performance of multicast and unicast transmission schemes, especially in limited bandwidth environments. This paper presents a simple stochastic Markov model for multicast communication over infrastructure wireless LANs. The model addresses configurations where a variable number of mobile hosts request access to one or more concurrent communication streams. The steady state transition probabilities are derived and used to obtain numerical results for average bandwidth used for streaming transmissions under typical wireless LAN conditions, under both unicast and multicast transmission. Parameters in the model include number of avialable streams, maximum permitted number of sessions, and arrival rates of mobile hosts. The stochastic model and quantitive results can have application to evaluation of proposed designs for multicast service models and protocols.

Keywords: Multicast, Markov chains, Wireless LANs.

1 Introduction

Multicast can be implemented on both a WAN or a LAN. In a WAN, such as the Internet, all routers along the path need to support multicast by implementing multicast routing protocols. Researchers have proposed many routing protocols which can be categorized as interior and exterior routing protocols. DVMRP [10,24], first proposed in 1988, was one of the earliest interior multicast routing protocols; it was physically deployed for multicast audio at an IETF meeting. Later MOSPF [17], a link state routing protocol, was proposed. Both deployed one shortest path tree per source which is not efficient. Then CBT [2] is proposed a single tree for each group. PIM [27,28] combined mechanisms of CBT and the shortest path algorithms, which can be run in dense mode [1] or sparse mode [5]. PIM can be deployed as either a center based tree or reverse shortest path tree. For exterior routing, BGMP [7,8] has been proposed for deployment between autonomous system, using center based tree.

K. Cho and P. Jacquet (Eds.): AINTEC 2006, LNCS 4311, pp. 75–89, 2006.
© Springer-Verlag Berlin Heidelberg 2006

Typically, a multicast routing protocol assumes that all routers along the path support multicast, which is not a realistic assumption. Multicast Backbone, MBone [11,22], proposed an alternate implementation that required only edge routers support multicast while the other routers along the path can be regular non-multicast routers. However, multicast routers are still needed. Some researchers [6,18,31] proposed that end stations perform all multicast functions so that multicast-aware routers are not needed; HMTP [3] is one such protocol.

In a LAN, multicast communications can be directly deployed by updating the driver of network cards to understand multicast frame. For deploying multicast over the wired network, such as regular Ethernet which is the contention based, frame losses can be occurred. This reliable problem can be tolerated if the system bandwidth is enough for all active communication sessions. The problems become more serious in deploying multicast over wireless LAN due to wireless characteristics such as bandwidth limitation, channel interference, and hidden terminal.

Most published work on multicast evaluation methods address issues in a WAN environment, such as complexity of the multicast routing algorithm [20,21] and link cost [12,15]. For LAN environments, most address the issue of multicast reliability [4,13,16,29,30]. Aaltonen, et al [14] present results of the multicast gain over unicast by using call blocking probabilities in cellular network.

In this paper, a stochastic model for multicast transmissions over a wireless LAN is presented, and used to compare the performance and availability of streaming transmissions between the unicast and multicast transmission modes. The analytical results of this study can be used to access bandwidth utilization, availability, and bandwidth per session of streaming media under a variety of real circumstances.

1.1 Multicast Fundamentals

Any host who wants to receive multicast information need to know the multicast address. Then it will send a request to its local multicast router to ask for joining the multicast group. Once the joining process success, all members in the group will be able to receive the same information from the sender though their multicast group address. Multicast routers will select paths based on the routing algorithms and decide to replicate data to one or multiple interfaces.

The Internet Group Management Protocol (IGMP) [25] is defined as a supporting protocol (number 2) for Internet Protocol (IP), the same way that ICMP is defined for unicast communication. IGMP is used for exchanging information among multicast routers and also for communicating between host and multicast routers in the network.

The format of an IGMP message is shown in Figure 1. The group IP address is defined as class D, ranging from 224.0.0.0 to 239.255.255.255. There are two types of IGMP messages: Report and Query. The IGMP Report message, sent by a host, is used for joining multicast groups. While the IGMP Query message, regularly sent by local routers, is used for discovering and maintaining multicast group membership.

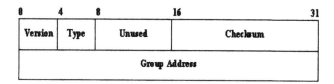

Fig. 1. IGMP message format

1.2 Multicast over Infrastructure Wireless LAN

wireless LAN is now widely deployed due to their ease of implementation and cost effectiveness, resulting in a dramatic increase in the number of wireless end users. The behavior of these wireless users is the same as regular wired line users including the use of multicast applications that cannot guarantee smooth success over a wireless LAN.

IEEE 802.11 is now the defacto standard for wireless LAN. Most implementations utilize infrastructure based topology. Mobile host (MH) in the basic service set (BSS) must associate to an access point to obtain network services. MH can only communicate with other hosts via an access point, which also acts as a bridge to the wired network, as illustrated in Figure 2.

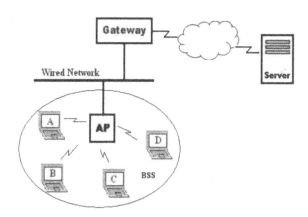

Fig. 2. Infrastructure Wireless LAN

To implement multicast over a wireless LAN, the multicast server location is significant. If the multicast server is located inside the BSS, the server sends multicast frames directly to its AP using unicast addressing. The AP will then send the received frame to all members in the group by using the group's multicast address. Unicast frames from the sender must be acknowledged to avoid retransmission; however, multicast frames from the AP to all members are not acknowledged. Therefore, no retransmission occurs in this manner which makes multicast communication becomes unreliable.

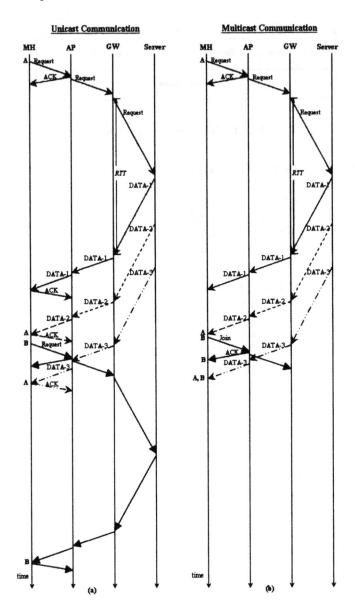

Fig. 3. Timing Diagram

In the case where the multicast server is located outside the BSS, all frames from the sender will be sent through the AP to all members in multicast frame format. No acknowledgement will be sent from any receiver which causes the same unreliable transmission.

To counter this problem, many reliable multicast protocols have been proposed, implementing acknowledgement based detection with retransmission (or Automatic Repeat request, ARQ) [4,29], Forward Error Correction (FEC) [19,23], and Channel Reservation [16,30].

1.3   Unicast and Multicast Time Diagram

A simple comparison between unicast and multicast communication is depicted in Figure 3. Mobile hosts A and B request the same data stream from the single sever located outside the BSS. For unicast communication, Figure 3(a), host B has to wait a substantial interval before the first data frame arrives, while for multicast communication, Figure 3(b), host B waits a much shorter period. The larger the number of mobile hosts, the longer the waiting period.

Even though the time diagram shows that multicast outperforms unicast communication, it does not provide any quantitative comparison.

The remainder of the paper is organized as follows. In section 2, a Markov model for both unicast and multicast is proposed. Section 3 shows the case study of the system evaluation. Section 4 describes numerical results of the system in term of average bandwidth and average number of simultaneous sessions. The paper, then be concluded in Section 5.

2   Stochastic Model

In this section, simple unicast and multicast queuing models in infrastructure wireless LANs are proposed.

Let M be the number of allowed live streaming media, such as TV channels, N be the number of simultaneously requested sessions, $M(t)$ and $N(t)$ are stochastic processes representing the allowed live streaming media and the simultaneous requested sessions, respectively, at time t.

2.1   General Assumptions

- The arrival of requested live streaming media is a Poisson process.
- $M(t)$ and $N(t)$ are independent.
- The limit on the number of MHs that an AP can serve, in real-world deployment, is at most 30 stations.
- No interference and hidden terminal effect.

2.2   Unicast Communication

Let the state variables of the Markov Chain be M, N, the arrival rate of the requested live streaming media be λ, and the departure rate of each session be μ. Hence, each session will be served for the time $1/\mu$.

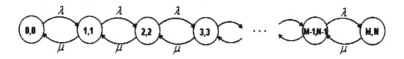

Fig. 4. Unicast Markov State Transition Diagram

The state transition diagram for the finite Markov chain is shown in Figure 4. Let $P_{i,j} = \lim_{t \to \infty} P\{M(t) = i, N(t) = j\}$ be the steady state probabilities, λ and μ are the arrival rate and departure rate at state (i, j). When the system is idle, the leftmost state becomes $M, N = 0, 0$. For an arrival of requested live streaming media $(0 \le i = j < N)$, the state will change to the right(from state (i, j) to $(i + 1, j + 1)$). When a session elects to leave or stop receiving the live streaming media $(i = j > 0)$, the state will change to the left (from state (i, j) to $(i - 1, j - 1)$). In the unicast case, when a new requested arrives, regardless of whether it is for the same or different live streaming media, a new data session must be created. Therefore, the state variables will always satisfy $M = N$. Once the number of the allowed live streaming media (bandwidth limitation) or the number of concurrent sessions reach the maximum, new requested sessions will be blocked. The parameter of the model can be defined as follows:

$$\lambda_{m,n} = \begin{cases} \lambda, & m = n = 0, 1, 2, ..., N - 1 \\ 0, & otherwise \end{cases}$$

$$\mu_{m,n} = \mu, \qquad m = n = 1, 2, ..., N$$

According to the diagram shown in Figure 4, we have drawn vertical boundaries between each adjacent pair of states. Each boundary actually separates the state transition diagram into two halves. A set of local balance equations can be obtained:

for $0 < i = j < N$

$$(\lambda + \mu)P_{i,j} - \lambda P_{i-1,j-1} - \mu P_{i+1,j+1} = 0 \tag{1}$$

for $i = j = 0$

$$\lambda P_{0,0} - \mu P_{1,1} = 0 \tag{2}$$

for $i = M, j = N$

$$\mu P_{M,N} - \lambda P_{M-1,N-1} = 0 \tag{3}$$

In addition,

$$\sum_{i=0}^{M} \sum_{j=0}^{N} P_{i,j} = 1 \tag{4}$$

2.3   Multicast Communication

For multicast, the model becomes more complex than the unicast case. The state transition diagram for the finite Markov chain is shown in Figure 5. When the system is idle, the leftmost state becomes $M, N = 0, 0$. At the first arrival of requested live streaming media, the state will change to state $1, 1$ for the same reason as the unicast case. However, when the next session request arrives, if it is a request to join the active requested stream (with probability p_c), the state will change to $M, N = 1, 2$ in the same level (state (i, j) to $(i, j+1)$). If it is a request

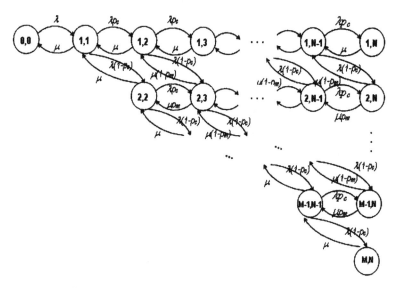

Fig. 5. Multicast Markov State Transition Diagram

for a new stream (with probability $1 - p_c$), the state will jump to $M, N = 2, 2$ at the second level of the Markov chain (state (i, j) to $(i + 1, j + 1)$). Subsequent transitions continue in the same manner, until the limit on the maximum number of concurrent live streaming media or sessions is reached. If any session decides to leave or stop receiving a particular live streaming media, we must differentiate between whether it is the last session of that active stream or not. Let the probability that a session is NOT the last one be p_m, in which case the state (i, j) will change to $(i, j - 1)$. If it is the last session, the state will jump to the previous level of the chain (from state (i, j) to $(i - 1, j - 1)$) with probability $1 - p_m$. Once the number of allowed live streaming media (bandwidth limitation) or the number of concurrent sessions reach the maximum, new session requests will be blocked. The parameters of the model can be stated as follows.

In the discrete-time Markov chain, the only non-null one step transition probabilities are:

$$
\begin{cases}
P\{i+1, j+1 | i, j\} = \lambda & i = j = 0 \\
P\{i, j+1 | i, j\} = \lambda p_c & i \in [1, M-1] \; j \in [1, N-1] \\
P\{i+1, j+1 | i, j\} = \lambda(1 - p_c) & i \in [1, M-1] \; j \in [1, N-1] \\
P\{i-1, j-1 | i, j\} = \mu & i = j \\
P\{i, j-1 | i, j\} = \mu & i = 1 \qquad\quad j \in [1, N] \\
P\{i, j-1 | i, j\} = \mu p_m & i \in [2, M] \qquad j \in [2, N] \\
P\{i-1, j-1 | i, j\} = \mu(1 - p_m) & i \in [2, M-1] \; j \in [2, N]
\end{cases}
$$

$$(5)$$

where

p_c = the probability that a MH joins a multicast group

p_m = the probability that a MH leaves a multicast group and is not the last session in that group

As in the previous subsection, the vertical boundaries in the transition diagram yield the following set of local balance equations.

for $1 < i < j < N$

$$(\lambda+\mu)P_{i,j}-\lambda(1-p_c)P_{i-1,j-1}-\lambda p_c P_{i,j-1}-\mu p_m P_{i,j+1}-\mu(1-p_m)P_{i+1,j+1} = 0 \tag{6}$$

for $i = j = 0$

$$\lambda P_{0,0} - \mu P_{1,1} = 0 \tag{7}$$

for $i = j = 1$

$$(\lambda + \mu)P_{1,1} - \lambda P_{0,0} - \mu P_{1,2} - \mu P_{2,2} = 0 \tag{8}$$

for $i = 1, j = N$

$$\mu P_{1,N} - \lambda p_c P_{1,N-1} = 0 \tag{9}$$

for $i = 1, 1 < j < N$

$$(\lambda + \mu)P_{i,j} - \lambda p_c P_{i,j-1} - \mu P_{i,j+1} - \mu(1 - p_m)P_{i+1,j+1} = 0 \tag{10}$$

for $1 < i < M, j = N$

$$\mu P_{i,j} - \lambda(1 - p_c)P_{i-1,j-1} - \lambda p_c P_{i,j-1} = 0 \tag{11}$$

for $1 < i = j < M$

$$(\lambda + \mu)P_{i,j} - \lambda(1 - p_c)P_{i-1,j-1} - \mu p_m P_{i,j+1} - \mu P_{i+1,j+1} = 0 \tag{12}$$

for $i = M, M < j < N$

$$(\lambda + \mu)P_{M,j} - \lambda(1 - p_c)P_{M-1,j-1} - \lambda p_c P_{M,j-1} - \mu p_m P_{M,j+1} = 0 \tag{13}$$

for $i = j = N$

$$\mu P_{N,N} - \lambda(1 - p_c)P_{N-1,N-1} = 0 \tag{14}$$

In addition,

$$\sum_{i=0}^{M}\sum_{j=0}^{N} P_{i,j} = 1 \tag{15}$$

3   Performance Analysis

In this section we derive some analytical results using the Markov model from the previous section. For simplicity, assume that each live streaming media requires 1 Mbps. The maximum concurrent number of the sessions is 5. The unicast and multicast modes will be compared in three example cases. All steady state probabilities were obtained using MATLAB.

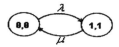

Fig. 6. Unicast Markov State Transition Diagram with $M=1$

Case 1: One Live Streaming Media, $M = 1$

The system bandwidth is available for only one live streaming media (1 Mbps). For unicast communication, only one session is allowed and the other later arriving session requests will be blocked. The state diagram is shown in Figure 6. The steady state probabilities can be obtained as

$$P_{0,0} = \frac{\mu}{\lambda+\mu} \qquad P_{1,1} = \frac{\lambda}{\lambda+\mu}$$

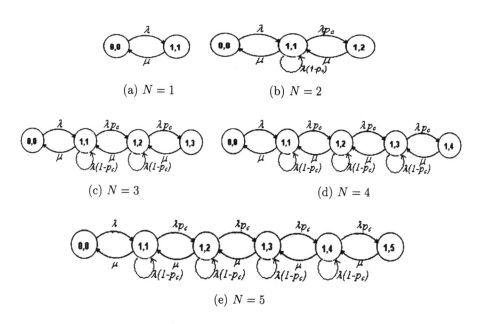

Fig. 7. Multicast Markov State Transition Diagram with $M=1$

For multicast communication, even though only one live streaming media is allowed, multiple session requests for the same stream will be granted. New requests will block only when the maximum number of session is reached (5, in our analysis). Figure 7(a) to (e) show the state transition diagram of the system in case of one to five sessions joining same live streaming media. The finite steady state transition probabilities for 1 session ($N=1$) is the same as unicast case, while 2 concurrent sessions ($N=2$) can be shown to be:

$$P_{0,0} = \frac{\mu^2}{\beta} \qquad P_{1,1} = \frac{\lambda\mu}{\beta} \qquad P_{1,2} = \frac{\lambda^2 p_c}{\beta}$$

where
$$\beta = \lambda^2 p_c + \lambda\mu + \mu^2$$

The finite steady state transition probabilities for 3 to 5 sessions can be solved with the same method.

Case 2: Two Live Streaming Medias, M = 2

In this case, the queueing system for unicast communication can accommodate at most a total of two concurrent live streaming media. Figure 8 displays the unicast state transition diagram. The steady state probabilities can be obtained as

$$P_{0,0} = \frac{\mu^2}{\delta} \qquad P_{1,1} = \frac{\lambda\mu}{\delta} \qquad P_{2,2} = \frac{\lambda^2}{\delta}$$

where
$$\delta = \lambda^2 + \lambda\mu + \mu^2$$

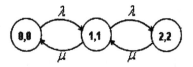

Fig. 8. Unicast Markov State Transition Diagram with $M{=}2$

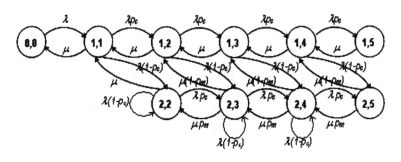

Fig. 9. Multicast Markov State Transition Diagram with $M{=}2$, $N{=}5$

For multicast communication, the system can accommodate up to 5 concurrent sessions for each stream, shown in Figure 9. The finite steady state transition probabilities for $N = 1$ to 5 can be solved from the governing equations using MATLAB, however, the expressions are not given here due to their length and complexity.

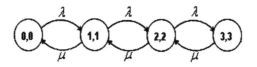

Fig. 10. Unicast Markov State Transition Diagram with $M=3$

Case 3: Three Live Streaming Medias, $M = 3$

In this case, three concurrent live streaming media are allowed in the system. Figure 10 shows the state transition diagram for unicast communication. The steady state probabilities can be obtained as

$$P_{0,0} = \frac{\mu^3}{\gamma} \qquad P_{1,1} = \frac{\lambda\mu^2}{\gamma} \qquad P_{2,2} = \frac{\lambda^2\mu}{\gamma} \qquad P_{3,3} = \frac{\lambda^3}{\gamma}$$

where

$$\gamma = \lambda^3 + \lambda^2\mu + \lambda\mu^2 + \mu^3$$

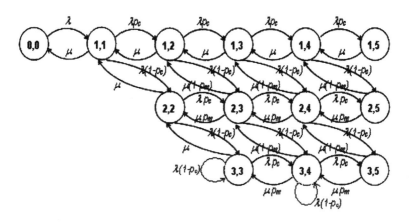

Fig. 11. Multicast Markov State Transition Diagram with $M=3$, $N=5$

For the multicast case, Figure 11 shows the state transition diagram for up to 5 concurrent sessions. The finite steady state transition can be solved with the same method.

4   Results and Discussion

In this section, a comparison of unicast and multicast performance is presented, using reasonable numeric values of the distribution parameters. The session departure rate (μ) is taken to be 1/30 min, corresponding to an average session time of 30 min, while the arrival rate (λ) is set to 2 requests per minute.

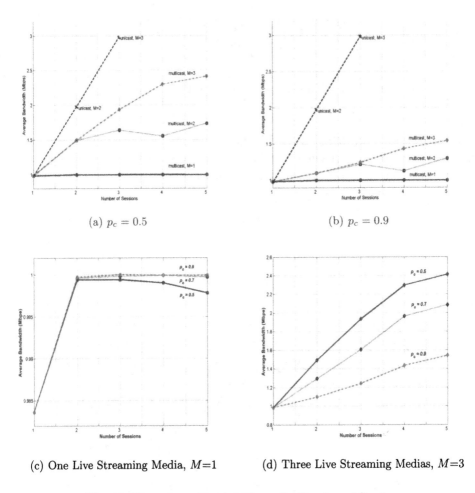

(a) $p_c = 0.5$ (b) $p_c = 0.9$

(c) One Live Streaming Media, $M=1$ (d) Three Live Streaming Medias, $M=3$

Fig. 12. The average Bandwidth vs. the Number of Sessions

4.1 Average Bandwidth Per Session

Figure 12 shows numerical results for the average bandwidth of each session. For unicast, the average bandwidth used (for cases $M =1$, 2 and 3) is simply the sum of the bandwidths of each requested stream (1, 2, and 3 Mbps). For multicast, the probability that an arriving request will join the active live streaming media, p_c, is set to 0.5 and 0.9, as shown in Figure 12 (a) and (b), respectively. For p_c = 0.5 and only one live stream, $M = 1$ (Figure 12 (a)), the average bandwidth for each session becomes approximately 1 Mbps for all numbers of concurrent sessions. By increasing the number of live streaming media to $M = 2$ and $M = 3$, the average bandwidth per session becomes lower than the unicast case due to many sessions receiving the same live streaming media without sending multiple sessions. The average bandwidth per session becomes much lower in the case of $p_c = 0.9$ or nearly one (Figure 12(b)).

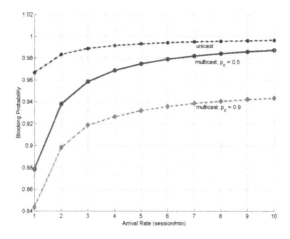

Fig. 13. The blocking probability with $M=2$, $N=30$, $\mu = 1/30$

Once the number of live streaming media is fixed due to the bandwidth limitation, as shown in Figure 12 (c) and (d), MHs with the high probability of joining the same stream will receive lower average bandwidth per session. Therefore, the behavior of MHs in the BSS greatly affects the system performance.

4.2   The Blocking Probability

In the unicast, each session will receive a separate live streaming media. When the utilized bandwidth reaches its maximum, all arriving requests will be blocked. However, for multicast with the same maximum number of allowed the concurrent streams, many more MHs can still receive the stream as long as they elect to join an active live streaming media. Hence, the blocking probability is much lower than the unicast case as shown in Figure 13.

5   Conclusions

In this paper, unicast and multicast communication modes for live streaming media have been quantitatively examined and compared with regards to performance. A simple bi-dimensional Markov model for both unicast and multicast was used to derive analytical expressions for the steady state behavior of the system. Numerical examples show that multicast outperforms unicast, with lower bandwidth per session and also a lower blocking probability. From the simple queueing model, the behavior of MHs can be easily understood and described in a manner that can be useful for future system design to make multicast more efficient, especially in the limited bandwidth situation like wireless LAN that users tend to share certain multimedia streams. The ongoing research is concentrated on developing a system that manipulates the unicast traffic for same requested streams to become a multicast stream without users' awareness.

References

1. A. Adams, J. Nicholas, and W. Siadak, Protocol Independent Multicast - Dense Mode (PIM-DM): Protocol Specification, RFC-3973 (January 2005).
2. A. Ballardie, Core Based Trees (CBT version 2) Multicast Routing, RFC-2189 (September 1997).
3. B. Zhang, S. Jamin, and L. Zhang, "Host Multicast: A Framework for Delivering Multicast To End Users", in:*Proceedings INFOCOM* (June 2002) pp. 1366-1375.
4. C.-W Bao and W. Liao, "Performance Analysis of Reliable MAC-Layer Multicast for IEEE 802.11 Wireless LANs", in: *Proceedings IEEE International Conference on Communications* (May 2005) pp. 1378-1382.
5. D. Estrin, D. Farinacci, A. Helmy, D. Thaler, S. Deering, M. Handely, V. Jacobson, C. Liu, P. Sharma, and L. Wei, Protocol independent multicast-sparse mode (PIM-SM): Protocol specification, RFC-2362, (June 1998).
6. D. Pendarakis, S. Shi, D. Verma, and M. Waldvogel, "ALMI: An application level multicast infrastructure", in:*Proceedings USENIX Symposium on Internet Technologies and Systems* (March 2001) pp. 49-60.
7. D. Thaler, D. Estrin, and D. Meyer, Border Gateway Multicast Protocol (BGMP): Protocol Specification, Internet draft (August 1998).
8. D. Thaler, Border Gateway Multicast Protocol (BGMP): Protocol Specification, RFC-3913 (September 2004).
9. D. Salyers, et al., "Wireless Stealth Multicast: Bandwidth Conservation for Last-Mile Wireless Clients", in:*Proceedings IEEE INFOCOM* (March 2005).
10. D. Waitzman and S. Deering, Distance Vector Multicast Routing Protocol, RFC-1075 (November 1988).
11. Hans Eriksson, MBONE: The Multicast Backbone, ACM Transaction Communications 37 (August 1994) 54-60.
12. G. Phillips, S. Shenker, and H. Tangmunarunkit, Scaling of Multicast trees: Comments on the Chuang Sirbu Scaling law", in:*Proceedings ACM SIGCOMM* (September 1999) pp. 41-51.
13. H. Fujisawa, K. Aoki, M. Yamamoto, and Y. Fujita, "Estimation of Multicast Packet Loss Characteristic due to Collision and Loss Recovery using FEC on Distributed Infrastructure Wireless LANs", in:*Proceedings Wireless Communications and Networking Conference* (March 2004) pp. 399-404.
14. J. Aaltonen, J. Karvo and S. Aalto, "Multicasting vs. Unicasting in Mobile Communication Systems", in:*Proceedings WoWMoM* (September 2002) pp. 104-108.
15. J. Chuang and M. Sirbu, Pricing Multicast Communications: A Cost-Based Approach. Telecommunication Systems 17 (July 2001) 281-297,
16. J. Kuri and S.K. Kasera, Reliable Multicast in Multi-Access Wireless LANs, Transaction on Wireless Network 7 (July 2001) 359-369.
17. J. Moy, Multicast extensions to OSPF, RFC-1584 (March 1994).
18. M. Castro, P. Druschel, A.-M. Kermarrec, and A. Rowstron, Scribe: A large-scale and decentralized application-level multicast infrastructure, IEEE Journal on Selected Areas in Communications 20 (October 2002) 1489-1499.
19. N. Nikaein, H. Labiod, and C. Bonnet, "MA-FEC: A QoS-based adaptive FEC for multicast communication in wireless networks", in: *Proceedings IEEE ICC* (June 2000) pp. 954-958.
20. P. Van Mieghem, G. Hooghiemstra and R. Van Der Hofstad, On the efficiency of multicast, IEEE/ACM Transactions on Networking 9 (December 2001) 719-732.

21. P. Van Mieghem and M. Janic, "Stability of a Multicast Tree", in:*IEEE INFOCOM* (June 2002) pp. 1099-1108.
22. S Casner and S. Deering, "First IETF internet audiocast", in:*ACM SIGCOMM Computer Communication Review* (July 1992) pp. 92-97.
23. S. Choi, Y. Choi, and I. Lee, IEEE 802.11 MAC-Level FEC with Retransmission Combining, IEEE Transaction on Wireless Communication 5 (January 2006) 203-211.
24. S. Deering, "Multicast routing in internetworks and extended LANs", in:*Proceedings ACM SIGCOMM* (August 1988) pp.55-64.
25. S. Deering, Host Extensions for IP Multicasting, RFC 1112 (August 1989).
26. S. Deering and C. David, Multicast Routing in Datagram Networks and Extended LANs, ACM Transactions on Computer Systems 18 (May 1990) 85-110.
27. S. Deering, D. Estrin, D. Farinacci, V. Jacobson, C. Liu, and L.Wei, "An architecture for wide-area multicast routing", in:*Proceedings ACM SIGCOMM* (October 1994) pp.126-13.
28. S. Deering, D. Estrin, D. Farinacci, V. Jacobson, C. Liu, and L. Wei, The PIM Architecture for Wide-Area Multicast Routing. IEEE/ACM Transactions on Networking 4 (April 1996) 153-162.
29. S. Floyd, V. Jacobson, S. McCanne, C.G. Liu, and L. Zhang, "A reliable multicast framework for light-weight sessions and application level framing", in: *Proceedings ACM SIGCOMM* (August 1995) pp. 342-356.
30. S.K.S. Gupta, V. Shankar, and S. Lalwani, "Reliable Multicast MAC Protocol for Wireless LANs", in: *Proceedings IEEE ICC* (May 2003) pp. 93-97.
31. Y.-H. Chu, S. G. Rao, and H. Zhang, "A case for end system multicast", in: *ACM SIGMETRICS international conference on Measurement and modeling of computer systems* (June 2000) pp. 1-12.

NAT-PT with Multicast

Maneenate Puongmanee, Robert Elz, Sinchai Kamolphiwong,
Thossaporn Kamolphiwong, Chatchai Jantaraprim, and Touchai Angchuan

Department of Computer Engineering
Faculty of Engineering
Prince of Songkla University
P.O. Box 2, Kohong, Hat Yai,
Songkhla 90112 Thailand
S4412038@psu.ac.th,
{kre, ksinchai, kthossaporn, cj, touch}@coe.psu.ac.th

Abstract. This work investigates Network Address Translation – Protocol Translation (NAT-PT) as an IPv4/IPv6 transition technique. NAT-PT is adequate for unicast communication, however, there is no provision for multicast address mapping. This paper presents a solution to improve NAT-PT by adding support for multicast. As a result, NAT-PT can provide multicast address translation, and applications using multicast can interoperate between IPv4 and IPv6. An application level gateway (ALG) for the Session Advertisement Protocol (SAP) is added to perform and announce group address mapping.

Keywords: IPv4, IPv6, NAT-PT, multicast.

1 Introduction

In the Internet, an IP address is used to identify each computer or device which is attached to a link of the network. There are millions of hosts, servers, mobile phones, communication devices, conference services and online electronic devices. Each of them needs an IP address in order to communicate. In addition, new technology, such as Mobile IP, Voice over IP, IP telephony and 3GPP are intending to use IP in their components.

However, the number of IPv4 addresses [1] is limited by their structure. Many are already assigned for nodes while other addresses cannot be assigned. The assignment hierarchy effectively ensures that many of the remaining addresses will never be assigned to actual nodes. As IP addresses have been rapidly used, address depletion will become a problem for the Internet in the near future.

These factors lead to the use of private IPv4 addresses within local domains. A short-term solution to allow this is the address reuse solution: IPv4 Network Address Translator (NAT) [2]. It allows the use of private IPv4 addresses within a local domain. NAT is placed the borders of the stub domain. Each NAT box has a table consisting of pairs of local IP addresses and globally unique addresses. The IP addresses inside the stub domains are not globally unique. They are reused in other domains that have deployed NAT to reduce the use of global addresses. However, some global addresses are still required by the organizations.

K. Cho and P. Jacquet (Eds.): AINTEC 2006, LNCS 4311, pp. 90–102, 2006.

The new Internet Protocol, IPv6 [3], was invented to replace the exhausted IPv4. An IPv6 address with 128-bits provides more than 3.40×10^{38} addresses to allow a very large number of nodes to be attached to the internet.

The original plan to transition to IPv6 was gradually to turn on IPv6 in every node that was attached to the Internet or upgraded. This technique is called Dual-Stack. Eventually every node would contain both IPv4 and IPv6. Each node would be able to communicate to other v4 and v6 nodes.

It now seems clear that even if all network modes were able to support IPv6 before the last IPv4 global address is allocated, not all, and perhaps not even most, IPv4 networks will enable parallel operation of IPv6. Once there are no more available IPv4 addresses, new networks joining the Internet will have no choice except to use v6 alone for external communications – private v4 addresses can still be used internally. Some other networks are likely to remain v4 only, even with new ones being v6 only. So the Internet is required to deploy a transition mechanism to allow communication between these worlds which have different IP versions.

Network Address Translation – Protocol Translation (NAT-PT) [4], a translation mechanism, was created to provide communication and applications between v4 and v6 worlds. It translates address, port and protocol between IPv4 and IPv6 which allows transparent communication between the protocols without changing anything at the end nodes. It can provide bidirectional unicast address translation and communication between IPv4 and IPv6.

Since NAT-PT was derived from NAT, they have the same features in some functions. NAT-PT program is available to implement for testing and it is expected to be used in the migration period. These advantages are a motivation to evaluate and enhance NAT-PT's features. There are other translation mechanisms available [5],[6],[7], we chose to evaluate NAT-PT because of its relationship to NAT which is very widely deployed. We found that NAT-PT has limitations inherited from NAT, as expected, and others caused by the effects of protocol translation. In addition, it provides unicast communication only. It drops multicast packets and does not perform multicast address translation. Thus v4 and v6 nodes cannot participate in a common multicast session. In the future, multimedia and multicast application are likely be used more. Not only v4 to v4 or v6 to v6 but these applications are also required between v4 and v6 worlds.

This work proposes a solution to improve NAT-PT to provide multicast communication between v4 and v6 worlds. It also presents a way to announce group addresses. This paper is organized as follows: review of NAT-PT transition techniques is in section 2. A solution to provide multicast address mapping is offered in section 3. The implementation and testing of the module are explained in section 4. The results are in section 5 with suggestions for future work in section 6. The conclusion of this work is in section 7.

2   Review NAT-PT

NAT-PT provides translation between IPv4-only and IPv6-only nodes. The IP address, port and protocol are translated from IPv4 to IPv6 and vice versa. Translated packets need to be passed through an enabled NAT-PT border router between the

IPv4 and IPv6 realms. During the connections NAT-PT must keep translation information to identify the end nodes and hold the mappings between the original and translated addresses. There will be a single point of failure if the NAT-PT router goes down. However, there can be more than one NAT-PT router with each handling a subset of all communications. Multi-NAT-PT or mNAT-PT [8],[9] has been offered to extend the scalability of NAT-PT.

NAT-PT breaks end-to-end security and cannot support Internet security protocols that contain IP address and port information in the payload such as the IP security protocol (IPsec) [10],[11],[12] – Authentication Header (AH) and IP Encapsulating Security Payload (ESP). Those prohibit modification of the IP header and payload. Because TCP, UDP and ICMPv6 checksums have a dependency on the IP source and destination addresses via the pseudo-header, they must be updated when the addresses are translated. These limitations are inherited from NAT.

Also, protocols that contain IP addresses inside their payload, for example ftp, DNS, cannot be handled by NAT-PT alone. It does not see the IP address inside these payloads and does not know which addresses must be translated. NAT-PT uses the concept of Application Level Gateways (ALG), for example Domain Name System – Application Level Gateway (DNS-ALG) [13], File Transfer Protocol – Application Level Gateway (FTP-ALG) to translate the payloads for those protocols that require it.

Normally, a node finds the IP address of a destination from the DNS [14],[15] server when it wants to connect to that node. For communication between v4-only and v6-only, the destination has an incompatible address in the DNS records. The DNS-ALG is used to allocate an appropriate address and provide the mapping between IPv4 and IPv6 addresses. The DNS-ALG intercepts and modifies the DNS reply for an A or AAAA record – it changes A to AAAA and vice versa. Then it adds the IPv6 and IPv4 addresses into a mapping table. The DNS-ALG tells NAT-PT about the mapped addresses in order to provide later address and packet translation when the address is used in packet headers.

3 Multicast Address Mapping

Multicasting is one-to-many communication. If a multicast application is available, the data packets need to be transmitted to every network that wants to participate in the session. Multicast routers handle this task. They duplicate the original packet and send the copies to every network attached to their interfaces as required.

The way to communicate between v4 and v6 nodes is similar to communication between nodes that have the same IP version. However, group address and packets must be adjusted to be the appropriate IP versions.

In order to provide a multicast application between v4 and v6 realms, the session must be identified with unique group addresses for each realm. The appropriate addresses must be known by v4 and v6 recipients of the session.

This section presents the assumption and plan to develop multicast address translation between IPv4 and IPv6 addresses. We assume:

a) Only a prototype implementation will be produced.
b) Only one NAT-PT exists between v4 and v6 multicast users.
c) Only global scope multicast addresses are handled.

We make these assumptions in order to determine whether multicast through NAT-PT is practical. This work is a prototype and needs implementation to test whether it is possible before focusing on performance. Having determined that we can later determine the effects of relaxing these assumptions. So we implement NAT-PT with multicast on a basic and simple isolated network in our laboratory. There is only one NAT-PT box to provide multicast communication between an IPv4-only and an IPv6-only networks. The simple testing network makes for easy checking whether our solution can provide multicast address translation on NAT-PT.

Multiple NAT-PT routers can be deployed as gateway on a network in order to perform load balancing. However, we must consider packet looping inside that network. In addition, the multiple boxes must coordinate address mapping between IPv4 and IPv6. The mapped address must not be duplicated by the other NAT-PT routers. Performance of NAT-PT or speed to process multicast packets needs to be measured and enhanced. These issues will be further studied and developed in future work.

When a v4 server provides a multicast v4 application, it sends multicast v4 packets to the world. These multicast packets must be delivered to all networks where they are required. When a v6 node wants to join this group, it needs to know an appropriate group address to join. This requires translation between IPv4 and IPv6 multicast addresses.

The v6 recipient uses the IPv6 group number to identify the application in order to send to the group. This IPv6 address must be translated back to the original IPv4 address corresponding to that session.

Provision of multicast NAT-PT can be accomplished by meeting three objectives.

1. A solution to provide multicast packet mapping between IPv4 and IPv6.
2. An algorithm to translate multicast addresses.
3. A solution to distribute multicast group information.

3.1 Solution to Provide Multicast Packet Mapping Between IPv4 and IPv6

First, the source address must be changed. It is a unicast address and is translated following the original algorithm of NAT-PT that translates unicast addresses. The destination address is multicast, and it is translated using the algorithm and method presented in section 3.2.

The packet header formats also must be translated. Because there is no difference between unicast and multicast packet formats, the packet translation mechanisms from unicast NAT-PT can be used. Transport protocols are also impacted. Most multicast transport protocols are layered above UDP as a basic transport layer. NAT-PT already handles UDP updates (port mapping if required, and checksum correction to allow for the altered pseudo-header.) It turns out that the most popular of the upper transport protocols used by multicast applications – the Real Time Protocol (RTP) [16] needs no further adjustment. Thus aside from the multicast destination mapping function, multicast translation needs no alteration to that used for unicast.

3.2 Algorithm to Translate Multicast Address

Multicast addresses, or group identifiers need to be translated between v4 and v6. Mappings must be bi-directional, however the same algorithm is not required when translating a group identifier created using IPv4 to IPv6 as is used for one created initially in IPv6.

Algorithm to Translate IPv4 to IPv6 Address

To translate multicast IPv4 to IPv6 address, a temporary IPv6 address is required. This address is the transient number for mapping from multicast IPv4 to IPv6 and vice versa. The simplest way to generate the temporary IPv6 address is to assign a particular multicast IPv6 prefix with IPv4 multicast address in the last 32 bits. This work assigns a new multicast IPv6 prefix for NAT-PT translation only. This prefix is assigned with the same scope as the v4 multicast address, which we assume to be global initially, in order to provide a multicast application to the Internet as shown in Fig. 1.

IPv4-mcast-addr(32bits)   =>   ff3e:ff00::0/96 + IPv4-mcast-addr

Fig. 1. Algorithm to translate multicast IPv4 to IPv6 address

Algorithm to Translate IPv6 to IPv4 Address

When a group exists with an IPv6 address, an IPv4 multicast address must be allocated. Unlike in the previous case, the multicast IPv6 address cannot be embedded as the suffix of the multicast IPv4 address.

In order to avoid using the identical IPv4 multicast addresses with the other applications and control packet looping, the simplest way is to allocate a dedicated block of multicast IPv4 addresses. However, the way to choose, and the size of, the dedicated address block for NAT-PT are important issues that we must consider. The address block should be reserved for NAT-PT only.

In the early stage of this enhancement, the temporary IPv4 address can be an arbitrary number in the multicast IPv4 block. We select a block of multicast IPv4 address and a random address in that range to map to IPv6 multicast address. The algorithm to translate multicast IPv6 to IPv4 address is presented in Fig. 2.

IPv6-mcast-addr => next-free(IPv4-mcast-addr)

Fig. 2. Algorithm to translate multicast IPv6 to IPv4 address

The procedures to translate a packet are shown in Fig. 3. In this diagram, the variables X and Y are used to represent the IP versions. Multicast packets are processed using the following steps:

1. When an IPvX source initiates a multicast IPvX application and sends IPvX packets, the multicast routing protocol in the IPvX network distributes the packets. NAT-PT, a function on an IPvX multicast router, participates in that multicast routing algorithm. Then all packets it needs get delivered to it.
2. The router checks the properties of the received packets and determines destination of the packet. Since the packet is multicast, it is processed like normal multicast packets. The packet is duplicated as required. The router forwards these packets via every appropriate IPvX network interface for IPvX recipients. The sending relies on multicast packet forwarding, RPF, and multicast routing protocol for IPvX to find the paths.
3. NAT-PT with multicast function looks for the IPvX group address of the packet in the mapping rules. The way to check and translate multicast packet for IPv4 and IPv6 groups are shown in Fig 4 and 5 respectively.
4. If the group address is in the list, the packet is translated to IPvY format with a new destination address from the mapping rule.
5. Packets that have been translated are treated as normal multicast packets that arrived from another node. They are sent via every IPvY network interface of NAT-PT to IPvY recipients. The router uses multicast routing protocol for IPvY to find the paths for sending the translated packet.

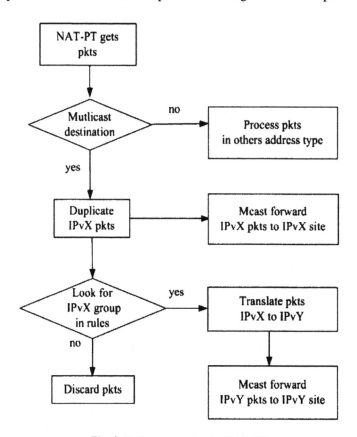

Fig. 3. Packet processing by NAT-PT

6. If the group address is not in NAT-PT's mapping rules, no packet translation is performed, and the packet is not forwarded to IPvY. There cannot be any useful purpose to dynamically generating a new mapping and using that, as there could not possibly be any members of the new group, if the group identifier were only created by NAT-PT after the packet arrived.

```
if (IN_MULTICAST(IP4-dest-addr))
{
    if  IP4-mcast-addr  match in mapping rules
        assign mcast IPv6 prefix to IP4-mcast-addr
        and send translated packet
    else
        not translate to the other protocol
}
```

Fig. 4. Packet processing to check IPv4 group address

```
if (IN_MULTICAST(IP6-dest-addr))
{
    if  IP6-mcast-addr  match in mapping rules
        assign IP4-mcast-addr  to  IP6-mcast-addr
        and send translated packet
    else
        not translate to the other protocol
}
```

Fig. 5. Packet processing to check IPv6 group address

3.3 Solution to Distribute Multicast Information

When a node provides multicast services, information of these applications should be available for the other nodes in network. Normally, multicast communication has protocols to describe a session and allow a recipient to find the group address used by the desired multicast session. They are the Session Description Protocol (SDP) [17] and Session Announcement Protocol (SAP) [18]. SDP is used to describe the properties of a multimedia session such as the group address, media type, time table to provide service. SAP, a multicast protocol, is the distribution protocol, used to carry SDP which contains group address inside its payload to listeners in the network. SAP uses a well known multicast address for each IP version.

In order to allow v4 and v6 recipients in each network to know the available multicast sessions from the other world, the SAP packet and its group address must be changed to be the appropriate value for the other IP version. Since SAP/SDP is like the DNS and FTP which contain IP addresses in the payload, NAT-PT does not see these addresses and cannot perform address translation.

An ALG for multicasting is necessary to be used to help NAT-PT like DNS-ALG and FTP-ALG. This work proposes an ALG to provide multicast address mapping to the group address in SAP/SDP. We call it the Session Announcement Protocol-Application Level Gateway (SAP-ALG). It is a function on the NAT-PT router or gateway.

The SAP-ALG module is presented in Fig. 6, an overview of the operation is as follows. The ALG gets an advertisement, an IPv4 SAP packet, from a v4 node. It looks for the IPv4 group address in the SDP packet. It allocates, if required, and maps the appropriate new multicast number to the original address. SAP-ALG uses the method from section 3.2 to allocate multicast address for group address mapping. The NAT-PT kernel code is informed of the mapping. Then a new IPv6 SAP packet is generated containing the mapped group number as a part of SDP payload of the new packet. The other descriptions such as application or media type, schedule, are unchanged from the original IPv4 SAP packet. After that the ALG sends the new IPv6 SAP packet to every v6 network. Mapping from IPv6 to IPv4 is done in the same way.

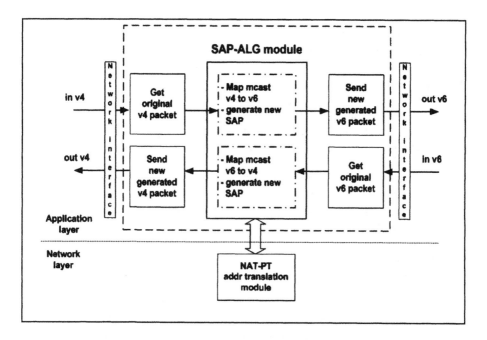

Fig. 6. SAP-ALG module

4 Implementation and Testing

The multicast module has been added into the existing NAT-PT system that works on FreeBSD-4.9 [19]. The original NAT-PT was implemented on this kernel by the KAME project [20]. The testbed network is shown in Fig. 7 which, while simple, is adequate to test for the case of a single NAT-PT.

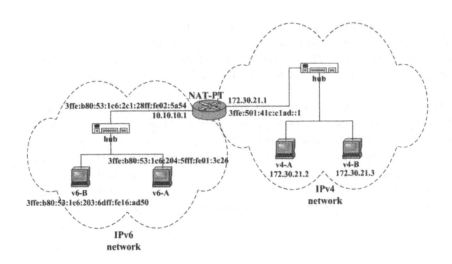

Fig. 7. Testbed network

The test consists of two parts: testing of address and packet translation, and, multicast address mapping by SAP-ALG. Each test has been implemented as follows:

4.1 Testing of Address and Packet Translation

The objective of this part is to test the extension multicast address module to provide multicast and packet translation. The multicast application, vic (Videoconferencing tool), is deployed to test in this part. It is easy to use, and generates a stream of multicast packets with no user input required.

The condition of this testing are that the multicast applications have been configured with global scope, and the only-one NAT-PT has been set up as a gateway between the networks. This testing uses manually configured address translation and the end nodes simply know the appropriate group addresses. The mapping rules are proposed in Fig. 8. The expected result is the multicast module must translate multicast address and packet following the mapping rules. Then the recipient in one network can use the multicast application to receive data from the other.

```
map from   ff3e:ff00::e0c8:c8c8   to  224.200.200.200
map from   224.200.200.200        to  ff3e:ff00::e0c8:c8c8
```

Fig. 8. The mapping rules

4.2 Testing of Multicast Address Mapping by SAP-ALG

The objective of this part is to test SAP-ALG to provide and advertise group address mapping. The program sdr (Session directory tool) is used to generate information about the available multicast applications. Sdr generates multicast announcements in the v4 and v6 networks. The expected result is for the SAP-ALG to provide group address mapping to allow v6 listeners know the available v4 multicast applications and vice versa.

5 Result

Address and Packet Translation Tests
On the v6 recipient, the application vic joins the v6 group, ff3e:ff00:e0c8:c8c8 as in Fig. 9. After the node joins the group, it transmits its own data (video packet), and receives video stream from any other members of the group which are transmitting. Vic uses RTP/RTCP to deliver data and control information. RTCP provides the description to present to the user about that session. There are two sessions shown on the vic menu. The first is the description from a v4 node the sender. It is generated by user root at the host which is identified by the IP address 172.30.21.2 though in RTCP this is just a string identifier. This application is encoded with technique h261. The second is the description of the session originated by this v6 node. It shows that this session is created by root at the host 3ffe:b80:53:1c6:204:5fff:fe01:3c26 by using technique h261 to encode data.

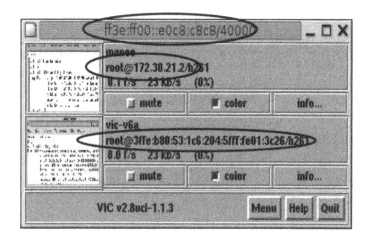

Fig. 9. vic on the v6 recipient

In each case the small (illegible in the figure) window to the left of the session description shows a dynamic thumbnail view of the transmitted video, which for our test purposes is merely an image extracted from the sending system's graphic display.

Testing of Multicast Address Mapping by SAP-ALG
On the v4 announcer, sdr generates session description for the available multicast v4 applications as in Fig.10. The description is advertised to v4 listeners.

SAP-ALG intercepts the SAPv4 announcements and provides group address mapping to IPv6 multicast addresses. It uses the method in section 3.3 to perform this task. Then it sends a new SAPv6 advertisement that contains the mapped IPv6 group addresses to the v6 network. The v6 recipient also runs sdr to get the advertisement. The program displays the session descriptions of the v4 multicast applications as shown in Fig. 11.

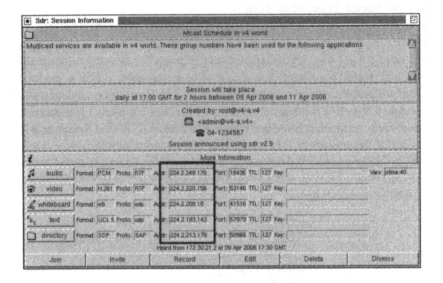

Fig. 10. sdr on the v4 announcer

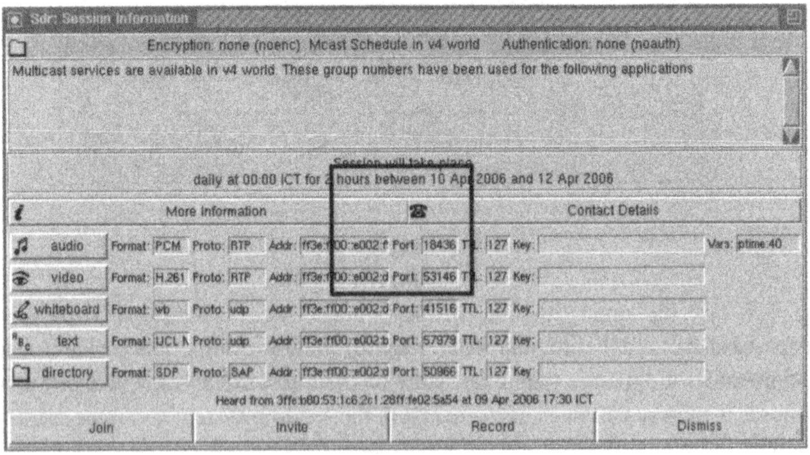

Fig. 11. sdr on the v6 recipient

6 Future Work

Although this enhancement can provide multicast application between IPv4 and IPv6, it works correctly for only one NAT-PT router. The following areas should be studied and explored to improve its features.

a) NAT-PT can be applied into multiple routers in the same network. However, the multiple routers must deal with packet looping of multicast packets inside the network. More research is required to solve this problem, probably by embedding more intelligence into the SAP-ALG.

b) When multiple NAT-PT boxes are installed between the same networks, a method is required for them to co-ordinate address mapping between IPv4 and IPv6. The addresses for mapping should not be duplicated with other NAT-PT boxes or other multicast applications. In order to do that, a better solution to allocate these addresses is required. Again, as it is the SAP-ALG that creates the mappings, co-ordination between the ALGs is required. It may be sufficient for each ALG to intelligently process advertisements from the other(s). More research is required in this case.

c) There are several areas where implementation improvements are required to allow a practical solution to be obtained.

7 Conclusion

This paper describes enhancement to NAT-PT to provide multicast between IPv4 and IPv6. It proposes a method to map group numbers for available multicast v4 and v6 applications.

Multicast sessions and communication can be provided between IPv4 and IPv6 by NAT-PT with the multicast function. Multicast addresses and packets are translated and allow recipients in the other network to join these sessions.

The recipients can obtain information of the available multicast sessions from network by using SDP/SAP. In order to allow the recipients from the other networks know of these sessions, SAP-ALG provides an appropriate multicast addresses to map the groups of these sessions and advertises the sessions using the mapped group identifiers. As a result, the recipients in each network know the available sessions in the other. They can join and use services from each of them.

Acknowledgments. This work is supported by National Electronics and Computer Technology Center (NECTEC), Contact Number: NT-B-06-4B-18-507.

References

1. J. Postel, "Internet Protocol", RFC 791 September 1981.
2. Deering, S. and Hinden, R., "Internet Protocol, Version 6 (IPv6) Architecture", RFC2460, December 1998.
3. P. Srisuresh, "Traditional IP Network Address Translator (Traditional NAT)", RFC3022, January 2001.

4. G.Tsirtsis, "Network Address Translation - Protocol Translation (NAT-PT)", RFC2766, February 2000.
5. R. Gilligan, "Transition Mechanisms for IPv6 Hosts and Routers", RFC2893 August 2000.
6. J. Hagino and K. Yamamoto, "An IPv6-to-IPv4 Transport Relay Translator",RFC3142, June 2001.
7. H. Kitamura, A. Jinzaki and S. Kobayashi, "A SOCKS-based IPv6/IPv4 Gateway Mechanism", RFC3089, April 2001.
8. S. Daniel Park, "draft-park-v6ops-multi-natpt-00", April 2003.
9. S. Daniel Park, "draft-park-scalable-multi-natpt-00", May 2003.
10. S. Kent, "Security Architecture for the Internet Protocol", RFC2401,November 1998.
11. S. Kent, "IP Authentication Header", RFC2402, November 1998.
12. S. Kent, "IP Encapsulation Security Payload (ESP)", RFC2406, November 1998.
13. P. Srisuresh, G. Tsirtsis, P. Akkiraju and A. Heffernan, "DNS extensions to Network Address Translators (DNS_ALG)", RFC2694, September 1999.
14. P. Mockapetris, "DOMAIN NAMES – COMCEPT AND FACILITIES", RFC1034, November 1987.
15. P. Mockapetris, "DOMAIN NAMES – COMCEPT AND FACILITIES", RFC1035, November 1987.
16. H. Schulzrinne, et.al, "RTP: A Transport Protocol for Real-Time Applications", RFC3550, Jul. 2003.
17. M. Handley and V. Jacobson, "SDP: Session Description Protocol",RFC2327, April 1998.
18. M. Handley, "Session Announcement Protocol", RFC2974, October 2000.
19. http://www.freebsd.org
20. http://www.kame.net

Network Processing Hardware

Mary Inaba and Kei Hiraki

Graduate School of Information Science and Technology
University of Tokyo
{mary, hiraki}@is.s.u-tokyo.ac.jp

Abstract. Speed-up of networks is faster than that of processors. For high-speed networks, general-purpose computers can no longer play the management role of network streams such as Intrusion Detection System, and hardware approaches are required. This paper introduces two approaches of network processing hardware; a *network processor* approach and a *middle hardware* approach.

1 Introduction

The speed-up of network is faster than that of processors. For example, since IEEE802.3 CSMA/CD was standardized in 1983, it took twelve years till 802.3u Fast Ethernet was standardized in 1995. Then, 802.3z 1000BASE-X in 1998, and 802.3ae 10Gbit/s Ethernet over fiber in 2003, that is, it becomes 100 times faster only in eight years. On the other hand, a typical processor speed is roughly 100MHz in 1997 and 4 to 6 GHz in 2005, following Moore's Law. As a result, general-purpose computers can no longer play the management role of network streams by processing network protocols at line speed such as a gateway and a network surveillance type Network Intrusion Detection System(IDS).

Backbone networks have rapidly expanded and become fatter. For example, in 1998, Internet2 started Abilene IP over SONET(Synchronous Optical Network) backbone network with OC-48, and now covers the whole U.S. with OC-192, and, recently announced a plan to shift to Lambda Network with testbed of 40 to 100Gbps speed in 2007. For backbone network infrastructure, new technologies such as WANPHY and LANPHY are also spreading, which realize very long-distance Ethernet networks. Although a worldwide L2 network is very convenient for users, there still remain a lot of problems to be solved. For example, well-known L3 tools such as "`traceroute`" command do not work with intermediate switches, and the only way to check connectivity is "`ping`" command to every intermediate switches. Furthermore, some switches can not remotely provide information even of the SONET layer. Actually, when we tried WANPHY network from CERN to Tokyo in 2003, the only way to locate an error was successive loop-back trials and human communication via E-mail, or worse, via telephone across several time zones and several organizations. In such situation, a demand for remote network testers becomes larger and larger.

It is well known that TCP/IP data transfer on Long Fat pipe Network(LFN) is difficult. To tackle with this problem, we have developed several types of network

K. Cho and P. Jacquet (Eds.): AINTEC 2006, LNCS 4311, pp. 103–112, 2006.

equipment for processing network protocols with hardware support, not only for improving communication performance but also for analyzing the cause of the problems.

To process network protocols, speed and flexibility are important factors. This paper introduces two approaches of programmable network processing hardware; a *network processor* approach which consists of a network stream processor and a rewritable state transition table, and a *middle hardware* approach which uses Field Programmable Gate Array (FPGA) and enables hardware parallel processing.

2   Network Processor Approach – Comet and Its Applications

2.1   Comet NP

The Comet protocol processing engine is a programmable network processor, which consists of Finite State Machine engine and State Transition Table. Comet Network Processor (Comet NP) uses 350nm CMOS technology and has two stream processors, two PCI-64bit/66MHz external buses(Fig. 1). It has function units of checksum, table lookup and DES/3DES, and executes parallel processing with horizontal microprogramming. For more detail, refer to [2].

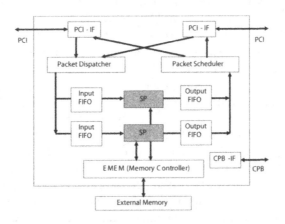

Fig. 1. Comet NP

Comet i-NIC(Network Interface Card) is a programmable intelligent NIC with two 10/100/1000Base-T ports, which has a pair of 64/32 bit 66/33MHz PCI buses for both external and host links. It has Comet NP for protocol processing and Strong Arm 1110 233MHz as a controll processor, with 256MByte SDRAM memory and 16MByte Flash memory. It can provide functions such as IPsec single DES, 3DES, protocol offloading, automatic forwarding and Interrupt Coalescing.

2.2   Comet i-NIC Applications

Here, we show our network equipment prototypes using Comet i-NIC.

Pseudo-LFN emulator, Comet Delay and Drop

Since real LFN environment is expensive, we developed pseudo-LFN environment emulator Comet Delay using Comet i-NIC as an L2 bridge. We can set a delay ranging from 0 to 127 seconds with granularity of 100 μs. Then, Comet Delay stores received packets in the buffer memory on the NIC for the specified time, and send them using the packet forwarding function. We also add a drop function to emulate packet losses, where we can program and try different packet drop models.

DR Giga-Analyzer

DR Giga-Analyzer is a packet analyzer which logs packet information adding GPS timestamps with 100ns accuracy[4]. It uses a pair of Comet i-NIC, receives tapped stream, adds timestamp and encapsulates it to UDP packets and sends them to eight IA servers to record. It can process packet at the full wire-rate, 2Gbps for both directions even for 64Bytes short packets, which requires more than 2,976,000pps processing capability. DR Giga-Analyzer merges packets and decreases the number of packets while using the packet forwarding function.

Comet-TCP

Comet-TCP is a variation of TCP optimized for long distance data transfer, which utilizes the Comet i-NIC functions. It work as a proxy by relaying TCP streams between a pair of Comet i-NICs at distant places, using a protocol which we call Long Fat Tunnel(LFT), in order to minimize the latency effects between Comet i-NICs. No modification is required for application programs because Comet-TCP has a compatible API to the conventional TCP protocol stack.

2.3   Experimental Results

Gigabit Ethernet NIC unstability

At SC02, we examined "Data Reservoir" file sharing system, between Baltimore and Tokyo, where the distance is 7,500 miles, RTT(Round Trip Time) is 200 ms, where APAN OC-12/POS was the bottle neck.

We attained 91% usage of the bottleneck bandwidth using a pair of 26 IA servers. But the performance of each stream was worse than we expected, and unstability and large deviations between streams troubled us. To investigate this strange phenomenon, we compared data transfer on the pseudo LFN with the real LFN, and using GbE(Gigabit Ethernet) NICs and Fast Ethernet NICs, monitored by DR Giga-Analyzer. Fig. 2 shows the number of packets received for 1 msec on GbE, which is bursty for every RTT. On the other hand, when a Fast Ethernet NIC is used, the number of packets are almost constant. This means, even if the congestion window size is same and the transfer rate of TCP is macroscopically same, the packet distributions are different depending on NIC speeds, and, when we use GbE on the real LFN with an OC-12/POS bottleneck, there occur a lot of avoidable packet losses because of microscopic bursts.

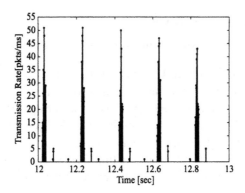

Fig. 2. Number of packets received in 1msec (GbE NIC)

Comet TCP with Comet Delay and Drop

Comet TCP is a proxy using the LFT protocol, for minimizing the latency effects. First, using Comet Delay and Drop, we compare effects of latency for TCP variations in the pseudo LFN environment.

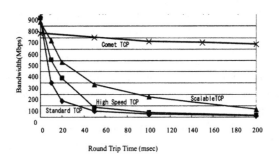

Fig. 3. TCP variations

Figure 3 shows the performance and latency graph for variations of TCP. Standard TCP and other TCP variations suffer from latency around 20msec, and around 50msec, the performance decreases down to 10 to 30 %. On the other hand, Comet TCP can keep 90% of its performance even with 200msec latency.

Comet TCP in SC03

On SC03 in Phoenix, we examined disk-to-disk data transfer for one and a half round trips between Tokyo and U.S.. The circuit is 24,000km(15,000mile), and the bandwidth bottleneck is 8.2Gbps.

Fig. 4 shows the network topology for the experiment and Fig. 5 shows the official record of Comet-TCP data transfer for SC03 Band Width Challenge. We used a pair of 16 IA servers and attained 7.56Gbps which is 92% usage of the available bandwidth. For first 1,000 seconds, circuit was rather unstable and some packets were lost, but, we can see Comet TCP recovers its throughput promptly.

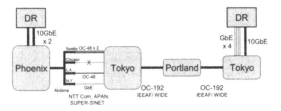

Fig. 4. 15,000miles Network, 3 different routes merged to 8.2Gbps

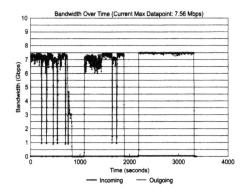

Fig. 5. Bandwidth Challenge Official Record of Comet-TCP

3   Middle Hardware Approach – MH-Box and an Application

As shown in the previous section, the network processor approach is effective to process network streams with 1Gbps speed. But, to deal with 10 to 100Gbps speed networks, parallel processing is required. For example, if we want to process a 40Gbps stream using a chip whose operating clock speed is 400MHz, at least 12 octet characters must be processed in parallel in each cycle. We proposed a programmable hardware framework to handle network streams at the wire-rate speed, on which we can realize a function by developing a firmware for FPGA. We call this as Middle Hardware approach.

3.1   Middle Hardware(MH)-Box

To attain wire-speed rate processing constantly, all program and data should fit in FPGA's on-chip memory. In addition, to handle TCP streams in the middle of a network path as required for IDS, the system requires light context switching with handling out-of-order packets efficiently and withdrawing retransmission inconsistency. We design a framework which recognizes each stream, and can be used as a network proxy to analyze and improve network performance and security.

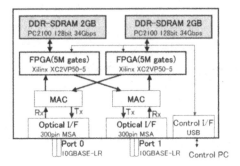

Fig. 6. MH-Box

We implemented MH-Box. Figure 6 shows its block diagram. MH-Box has a pair of 10GbE LR optical interfaces, port 0 and port 1, and there are two data paths. Each path has its own FPGA; Xilinx XC2VP50-5 which has 5 million gates inside and 2Giga bytes DDR-SDRAM memory; PC2100 128bits 34Gbps. Each FPGA works independently. Since there is no buffer memory between Rx and FPGA, from Rx to FPGA, it accurately takes a constant time.

3.2   An Application: TAPEE

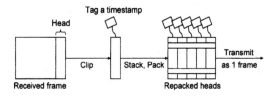

Fig. 7. TAPEE

On MH-Box, we implemented FPGA firmware to support (1) Network Analyzer, (2) LFN emulator, (3) TCP hamonizer, (4) packet pacing, (5) string matching, and (6) encryption and decryption. Here, we introduce Network Analyzer, TAPEE(Traffic Analysis Precise Enhancement Engine).

TAPEE aims to collect packet header logs with 10Gbps speed. It consists of a MH-Box, a recorder, and a tap. For packet logging, MH-Box captures a packet, clips its head, tags a timestamp, merges heads to a "repacked heads" and transmits it to the recorder as one frame(Fig.7). The recorder is IBM eServer x345 with dual Intel Xeon 2.4GHz 2GByte memory and Chelsio T110 10GbE NIC, which receives repacked heads, stores them, analyzes, and visualizes them. TAPEE also has a function to generate packets by itself for load test of network.

3.3   Experimental Result of 10G Packet Analyzer

Here, we show one example data using TAPEE. We used a real LFN circuit Tokyo – Chicago – Amsterdam – Seattle – Tokyo network with RTT 498ms. We

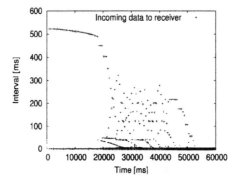

Fig. 8. Intervals of incoming data packets to the receiver

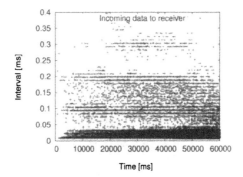

Fig. 9. Intervals of incoming data packets to the receiver

used dual AMD Opteron 250 with memory 2GByte, Rioworks HDAMA mother board with PCI-X 1.0 64bit 133MHz buses, and Chelsio N210 GbE NIC with Linux 2.14.7 original TCP stack. Here, the bottleneck was the PCI-X bus of about 8Gbps speed. We executed IPv6 memory to memory data transfer using 9,208Byte jumbo frames with "iperf" command. Figure 8 shows the interval of data arrival at the receiver side. As for long intervals, they start about RTT 500ms, for first 20 seconds, gradually decrease, then, disperse for a while, and finally, around 50 seconds (50,000ms) converge to short interval about 15 μseconds, which result in about 7Gbps. Fig. 9 is a magnification of fig. 8 to show intervals shorter than 0.4ms. Around 15 μsec, thick part is observed as expected. In addition, we can observe dense lines around 0.1ms, 0.2ms, and 0.3ms, which might be caused by time slice of TICK of the operating system.

Fig. 10 and Fig. 11 shows the frequency of intervals of outgoing ACK from the receiver and incoming ACK to the sender, respectively. Fig. 12 shows incoming ACK back to the sender of the same experiment on a pseudo-LFN with artificial delay of 500msec. As for outgoing ACK, we can observe periodical peaks in addition to the 15 μsec high peak, and so as incoming ACK on pseudo-LFN. On the other hand, incoming ACK on the real LFN environment, it has two peaks;

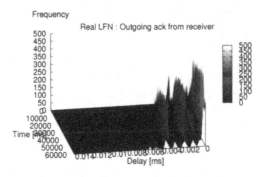

Fig. 10. Outgoing ACK distribution

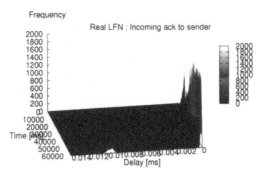

Fig. 11. Incoming ACK Distribution

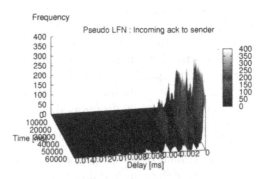

Fig. 12. ACK Distribution on Pseudo LNF environment

one is almost 0μsec with very high frequency, and the other is about 120 μsec, i.e., several ACKs are merged periodically, which might be one of the causes of microscopical burst on the real LFN.

4   Concluding Remarks

As the backbone networks grows, tools for network security and analysis become more and more important, which process network protocols at the wire-rate speed. In addition, to follw the rapid growth of network technologies, programmability for prompt development and easy update is strongly desirable. We show two programmable network processing hardware aproaches; a network processor approach using a stream processor with a State Transition Table, and a middle hardware approach using an FPGA. These frameworks enable easy and prompt developments of what we want when we need. This paper shows some results of our experiments using applications on those frameworks.

The network middle hardware can be used as an off-the-shelf hardware and firmware for GRID and other global applications without any special modifications on the end-node computers.

Acknowledgement

Special thanks to Prof. Akira Kato of University of Tokyo for useful discussions and networking coordination. Comet network equipments are developed by joint work with Fujitsu Laboratories Ltd., and we thank Mr. Akira Jinzaki for useful discussions. MH-Box and TAPEE are joint work with Dr. Yutaka Sugawara, and Mr. Tsuyoshi Yoshino. We thank Mr. Seiichi Fujishiro of Sansei Electric Co. Ltd., for developing MH-Box boards with FPGA and 10GbE. We also thank Prof. Don Reilly, Dr. Yamamoto, Mr. Hasebe, Mr. Kobayashi, Mr. Tanaka, Mr. Sekiya, Mr. Hattori, Mr. Watanabe, and Mr. Kurokawa for network support. We also thank organization and people StarLight, Tyco Telecommunications, IEEAF, Pacific Northwest Gigapop, SURFnet, CA*net4networks, JGN and WIDE project.

This research is partially supported by the Special Coordination Fund for Promoting Science and Technology, and Grant-in-Aid for Fundamental Scientific Research B(2) #13480077 from Ministry of Education, Culture, Sports, Science and Technology Japan, Semiconductor Technology Academic Research Center (STARC) Japan, CREST project of Japan Science and Technology Corporation, and by 21st century COE project of Japan Society for the Promotion of Science. We acknowledge the support of Global Crossing, Industry Canada, NTT Communications, and ITC of the University of Tokyo.

References

1. K. Hiraki, M. Inaba, J. Tamatsukuri, R. Kurusu, Y. Ikuta, H. Koga, A. Zinzaki: Data Reservoir: Utilization of Multi-Gigabit Backbone Network for Data-Intensive Research, *SC2002*, http://www.sc-2002.org/paperpdfs/pap.pap327.pdf, (2002)
2. A. Jinzaki: Stream Processor Comet, *Proc. JSPP2000*, pp. 205–212,(2000). (in Japanese)
3. M. Nakamura, M. Inaba, K. Hiraki: Fast Ethernet is sometimes faster than Gigabit Ethernet on LFN — Observation of congestion control of TCP streams, *Proc. PDCS*, pp. 854–859, (2003).

4. S. Nakano, K. Torii, S. Yoshida, T. Yanagisawa, K. Mizuguchi, Y. Ikuta, A. Zinzaki, J. Shitami, J. Tamatsukuri, M. Nakamura, M. Inaba, and K. Hiraki: DR Giga Analyzer, Symp. on Global Dependable Information Infrastructure, pp. 199-202, (2004). (in Japanese)
5. H. Kamezawa, M. Nakamura, J. Tamatsukuri, N. Aoshima, M. Inaba, K. Hiraki, J. Shitami, A. Jinzaki, R. Kurusu, M. Sakamoto, and Y. Ikuta Inter-layer coordination for parallel TCP streams on Long Fat pipe Networks Super Computing 2004, High Performance Networking and Computing, SC2004
6. Y. Sugawara, M. Inaba, and K. Hiraki, "Over 10Gbps String Matching Mechanism for Multi-Stream Packet Scanning Systems" FPL2004, (2004)

Channel Status Aware Proportional Fair Scheduling Algorithm for IEEE 802.15.3 WPAN*

Sung-Don Joo and Chae-Woo Lee

School of Electrical and Computer Engineering, Ajou University
SSan 5 Woncheon-Dong, Youngtong-Gu, Suwon 442-749, Korea
sungdon@ajou.ac.kr, cwlee@ajou.ac.kr

Abstract. IEEE 802.15.3 High-Rate WPAN(Wireless Personal Area Network) which is operated in ISM unlicensed frequency band is easily affected by channel errors. In this paper, we propose a scheduling algorithm which takes channel errors into consideration in scheduling asynchronous data traffic. The proposed scheduling algorithm can allocate CTA(Channel Time Allocation) proportionally in accordance with the requested channel time of each device. It also prevents the waste of channel time by allocating CTA of the devices that are in channel error status to other devices and preserves the fairness among the devices by compensating the channel time to the devices recovering from channel error. Simulation results show that proposed scheduling algorithm is superior to existing SRPT(Shortest Remain Processing Time) and RR(Round Robin) in throughput and fairness aspects.

1 Introduction

IEEE 802.15.3 HR-WPAN(High Rate - Wireless Personal Area Network) is an ad-hoc communication technology which can support data rate up to 55Mbps and connect computers, mobile devices or appliances within 10 meter range. It is also able to minimize power consumption to support low power mobile devices by using power management [2].

Wireless channels are susceptible to various errors [3]. Especially, HR-WPAN is easily affected by interference because it operates with other wireless technology such as Bluetooth and WLAN(Wireless LAN) in ISM unlicensed frequency band. Channel error decreases the network performance such as throughput and packet loss. Thus wireless MAC scheduling algorithm should consider channel error status to improve its performance. Many of the wireless packet scheduling algorithms assume that they know exact queue status of the mobile nodes [4-8].

It is possible for SRPT(Shortest Remain Processing Time) and RR(Round Robin) algorithms to schedule asynchronous data in HR-WPAN [9]. SRPT algorithm prefers to allocate channel time to the device which requests the smallest channel time. In the algorithm, the mean waiting time to access wireless channel becomes the shortest, but the maximum waiting time may become very long.

---

* This work was supported by the grant No.R01-2003-000-10724-0 from Korea Science & Engineering Foundation.

K. Cho and P. Jacquet (Eds.): AINTEC 2006, LNCS 4311, pp. 113–127, 2006.
© Springer-Verlag Berlin Heidelberg 2006

RR algorithm allocates the channel time to the devices in round robin manner, thus it is simple to operate. However, since the two algorithms do not consider the channel status, the network performance such as throughput decreases when channel errors are prone to occur. Furthermore they do not allocate the channel time in accordance to the requested channel time by each device. In this paper, we propose an efficient asynchronous data scheduling algorithm which can prevent the waste of channel time due to the channel error and guarantee proportional fairness among devices by allocating channel time according to the requested channel time by each device. When channel status of a specific device is in error, PNC which is responsible for scheduling allocates the channel time to those devices which are not in channel error status. After recovering from the channel error status, it compensates relinquished channel time to preserve proportional fairness among devices.

This paper is organized as follows. Section 2 explains the basic operation of HR-WPAN to understand the scheduling in HR-WPAN. Section 3 describes our proposed scheduling algorithm. In section 4, we evaluate proposed algorithm by simulation results. And in section 5, we summarize the paper.

2   The Basic Operation of IEEE 802.15.3 HR-WPAN

Now, we explain the basic operation to understand scheduling in HR-WPAN. HR-WPAN makes a network called piconet which is centralized ad-hoc network similar to Bluetooth as shown in figure 1. However, each device in HR-WPAN communicates peer to peer (P2P). PNC(Piconet Coordinator) broadcasts the beacon that contains synchronization information and channel access time. Devices in piconet are synchronized to piconet using received beacon message and access channel time to transfer data using allocated CTA(Channel Time Access) by PNC [2].

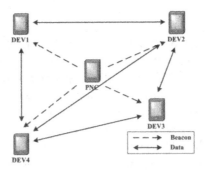

Fig. 1. Network architecture of IEEE 802.15.3 HR-WPAN

Channel time of HR-WPAN consists of basic unit of superframe as shown in figure 2 [2]. The superframe consists of three parts which are beacon message, CAP(Contention Access Period) and CTAP(CTA Period). CAP is used to transfer asynchronous data or commands such as channel time request and network management and uses CSMA/CA for medium access. PNC can use this period optionally. CTAP is divided into MCTA(Management CTA) and CTA. MCTA is used to transfer commands such as association, channel time request and management. CTA is utilized to transmit isochronous or asynchronous data.

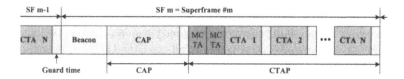

Fig. 2. Superframe structure of IEEE 802.15.3 HR-WPAN

Devices in piconet send CTRq(Channel Time Request) message to access wireless medium. This command is transferred to PNC in CAP or MCTA period. PNC schedules channel time based on requested channel time by each device. There are two methods, asynchronous and isochronous channel time request, to request channel time according to the type of traffic. If device needs channel time on a regular basis to transfer multimedia stream, it makes a request for isochronous channel time. This method transfers minimum channel time which guarantees QoS requirement and desired channel time using CTRq message. However, if device needs to transmit asynchronous data, it sends asynchronous channel time request which requests a total amount of time to be used to transfer its data. More detailed information or operation process is obtained in [2].

3 Proposed Algorithm

Fair scheduling algorithms are based on FFQ(Fluid Fair Queueing) model. FFQ is an ideal model which guarantees the service during time $(t1, t2)$ according to the weight of flows where $W_i(t1, t2)$ and ϕ_i are the amount of received service and the weight of each flow i [10].

$$\frac{W_i(t_1, t_2)}{\phi_i} = \frac{W_j(t_1, t_2)}{\phi_j} \tag{1}$$

To improve the performance of FFQ, various algorithms are suggested such as WFQ, WF2Q, SCFQ [11-13]. However, these algorithms can not be apply to the wireless environment, because they do not consider wireless channel errors. Many algorithms have been proposed to take the wireless channel errors into consideration. Some of them are IWFQ, W2F2Q, CIF-Q, and WFQ [4-8]. These algorithms assume to know the queue status, however PNC in HR-WPAN is not able to know the queues' exact status which are located in each device. Thus they can not applied to the HR-WPAN system. In this paper, we introduce a new asynchronous data scheduling algorithm that is able to operate in HR-WPAN and guarantee fairness.

3.1   Scheduling Architecture

To describe the proposed algorithm, we explain the scheduling architecture first in this section. Then, because PNC is not able to know the channel status between the communicating devices due to the P2P nature of HR-WPAN [2][13], we introduce a simple method how PNC infers the channel status.

Proposed Scheduling Architecture. Figure 3 shows the proposed scheduling architecture which consists of scheduler, imaginary queues, channel predictor and lag counters. The scheduler is responsible to allocate the CTA in proportional to the requested channel time by each device. The imaginary queue is used to store the requested channel time of each device. PNC can aware the channel status between devices by the information which is sent by each device. The lag counter shows the service degree of the device. If the lag counter is negative, this means the device is served less than the requested, which state is called lagging. If lag counter is positive, this indicates devices is received more service than requested, which state is called leading [4].

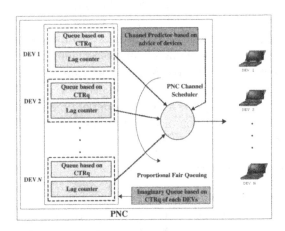

Fig. 3. The scheduling architecture of PNC in proposed algorithm

Channel Status Awareness in PNC. PNC is not able to recognize the channel status between the communicating devices directly, because the devices transfer data peer to peer [2][13]. To inform the channel error status, when the device can not transmit the data to its peer device, it informs this to PNC using using an unused field of CTRq message. Even though the device may not communicate with its peer device, it is always able to communicate with PNC. Otherwise, it can not request the channel time to PNC and the channel time will be utilized by other devices.

Assume that device i is not able to transmit the data because of channel errors. Device i tries to transfer data using the allocated CTA in n^{th} superframe but it is not able to receive Imm-ACK message for the transmitted packet even after seven retransmissions. Then device i interprets that the channel error occurs between source and destination devices. Then, device i stops transmitting the packet. Device i inspects the channel status once more using Channel Status Request/Response which are defined in the standard at allocated CTA in $(n+1)^{th}$ superframe. If the channel status is still error as before, device i sends CTRq message to PNC to report that the channel status is error. After receiving CTRq message, PNC marks that device i is in channel error state and does not allocate CTA to it from the next superframes. However PNC allocates device i with CTA just enough to investigate channel status and inform the result to PNC using Channel Status Request/Response and CTRq messages. This testing period is about 90 us except preamble signal that is a time to transfer these three messages. This period is 3-4 times smaller than default TU(Time Unit) that uses 1500Bytes or 2048Bytes.

If channel status is error-free in $(n+k)^{th}$ superframe, the device reports the channel status using CTRq message which indicates the channel status is error-free. Then PNC reallocates CTA from the next superfrmae. Figure 4 shows the process.

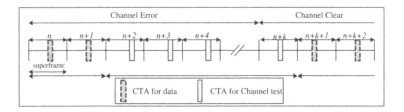

Fig. 4. The channel status awareness method in the proposed algorithm

When the channel status is error, by allocating CTA to the other devices that is error-free PNC can prevent the waste of CTA and increase the throughput. We explain operation of proposed algorithm in the next section.

3.2   The Operation of Proposed Algorithm

In this section, we explain how our algorithm achieves proportional fair scheduling and preserve the fairness even when channel errors occurs frequently. Proportional fair scheduling algorithms must allocate the service in accordance with the weight of each device. To do that, the proposed algorithm determines the weight of each device in each superframe and allocates CTA in proportional to the weight. The algorithm determines the weight in accordance with the amount of traffic to transfer.

Proposed MAC scheduling is operated as the flow chart shown in figure 5. First, PNC allocates CTA to achieve the proportional fairness. If the channel is in error state, then PNC withdraws allocated CTA and reallocates it to other devices. After the error is recovered, PNC must allocate more CTA to the device if PNC want to achieve the proportional fairness faster. When such compensation is needed, PCN may use full compensation or graceful compensation methods. More detailed operation is explained in the next section.

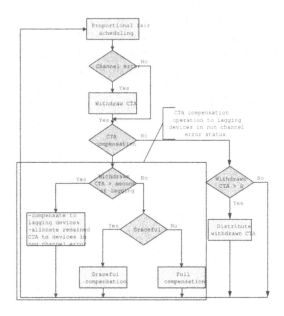

Fig. 5. Flow chart of the proposed algorithm

Proportional Fair Scheduling. To receive CTA according to the amount of traffic to transfer, each device makes a request by sending CTRq message to PNC. The weight of device i (ϕ_i) is determined as follows.

$$\phi_i = \frac{CTRq_i}{\sum CTRq_j} \tag{2}$$

PNC allocates CTA in proportion to the weight using the available channel time for asynchronous data ($CTAP_{async}$) as follows.

$$CTA_i = \lceil \phi_i \times CTAP_{async} \rceil \tag{3}$$

Scheduling in Channel Error Status. If PNC is reported from the device that the channel is in error state, then it withdraws the allocated CTAs. Thus total sum of withdrawn CTAs from devices in channel error status can be written as follows.

$$CTA^{error} = \sum_{\substack{k \in \{\text{channel} \\ \text{error devices}\}}} CTA_k \tag{4}$$

Since PNC does not allocate CTA, it increases the lag counter as much as the withdrawn CTA. The lag counter is set as follows.

$$Lag_i = Lag_i + CTA_i, \; i \in \{\text{channel error devices}\} \tag{5}$$

Withdrawn CTA is allocated first to the devices which are lagging and non-channel error status for CTA compensation. Remained withdrawn CTA after compensation is distributed to all non-channel error devices in accordance with their weights. This operation is explained in the next section.

CTA Compensation for Lagging Devices. After a lagging device is recovered from the channel error status, it should receive the withdrawn CTA. To compensate it, in each superframe PNC allocates additional CTA to it. In our algorithm, there are two ways to compensate lagging devices: one method is full compensation which gives absolute priority to the recovered device and the other method is graceful compensation that gives relative priority to it.

The amount of CTA which PNC should compensate is the sum of the lag counters of the lagging devices that are not in the channel error status. It is written as follows.

$$Lag^{compensate} = \sum_{\substack{k \in \{\text{lagging and} \\ \text{channel error free devices}\}}} Lag_k \tag{6}$$

To compensate CTA for the lagging devices, the devices that receive more CTA than their shares, which are called leading devices, must give their CTA to the lagging devices. As much as the amount of CTA that they yield, the amount of leading will be decreased. The total available CTA from the leading devices in a superframe is obtained as follows.

$$CTA^{available} = \sum \min\{|Lag_j|, CTA_j\}, j \in \{\text{leading devices}\} \tag{7}$$

Total amount of CTA which PNC can use for compensating the lagging devices is the sum of withdrawn CTA by the channel error and relinquished CTA by the leading devices, i.e.,

$$\Delta CTA = CTA^{error} + CTA^{available} \tag{8}$$

Full Compensation. PNC use some or all of ΔCTA in compensating the lagging devices which are in non channel error status. Full compensation of proposed algorithm allocates CTA according to the following three cases.

1. case 1: $(CTA^{error} > Lag^{compensate})$

   In this case, withdrawn CTA during channel error status is larger than the amount of CTA which should be compensated. PNC compensates CTA to the lagging device as much as amount of the lag counter indicates. PNC additionally allocates the remained CTA after compensation to the devices that are not channel error status in proportion to their weights.

2. case 2: ($CTA^{error} < Lag^{compensate} < \Delta CTA$)

In this case, the amount of CTA which should be compensated is larger than withdrawn CTA by channel error but smaller than the available CTA to compensate. PNC compensates CTA as much as amount of lag counter. Leading devices must relinquish some of their CTA but still receive CTA.

3. case 3: ($\Delta CTA < Lag^{compensate}$)

The amount of CTA which should be compensated is larger than the available CTA for compensation. PNC allocates ΔCTA to lagging devices in proportion to the lag counters. In this case leading devices relinquish CTA unless they become lagging devices after relinquishing CTA.

In the case 1, PNC compensates to the lagging devices using the withdrawn CTA during channel error. After compensation the lag counter becomes zero. The amount of CTA given to the lagging device i is

$$CTA_i = CTA_i + Lag_i, \ i \in \{\text{lagging and channel error free devices}\}. \quad (9)$$

Remained CTA (CTA^{error} - $Lag^{compensate}$) after compensating the lagging devices is distributed to the devices which are not in channel error status in proportion to their weights and the lag counters of them decrease by the additionally allocated CTA. We can write it as follows.

$$\Delta CTA_j = \left\lceil \frac{\phi_j}{\sum \phi_k} \times (CTA^{error} - Lag^{lagging}) \right\rceil$$
$$Lag_j = Lag_j - \Delta CTA_j, \ j,k \in \{\text{channel error free devices}\} \quad (10)$$

Thus the total CTA allocated to each non-error device is given as follows.

$$CTA_j = CTA_j + \Delta CTA_j, j \in \{\text{channel error free devices}\} \quad (11)$$

In the case 2, the leading devices concede some of their CTA in proportion to their weight to compensate lagging devices. After compensation, the amount of CTA that the leading devices receive is as follows.

$$CTA_j = CTA_j - \left\lceil \frac{\min(|Lag_j|, CTA_j)}{CTA^{available}} \times (Lag^{compensate} - CTA^{error}) \right\rceil,$$
$$j \in \{\text{leading devices}\} \quad (12)$$

In the case 3, PNC compensate CTA to the lagging devices in proportion to their lag counters. Thus the received CTA by the lagging devices is the sum of allocated CTA by equation (3) and compensated CTA by the following equation.

$$CTA_i = CTA_i + \left\lceil \frac{Lag_i}{Lag^{compensate}} \times \Delta CTA \right\rceil,$$
$$i \in \{\text{lagging and channel error free devices}\} \quad (13)$$

Allocated CTA to leading devices is deducted relinquished CTA from determined CTA by equation (3) and their lag counters increase as much as relinquished CTA.

$$CTA_j = CTA_j - \min(|Lag_j|, CTA_j), j \in \{\text{leading devices}\} \quad (14)$$

In full compensation, PNC compensate the lagging devices first and this continues until there remains nothing to compensate.

If the full compensation is used, the lagging device recovered from channel error status can be compensated rapidly but the leading devices may not access the channel for a while when the amount of compensation is large. To prevent such a situation, we propose a graceful compensation method.

Graceful Compensation. In this method, the leading device does not relinquish all of its allocated CTA to the lagging devices. Thus when PNC is compensating the lagging devices, the leading devices can still transmit the data. Using this method, we can solve the lack of CTA in the leading devices even if $Lag^{compensate}$ is very large. In graceful compensation, we use ROC(Ratio of CTA) parameter to determine how much the leading devices relinquish CTA to the lagging devices. ROC is defined as follows.

$$ROC = \frac{CTA^{available}}{Lag^{compensate} - CTA^{error}} \tag{15}$$

If ROC is larger than 1, this situation is same as the case 2 of the full compensation. If ROC is smaller than 1, the leading devices relinquish some portion of $CTA^{available}$. If ROC is close to 1, it mean that PNC can complete the compensation for the lagging devices within a few superframes. If ROC is small, it means that PNC needs many superframes to complete the compensation. In our graceful compensation method, if ROC is smaller than a threshold(α), the leading devices relinquish CTA by fixed probability so that they can some portions of CTA during compensation. If as ROC becomes larger than the threshold, the leading devices relinquish larger portions of CTA. In our method, the probability of relinquishment is determined by equation (16) or by figure 6.

$$p = \begin{cases} p_{min} & ROC < \alpha \\ 1 - \frac{(1-p_{min})}{(1-\alpha)\cdot e^{2\alpha}} \cdot (1 - ROC) \cdot e^{2ROC} & \alpha \le ROC \le 1 \end{cases} \tag{16}$$

When the graceful compensation is applied, there are three cases to consider.

1. case 4: ($CTA^{error} \ge Lag^{lagging}$)
   It is the same as the case 1 of the full compensation because the withdrawn CTA is larger than CTA that should be compensated.
2. case 5: ($ROC > 1$)
   It is the same as the case 2 of the full compensation because the available CTA is larger than CTA that should be compensated.
3. case 6: ($ROC \le 1$)
   In this case, CTA that should be compensated is larger than the available CTA. Thus PNC compensate CTA in proportion to the lag counter of each lagging devices. The leading device receives CTA after relinquishing some of its CTA to the lagging devices.

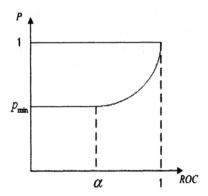

Fig. 6. Probability of CTA relinquishment by the leading devices

In case 6, the amount of CTA that each lagging and error free device receives is given as follows.

$$CTA_i = CTA_i + \left\lceil \frac{Lag_i}{Lag^{compensate}} \times \left(CTA^{error} + CTA^{available} \times p\right) \right\rceil, \quad (17)$$
$$i \in \{\text{lagging and channel error free devices}\}$$

CTA that is allocated to a leading device is determined by the following equation.

$$CTA_j = CTA_j - \lceil \min\{|Lag_j|, CTA_j\} \times p \rceil$$
$$Lag_j = Lag_j + \lceil \min\{|Lag_j|, CTA_j\} \times p \rceil, \ j \in \{\text{leading devices}\} \quad (18)$$

In the graceful compensation, the leading devices can receive CTA by relinquishing some portion of $CTA^{available}$ for CTA compensation. Thus they do not experience the lack of CTA to transfer data. However, to compensate the lagging devices it needs longer time than the full compensation.

4   Performance Evaluation

In this section, we evaluate our algorithm in the aspects of fairness and network throughput by comparing it with existing RR, SRPT.

4.1   Assumptions

For simulation, we use discrete two state Markov chain to model location dependent channel error. Let P_e denote the transition probability of the error-free state to to error state and P_g from the error state to the error-free sate. In steady sate, the channel error probability is $P_e/(P_e + P_g)$[3]. Figure 7 show the simulation environment that four devices try to transfer data to each destination device. Four source devices generate traffic as shown in table 1. Devices request CTA to PNC based on the unit of 1500 bytes packet. The length of superframe for asynchronous data transfer is set 10ms. When devices request CTA to PNC,

Table 1. Traffic generation of each device

Device Name	Traffic Generation
DEV1	1Mbps
DEV2	2Mbps
DEV3	3Mbps
DEV4	4Mbps

they use unit time(T) which is set one second. The parameter α, P_{min} which determine how much CTA is relinquished for compensation by tge leading devices in graceful compensation are both set to 0.5. Table 2 summarize simulation parameters.

Table 2. Simulation parameters

Parameters	Value
$CTAP_{async}$	10 ms
Unit Time	1 second
P_{min}	0.5
α	0.5
P_e	0.07
P_g	0.03

4.2   Simulation Results

We evaluate the performance of proposed algorithm by comparing with existing RR, SRPT and analyze results of full and graceful compensation. We compare

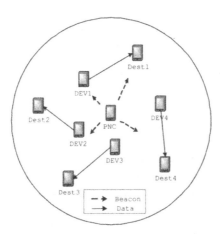

Fig. 7. Network architecture for simulation

the amount of transmission during 6000 superframes to evaluate the fairness of RR, SRPT, and the proposed algorithm.

Figure 8 shows the number of transmitted packets when there is no channel error. As shown in the figure, RR and SRPT can not provide proportional fairness among devices. However, allocated CTA by the proposed algorithm is the same as the ideal results.

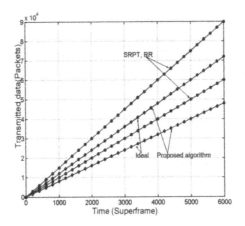

Fig. 8. The number of packets transmitted by DEV2 and DEV3: no channel errors

Figure 9-(a) shows the result when channel error exits in DEV 3. We can find from the figure that the fairness is maintained preserved although channel status is error in DEV 3. The transmission amount of DEV 3 is smaller than the ideal case because some of CTA are wasted for detecting and reporting the channel error during.

We compare the normalized goodput to evaluate network throughput. Figure 9-(b) shows the result. In the proposed algorithm, the waste of CTA occurs only when detecting channel error status and reporting it to PNC. Thus normalized goodput of the proposed algorithm is 0.98 which is the highest. However, the normalized goodput of SRPT and RR is lower than the proposed algorithm because they allocate CTA even if the device is in the channel error status. SRPT allocate CTA to device 3 in every superframe. Because RR allocates CTA to devices in turns, it is possible that PNC does not allocate CTA to DEV 3 during channel error status. Thus, the normalized goodput of RR is higher than that of SRPT in the simulation.

To show the effectiveness of the full and graceful compensation methods, we generate channel error to DEV 3 in the first fifteen superframes. To control the degree of graceful compensation, we set both P_{min} and α to 0.5. Figure 10 shows the results of the simulation. As seen from the figure, CTA compensation is started at the seventeenth supefraeme because DEV 3 reports that the channel status is error-free to PNC in sixteenth superframe and PNC allocates CTA

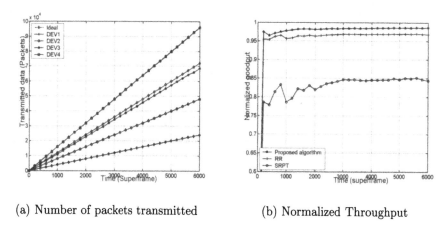

(a) Number of packets transmitted   (b) Normalized Throughput

Fig. 9. Comparison of each algorithm under channel error

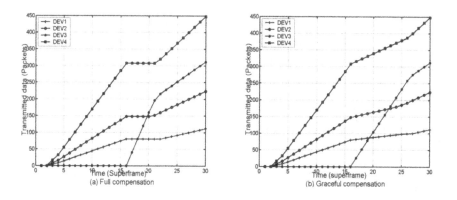

Fig. 10. Service compensation under channel error

to transfer data in the seventeenth superframe. In the full compensation, CTA compensation is completed at the twenty first superframe. During this period, the leading devices can not transfer data because all of CTA period was allocated to DEV 3. When the graceful compensation is used, the leading device relinquishes 50 % of their CTA to compensate the lagging devices . The graceful compensation method takes two times more time to complete CTA compensation comparing with the full compensation. However, in this time, the leading devices can transfer data because they only relinquish 50% of CTA. The proposed algorithm also prevents the waste of CTA by withdrawing CTA that is allocated to the device in channel error status and distributes it to the devices which are not experiencing channel error. From the simulation, regardless of compensation methods, we can observe that fairness is preserved under channel error condition.

5 Conclusion

HR-WPAN operates in ISM unlicensed frequency band so it is affected by other wireless technology or same one. Thus it needs efficient scheduling algorithm to maintain high performance. In this paper, we proposed a scheduling algorithm that is aware of channel error status between devices and allocate channel time in proportion to the requested channel time. Proposed algorithm can provide proportional fairness among devices and it can also preserve high network throughput by distributing withdrawn channel time from the devices in channel error status to the non-channel error devices. We show that the proposed algorithm can preserve fairness among devices by compensating to lagging devices using full compensation and graceful compensation.

In the future, various wireless technologies will coexist and the interference between wireless devices will increase, especially when they use ISM bands. In this wireless environment, it is very important to schedule efficiently by considering channel errors. HR-PAN(IEEE15.3) is not likely be used as much as projected before. However, the scheduling algorithm we proposed in the paper are quite general. If MAC access is controlled by by the central controller such as PNC or AP. we believe the proposed algorithm can be applied without much modification.

References

1. Karaoguz. J.: High Rate Wireless Personal Area Networks. IEEE Communications Magazine, Vol. 39, Issue 12, Dec. (2001)
2. Wireless Medium Access Control (MAC) and Physical Layer(PHY) Specifications for High Rate Wireless Personal Area Networks(WPAN), IEEE, Std 802.15.3, Sept. (2003)
3. Bai, H., Atiquzzaman, M.:Error Modeling Schemes for Fading Channels in Wireless Communications: A Survey. IEEE Communications Surveys, Vol.5, No.2, Fourth Quarter, (2003)
4. Nandagopal, T, Lu, S. Bharghavan, V.: A Unified Architecture for the Design and Evaluation of Wireless Fair Queueing Algorithms. ACM Mobicom'99, Aug. (1999)
5. Lu, S., Bharghavan, V., Strikant, R.: Fair Scheduling in Wirelss Packet Networks. IEEE/ACM Transaction on Networking Vol. 7, No. 4, Aug. (1999) 473–489
6. Yi, Y., Seok, Y., Park, J.: W2F2Q: Packet Fair Queuing in Wireless Packet Networks. WowMom'00, Aug. (2000) 2–10
7. Lu, S., Nandagopal T, Bharghavan, V.: A Wireless Fair ervice Algorithm For Packet Cellular Networks. IEEE Mobicom'98, (1998) 10–20
8. Ng, T., Stocia, I., Zhang, H.: Packet Fair Queuing Algorithms for Wireless Networks with Location-Dependent Errors. IEEE INFOCOM'98, Vol. 3, Mar. (1998) 1103–1111
9. Mangharam, R., Demirhan, M.: Performance and simulation analysis of 802.15.3 QoS. IEEE 802.15-02/297r1, Jul. (2002)
10. Demers, A., Keshav, S., Shenker, S.: Analysis and simulation of a fair queuing algorithm. Proc. ACM SIGCOMM'89, (1989) 3–12
11. Bennett, J., Zhang, H.: WF2Q:Worst-Case Fair Weighted Fair Queuing. IEEE INFOCOM'96, Mar. (1996)

12. Golestani, S.: A Self-Clocked Fair Queueing Scheme for Braocadband Appliacation. IEEE INFOCOM'94, (1994) 636–646
13. Bhagwat, P., Bhattacharya, P., Krishna, A., Tripathi, S.: Enhancing throughput over wireless LANs using Channel State Dependent Packet Scheduling. IEEE IN-FOCOM'96 vol.3, Mar. (1996) 1133–1140
14. Liu, C., Yeung, K., Li, V.: A Novel MAC Scheduling Algorithm for Bluetooth System. IEEE GLOBECOM'03, Vol. 1, Dec. (2003) 86–91

Application Performance Assessment on Wireless Ad Hoc Networks

Răzvan Beuran[1,2], Ken-ichi Chinen[2,1], Khin Thida Latt[2], Toshiyuki Miyachi[2,1], Junya Nakata[2,1], Lan Tien Nguyen[2], Yoichi Shinoda[2,1], and Yasuo Tan[2,1]

[1] National Institute of Information and Communications Technology, Hokuriku Research Centre, 2-12 Asahidai, Nomi, Ishikawa, 923-1211 Japan
[2] Japan Advanced Institute of Science and Technology, 1-1 Asahidai, Nomi, Ishikawa, 923-1292 Japan
razvan@nict.go.jp

Abstract. Using ad hoc networks as alternative means of communication in disaster situations is a salutary solution. However, analysing application performance is mandatory for evaluating such a possibility. In this paper we present the two aspects of our approach to application performance assessment on wireless ad hoc networks. The first aspect refers to real-world tests in which we quantify objectively the relationship between network conditions and application performance. The second aspect is represented by the wireless network (WLAN) emulator that we design to run on StarBED, the large-scale network experiment environment of the Hokuriku Research Centre in Ishikawa, Japan. By combining these two aspects we perform experiments with real applications, while having full control of the network conditions in which the application is tested (when using emulation).

Keywords: Emergency networks, ad hoc networks, application performance assessment, WLAN emulation.

1 Introduction

Emergency communication systems are required in the preceding phase of disaster situations to issue warnings and evacuation instructions. However they are equally decisive during catastrophes and after their occurrence to coordinate the activity of rescue teams. Dependable communication is also essential in mission-critical and safety-critical systems, or even in normal business environments that require "anytime, anywhere" access to network resources.

According to a study in [1] the requirements for emergency services' mobile communication are: resilience, coverage, access and capacity, security, regulation, group communication, fast call set-up, priority, direct mode/repeaters and gateways, integration with control room, and voice quality. The conclusion of this study is that public mobile networks, such as the GSM (Global System for Mobile Communications) standard, even with the latest proposed modifications, cannot fulfil all of the above requirements.

Public safety agencies have used specialized radio communication systems for many decades. TETRA (TErrestrial Trunked Radio) [2] is a specialist professional

K. Cho and P. Jacquet (Eds.): AINTEC 2006, LNCS 4311, pp. 128–138, 2006.
© Springer-Verlag Berlin Heidelberg 2006

mobile radio used by emergency workers, such as police, fire departments, ambulance and military. Although this system was designed to meet the cited requirements, it still has several disadvantages, such as low rates of 4.8 kb/s, expensive handsets, etc. In addition its deployment is predominant only in Europe for the moment.

Unfortunately recent disasters such as the Indian Ocean tsunami in 2004, or the 2005 hurricanes Katrina and Rita in U.S.A. have shown that current communication systems, both professional and public, fail too easily under emergency conditions. Therefore new alternative means of communication are needed for emergency or calamity situations. Given the current spread of Internet one such alternative is to make a more extensive use of the technologies associated with Internet, and in particular of ad hoc wireless LANs (WLANs).

The U.S.A. federal government report on the response to hurricane Katrina [3] proposes the creation of a National Emergency Communication Strategy. One of the recommendations included in this report mentions that "there is a strong need for rapidly deployable, interoperable, commercial, off-the-shelf equipment". The same event showed how Internet-based technologies could be used to establish links with the outside world. As an anecdotal example, the only communication means between the mayor of New Orleans and the outside world, including phone calls with U.S.A. President George Bush, was a wireless Internet connection and an Internet phone account [4]. Although we will not make here a full analysis, it is easy to notice that some of the key requirements for emergency communication systems find indeed built-in support in the WLAN technology. Capacity, security, regulation, priority, direct-mode communication are all available at present in wireless LANs.

Using converged WLANs makes it possible to transmit both audio and video information, so that rescuers can communicate with each other and with remote experts. Moreover, by using WLANs emergency workers can receive data, such as street maps or building floor plans. All these means of communication that make use of a unique network infrastructure are crucial for saving lives and preventing losses.

Wireless LANs are more stable than other communication infrastructures given the fact that they are decentralized. As their potential failure is independent, ad hoc WLANs can continue functioning in emergency conditions. The nodes of WLANs have low costs, and they require little power to operate. In addition, the potential of using advanced features on WLANs that are not available in traditional public communication systems makes it possible to provide probabilistic guarantees of service for emergency responders. Using a priority-enforcement system such users could be given an assured service level, independently of the activity of regular users.

In this paper we present our approach to assessing application performance in WLAN environments, in ad hoc mode, as well as in "infrastructure" mode (i.e., access point based deployments). An objective performance assessment is a mandatory step in analyzing the dependability of applications on WLAN in view of their use as alternative means of communication in emergency situations. According to the survey we did in [5] there are several factors that currently impede application performance on wireless LANs:

1. WLAN QoS parameters (bandwidth, packet loss, delay & jitter) have a high variability in real-world environments;
2. Existing WLAN QoS mechanisms are only of limited use for managing contention when applications with different QoS requirements, such as VoIP (Voice over IP) calls and TCP-based data traffic, share the same communication channel;

3. Real-time applications such as VoIP or video communication require timely servicing of the traffic; this is a challenging task in WLANs, even when using QoS enforcement, since most currently-implemented QoS mechanisms focus only on bandwidth provisioning;
4. Roaming between access points introduces communication gaps that may even be of the order of seconds, an unacceptable situation for real-time applications.

The paper is structured as follows. First we present the analysis methodology that we propose for the study of application performance over wireless LANs. This includes tests in real-world environments as well as the use of WLAN emulation, which is a key complementary element of our approach. Following that we give some illustrative results for our study of VoIP performance on WLAN, since reliable voice communication is one main requirement for emergency communication systems. The paper ends with a section of conclusions and future work.

2 Performance Assessment Methodology

The first step to take in studying IP application performance and dependability on WLANs is to define a test methodology that allows assessing objectively application performance, and understanding its dependence on network conditions. The methodology that we propose can be employed for any network application, but for each application under test specific metrics have to be used to assess performance. Objective performance assessment is important since users of WLANs, in either regular or special environments, such as emergency or disaster conditions, require that applications run at a satisfactory performance level. The approach we propose makes it possible to analyse application performance in a wide range of controllable network conditions. By correlating an objective assessment of the User-Perceived Quality (UPQ) for the applications under study with the corresponding network conditions one can determine the reasons of application performance degradation and investigate mechanisms to ensure satisfactory performance. Our approach has two aspects that will be detailed next: real-world tests and WLAN emulation.

2.1 Real-World Tests

Tests in real-world environments are one aspect of our approach to application performance assessment. They permits us to capture and analyse the behaviour of real applications in real network conditions. Another use is in the calibration of the emulation system that we develop, which will be described in Section 2.2. Below is a typical experimental setup for real-world WLAN tests. We show here the case when access points are used, but for ad hoc networks the measurement side is identical.

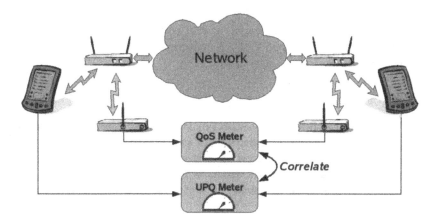

Fig. 1. Experimental setup for application performance assessment on WLAN

The setup in Figure 1 is adapted from the system we previously used to study VoIP performance on wired networks [6]. Using this setup we carry out a two-level analysis. At the level of the network we investigate the performance issues of WLANs, such as the dependency on signal strength, on the number of access points or peer ad hoc nodes, on quality degradation management techniques, etc. At this level there are two classes of metrics we use: (i) physical environment metrics, such as the power of the received signal, Pr, and the Signal to Noise Ratio, SNR; (ii) generic network metrics, which are the three inter-dependent QoS parameters: bandwidth, packet loss, and delay & jitter. These parameters are computed by the "QoS Meter" block that uses as input monitored WLAN traffic traces. For capturing the traffic we use the AiroPeek software of WildPackets, Inc. [7], in connection with wireless probes, such as RFGrabber of the same company, or high-end WLAN adapters, such as ORiNOCO 11a/b/g Gold or Cisco Aironet 802.11a/b/g. Special drivers are required to capture both data, and control & management packets, as well as signal and noise levels in the WLAN.

Simultaneously, at application level, we measure the User-Perceived Quality (UPQ) for the application under study. In the case of VoIP we use methods such as the ITU-T recommendations G.107 [8] and P.862 [9]. For file transfers, metrics such as the goodput and the transfer time performance are well suited [10]. In the case of video communication one can use a tool such as the Psytechnics Video Agent for Communications, from Psytechnics, Ltd. [11]. In our setup the function of measuring user-perceived quality is conceptually performed by the "UPQ Meter" block.

Correlating the WLAN-level and application-level performance permits us to establish objectively what are the requirements of a network application in order to ensure user satisfaction, as well as determine what type of mechanisms are needed to meet these requirements on WLANs.

One important aspect of this setup is its ability to capture the dynamic behaviour of the tested systems, which is made possible through the use of the above-mentioned WLAN traffic monitors (sniffers). Running averages and global assessments are not meaningful for short-term performance issues, which are nevertheless critical in disaster situations. Moreover WLANs are dynamic environments by definition: signal reception conditions fluctuate, the number of nodes and their position vary, the access points with which the nodes communicate, or their peers in ad hoc networks, change. By capturing the dynamic behaviour of the network we can follow and understand application performance fluctuations over time.

2.2 WLAN Emulation

Real-world experiments are only one aspect of our research. Such experiments are very useful for understanding the behaviour of real WLAN systems. However the range of conditions that can be tested in real-world experiments is limited and difficult to control. Therefore we proceeded to design a WLAN emulator that gives us direct control over the network conditions which we use to assess application performance.

The WLAN emulator that we develop makes use of StarBED [12]. StarBED is the large scale network experiment environment of National Institute of Information and Communications Technology (NICT), Hokuriku Research Centre in Ishikawa, Japan. This experiment environment is a cluster-based testbed currently employing about 700 PCs. The use of a custom-designed experiment-support software, nicknamed SpringOS, makes it possible to define complex experiments on StarBED in a straightforward manner.

A survey of existing WLAN-related real-world and simulation testbeds is available in [13]. General characteristics of WLAN emulators are summarized in [14]. Our design addresses these requirements through a scenario-driven two-stage approach inspired by [15] and [16]. The novelty of our work consists in the quality degradation view we take, the emphasis we lay on emulation realism, as well as the use of a large-scale testbed for experiments.

The setup we use when testing application performance through WLAN emulation is presented in Figure 2. Notice the similarity that exists with the test setup discussed in Section 2.1.

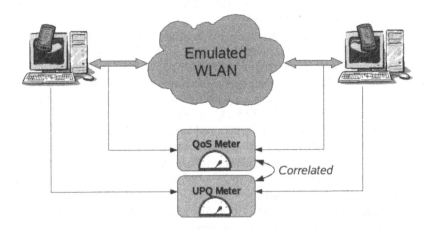

Fig. 2. WLAN emulation for application performance assessment

In the setup depicted in Figure 2 we use PCs to play the role of the mobile nodes in the emulated WLAN. The applications that run on the end PCs are of the same type with those running on a PDA, or a wireless phone. Therefore by using this setup we can test the performance of the same applications as those in the real-world experiments. Note that in the context of emulation too we measure the QoS parameters and the UPQ. Correlating these two measures permits in this case also to determine objectively the relationship that exists between application performance and network quality degradation under varying network conditions. The difference with respect to the real-world tests is that in this setup the full control over the scenarios and conditions that we use during the tests is readily possible.

There are several key requirements for such a methodology to be effective, and our approach addresses them. Realism of the emulation is important because it allows drawing conclusions that are thereafter useful in real-life deployment. Most application performance studies focus on data-transfer applications, typically based on TCP/IP. Models used are oversimplified in a bandwidth-oriented perspective, hence do not adequately reflect real network conditions as experienced by users, and only reproduce a simplified theoretical behaviour of WLANs. However the edge effects that do occur in reality are generally overlooked, for example between rate changes, as the WLAN cards automatically adapt operation rate to signal reception conditions using a mechanism such as Auto-Rate Fallback (ARF) [17]. Nevertheless these effects have significant consequences at application level, as our example in Section 3 shows. Such aspects are taken into account by the WLAN operation models that we employ. Moreover, in order to achieve an even higher degree of realism we propose to calibrate our system by combining observations and traffic traces of real WLANs with our analytical model of the WLAN environment, so that the calibrated model accurately describes the observed network behaviour.

The scenario-driven architecture we propose here has two stages. In the first stage, from a real-world scenario representation we create a network quality degradation (ΔQ) description which corresponds to the real-world events (see Figure 3). The ΔQ description represents the varying effects of the network on application traffic. Computing the ΔQ description is the key element of our system. This step is achieved by using a model of the WLAN communication, in particular by taking into account the properties of the physical layer and the data link layer (more specifically the MAC sub-layer) of the WLAN technology. For the physical layer the main model used is the log-distance path loss model [18]. For the MAC sub-layer we deploy several models for determining first frame error rates, and then packet loss rates, delay and jitter, as well as bandwidth variation according to the ARF mechanism.

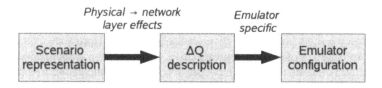

Fig. 3. Two-stage scenario-driven emulation

Subsequently the ΔQ description is converted into an emulator configuration which is used during the effective emulation process to replicate the user scenario. This allows the study of scenario effects on the real application under test, all this under realistic conditions.

As an example, assume that the scenario representation describes how, from an initial position, two mobile nodes move with respect to each other. As a consequence of the motion, the received radio signal strength will change. This is the WLAN physical layer effect, and it is quantified by means of the received signal power, Pr. We model the dependency of Pr on the distance between transmitter and receiver using the log-distance path loss model. At the moment attenuation in only considered from the point of view of path loss due to distance and shadowing. We are now working on integrating models of fading (e.g., Rayleigh fading) into our system.

WLAN performance is not only affected by the received signal power, Pr, but also by the environmental noise, which is quantified by means of the Signal to Noise Ratio, SNR. The effects of the received signal power and the noise are accounted for by using error models for the corresponding signal encodings, models which allow us to compute the corresponding bit error rate and frame error rate. These error models are based on typical receive sensitivities of WLAN adapters, as well as experimentally-determined characteristics of some widely-used WLAN-adapter components, such as the Intersil HFA3861B Direct Sequence Spread Spectrum Baseband Processor [19].

The variation of Pr and SNR causes quality degradation at the data-link layer as follows. The weaker signal first induces higher error rates and consequently packet loss. Simultaneously there is an increase in delay as the number of retransmissions becomes larger. Finally the WLAN adapters change the channel encoding and rate, according to a mechanism such as ARF, and the available bandwidth diminishes. These effects are modelled by taking into account the specific 802.11 MAC sub-layer, as well as the behaviour of ARF; the result is the ΔQ description associated to the emulated scenario.

The second stage of our approach is emulator specific. In this stage the generic ΔQ description calculated previously is converted into an emulator configuration. Initially the conversion target is the *dummynet* network emulator [20]. However by decoupling the two conceptually-independent emulation stages we make it possible that later on other wired-network emulators can be used as well, that are more accurate than *dummynet* and that have a richer set of features. Note that the possibility of using various network emulators running on Linux or FreeBSD is a feature that has been recently added to StarBED.

3 Experimental Results

In this section we show some illustrative results for VoIP performance over WLAN. We chose to study VoIP as a representative real-time application, since voice communication is one of the most important forms of communication in emergency situations.

As mentioned before, two methods are more appropriate to measure VoIP UPQ: the R-value score, which is the result of the E-model described in the ITU-T

Recommendation G.107, and the PESQ score, proposed by the ITU-T Recommendation P.862. A detailed comparison between the two metrics is available in [5]. For the purpose of this paper it is important to note that the R-value is computed uniquely based on traffic measurements, therefore it is only a *prediction* of what the user satisfaction would be if using the corresponding connection. On the other hand the PESQ score is calculated using voice recordings for the measured connection; hence it is a more accurate *estimate* of the VoIP UPQ for that connection. Note that the R-value can be converted to the Mean Opinion Score (MOS) scale [21], which is also used by the PESQ score. This makes it easy to compare results obtained using the two metrics. A value of 4.5 on the MOS scale indicates optimum quality, with good quality being associated to scores higher than 3. Quality is considered acceptable for scores between 2 and 3, whereas scores lower than 2 indicate unacceptable quality.

The results presented below were obtained using the setup in Figure 2. For simplicity reasons we consider a scenario with only two nodes. However it is possible to use the current system to study multi-hop environments as well.

In our scenario example the two nodes are at an initial distance of 10 m with respect to each other. One of them starts moving on a perpendicular direction with a speed of 0.5 m/s for a time interval of 30 s. This is a scenario fragment representative for the communication between an ad hoc network user moving in a building while making a VoIP over WLAN phone call to another user.

With the parameters $\alpha = 5.5$ (difficult reception conditions) and $Pr0 = -20$ dB in the log-distance path loss model we obtain the power of the received signal, Pr, shown in Figure 4 together with the distance between the mobile nodes. Horizontal dashed lines indicate the thresholds between minimum signal power levels for different operating rates of 802.11b (from top to bottom, the limit between 11 and 5.5 Mb/s, and the limit between 5.5 and 2 Mb/s, respectively). Note that Pr falls under the 11 Mb/s threshold after $t \approx 17.5$ s, and below the 5.5 Mb/s threshold at $t \approx 26$ s. The consequences of the Pr variation on the quality degradation were computed as ΔQ descriptors. Using them as the input of the ITU-T E-model we calculated the R-value, and predicted what the user satisfaction would be if communicating under such circumstances.

The next step was to use the same ΔQ descriptors to drive the network emulator *dummynet* while real voice data was sent through the network. We used a customized version of the SpeakFreely 7.6a application [22] that we modified to save the output voice signal. For this test SpeakFreely was configured to make use of the codec G.711 [23]. The voice input consists of standard voice test files supplied with the ITU-T P.862 recommendation. Based on the input and output voice signals we computed the PESQ score. Both the PESQ score and the MOS R-value (the MOS score obtained analytically from the previously computed R-value) are represented in Figure 5.

We can observe in Figure 5 that the MOS R-value has generally higher (i.e. more optimistic) values than the PESQ score, which is deemed to be more realistic. In the case when $t < 17$ s signal conditions are good, therefore the average packet loss was considered low (1%). Hence the MOS R-value is stable around a value of 4.3. However the PESQ score has a much more evident variation over the same interval. The explanation consists in the fact that while average packet loss values over a long period might be 1%, over shorter timescales and for a small number of packets the loss values change significantly, and this change leads to a important perceived quality variation, as it would be observed in a real situation.

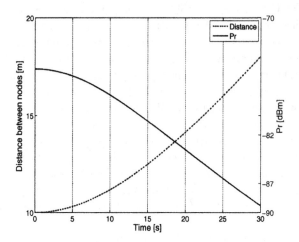

Fig. 4. Distance between mobile nodes and the power of the received signal versus time

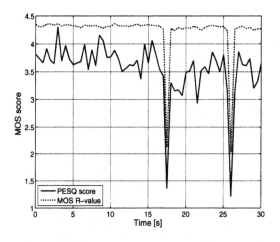

Fig. 5. PESQ score and the MOS R-value versus time

As remarked previously, at times $t \approx 17.5$ s and $t \approx 26$ s the decreasing level of the received signal power triggers rate transitions, with obvious effects on VoIP UPQ. At these moments the quality drops under the threshold of acceptable quality (MOS value = 2). However these effects are not caused by the rate change in itself (which only goes down to 2 Mb/s in the worst case, largely sufficient for the roughly 80 kb/s stream generated by the G.711 codec). On the contrary, these effects are produced by the packet loss and delay variation that occur just before and during the rate transition, and that are ignored in most WLAN emulation implementations. Moreover, once Pr falls under the optimum reception threshold for 11 Mb/s, the auto-rate fallback mechanism in 802.11 is triggered, and this causes a slight additional quality degradation, which is noticeable after the first rate transition.

4   Conclusions

Disaster situations impose strong requirements on communication systems, and in such cases dependability and performance guarantees are essential. This need is addressed by our research in the area of application performance on ad hoc and infrastructure mode WLANs. The two directions of our research are application performance analysis and assurance.

As a first step we started using real-world tests and a WLAN emulated environment to determine the relationship between the events in the physical world associated with WLANs, the corresponding network quality degradation and in the end the user perceived quality variation for network applications. Our methodology lays emphasis on dynamic behaviour capture and emulation realism.

The approach we propose for WLAN emulation allows the transformation of a user-meaningful real-world representation of a WLAN environment (termed "scenario representation") into a network quality degradation description (termed "ΔQ description"). The ΔQ description is sufficient to subsequently configure a wired-network emulator and effectively reproduce an environment that corresponds accurately at network level to the emulated WLAN scenario.

We illustrated the practical use of our approach through a simple real-world scenario, for which we determined the induced network quality degradation. The selected application for this experiment was VoIP, since speech is one of the most important forms of communication in emergency situations. We quantified the influence of the quality degradation on VoIP UPQ in an objective manner using ITU-T recommendations concerning expected user satisfaction for VoIP communication.

As a second step of our future research we will investigate application performance assurance. We intend to use the same setup to study the issue of application performance assurance in WLAN environments, which is vital in emergency conditions, such as disaster rescue operations and other critical situations. The framework and the specific techniques that we plan to develop will allow the creation of ad hoc WLANs under critical conditions, and the assurance of quality guarantees even under such circumstances for high-priority users (e.g., public safety teams, hospitals, etc.). The IEEE 802.11e standard for QoS on WLAN will be analysed first to determine whether it is suited for use in the context of emergency communication systems.

References

1. Swan, D.: Analysis in the ability of Public Mobile Communications to support mission critical events for the Emergency Services. White paper, Mason Communications Ltd, Manchester England, (March 2003)
2. TETRA: TETRA Memorandum of Understanding. http://www.tetramou.com
3. Towsend, F.F. (ed.): The Federal Response to Hurricane Katrina – Lessons Learned. U.S.A. Federal Government Report (February 2006)
4. Rhoads, C.: After Katrina, city officials struggled to keep order, In: The Wall Street Journal, (9 September 2005)
5. Beuran, R.: VoIP over Wireless LAN Survey. Research report, IS-RR-2006-005, Japan Advanced Institute of Science and Technology (JAIST), Ishikawa, Japan (April 2006)

6. Beuran, R., Ivanovici, M.: User-Perceived Quality Assessment for VoIP Applications. Technical report (delivered to U4EA Technologies), CERN-OPEN-2004-007, CERN, Geneva, Switzerland (January 2004)
7. WildPackets, Inc.: http://www.wildpackets.com
8. ITU-T: ITU-T Recommendation G.107: The E-model, a computational model for use in transmission planning (March 2005)
9. ITU-T: ITU-T Recommendation P.862: Perceptual evaluation of speech quality (PESQ), an objective method for end to end speech quality assessment of narrow-band telephone networks and codecs (February 2001)
10. Beuran, R., Ivanovici, M., Dobinson, B., Davies, N., Thompson, P.: Network Quality of Service Measurement System for Application Requirements Evaluation. In: Proc. of International Symposium on Performance Evaluation of Computer and Telecommunication Systems, SPECTS'03, Montreal, Canada (July 2003) 380-387
11. Psytechnics, Ltd.: http://www.psytechnics.com
12. Miyachi, T., Chinen, K., Shinoda, Y.: Automatic Configuration and Execution of Internet Experiments on an Actual Node-based Testbed. In: Proc. of Tridentcom2005, Trento, Italy (February 2005) 274-282
13. Kropff, M., Krop, T., Hollick, M., Mogre, P.S., Steinmetz, R.: A Survey of Real-World and Emulation Testbeds for Mobile Ad hoc Network. In: Proc. of TridentCom2006, Barcelona, Spain (March 2006)
14. Kojo, M., Gurtov, A., Manner, J., Sarolahti, P., Alanko, T., Raatikainen, K.: Seawind: a Wireless Network Emulator. In: Proc. of 11th Conference on Measuring, Modelling and Evaluation of Computer and Communication Systems (MMB), Aachen, Germany (September 2001)
15. Bateman, M., Allison, C., Ruddle, A.: A Scenario Driven Emulator for Wireless, Fixed and Ad Hoc networks. In: Proc. of PGNet2003, Liverpool, U.K. (June 2003) 273-278
16. Perennou, T., Conchon, E., Dairaine, L., Diazet, M.: Two-Stage Wireless Network Emulation. In: Proc. of WCC2004, Toulouse, France (August 2004)
17. Kamerman, A., Monteban, L.: WaveLAN-II: A High-performance wireless LAN for the unlicensed band. In: Bell Lab Technical Journal (summer 1997) 118-133
18. Rappaport, T.S.: Wireless Communications – Principles and Practice. Prentice Hall PTR, 2nd edition (2002)
19. Intersil: HFA3861B Direct Sequence Spread Spectrum Baseband Processor (2000)
20. Dummynet: FreeBSD network emulator. http://info.iet.unipi.it/~luigi/ip_dummynet
21. ITU-T: ITU-T Recommendation P.800: Methods for subjective determination of transmission quality (August 1996)
22. Wiles, B.C., Walker, J.: Speak Freely 7.6a. http://www.speakfreely.org
23. ITU-T: ITU-T Recommendation G.711: Pulse Code Modulation (PCM) of voice frequencies (1993)

Proactive Resilience to Dropping Nodes in Mobile Ad Hoc Networks

Ignacy Gawędzki and Khaldoun Al Agha

Laboratoire de Recherche en Informatique, CNRS
Université Paris-Sud 11, F-91405 Orsay, France
{i, alagha}@lri.fr

Abstract. Proactive routing protocols for mobile ad hoc networks currently offer few mechanisms to detect and/or counter malevolent nodes. Stability and performance of most, if not all, emerging standard proactive protocols rely on cooperation between nodes. While cryptographic methods may be a solution to secure control messages, nodes not willing to cooperate may still decide not to forward data packets. In this paper, a method to enable resilience to such malevolent nodes is presented. It is non-intrusive with respect to the packet forwarding mechanisms (e.g. TCP/IP kernel stack) and particularly well suited for integration with proactive routing protocols.

Keywords: proactive routing, ad hoc networks, malicious nodes, resilience.

1 Introduction

Currently emerging standardized routing protocols for mobile ad hoc networks (MANETs for short) [1,2,3] are distributed algorithms relying on cooperation between participating nodes to achieve efficient routing. Unfortunately, there are applications of MANETs where the assumption of benevolent collaboration is too strong and in fact nodes may be expected to behave in any conceivable way. Such potentially malevolent nodes are called *Byzantine processes* [4] in the jargon of distributed computing.

If Byzantine processes are to be expected among the participating nodes of a MANET, there are many imaginable ways by which such nodes could undermine the operation of the network as a whole (data flooding, packet dropping, ...) or a proactive routing protocol in particular (sending fake control messages, modifying control or data packets before retransmitting them, ...).

In Sect. 1.1 and 1.2, the problem at hand is presented and previous work resumed. In Sect. 2, the basis of the proposed idea is stated and then in Sect. 3, it is applied for the detection of cheaters. A few remarks about its practical implementation are given in Sect. 4. Evaluation results are analyzed in Sect. 5 and we finally conclude in Sect. 6.

K. Cho and P. Jacquet (Eds.): AINTEC 2006, LNCS 4311, pp. 139–158, 2006.
© Springer-Verlag Berlin Heidelberg 2006

1.1   Problem Statement

The general question of how to make a MANET resilient to Byzantine processes is a very difficult problem. Because of the complicated and compound design of MANETs, there are many weak points that could be exploited by malicious nodes to hinder network operations. At the physical level, because of the very nature of the radio medium, plain old jamming may forbid successful network communications. At the logical link level, the lack of scheduling facilities in current wireless MAC layers makes it possible to perform Denial of Service attacks. At the network level, a node may poison routing control messages to either get more resources for itself or simply, in a non-egoistic way, sap others' communications.

Some of the these issues may be addressed using cryptographic methods which enable to ensure no packet gets forged or altered and/or no data payload disclosed. Furthermore, depending on the routing protocol used, some methods enable surrounding nodes to verify that routing information diffused by a given node is correct. Consequently, in the present paper, we will focus on a more basic problem: the resilience to nodes that drop others' traffic instead of forwarding it towards their intended destination. The proposed solution relies on a simple and yet easily satisfied assumption, namely that those dropping nodes — let's call them *cheaters* — are isolated (no two of them are neighbors) and do not collude with each other.

1.2   Previous Work

Byzantine robustness of routing protocols have been actively studied for quite some time. The more and more decentralized aspect of network administration of the Internet made routing more prone to attacks. The emergence of wireless ad hoc networks called for a similar concern, but existing solutions for wired networks could not be applied directly, as was already the case with routing protocols proper.

The most trivial attack, and yet the most likely in a public network, is that of *selfish nodes*: nodes that don't want to spend their energy resources on behalf of other nodes. In [5], Marti et al. propose a solution to detect selfish nodes in a passive way, relying on the ability of neighbors to overhear a node's transmissions on the medium, it is expected to work on the condition that all nodes have only one wireless network interface, omnidirectional antennae and equal transmission power. Other approaches, based on prevention of selfish behavior by encouraging cooperation have also been proposed. The use of a virtual currency has been proposed in [6] and [7] with different rewarding rules for nodes that forward others' packets and different ways to ensure no node cheats on the currency. The downside of these solutions is that nodes on the extremities of a network have less chance that those in the center to forward others' packets and eventually go bankrupt, while having acted in a legitimate way. Solutions based on active probing of nodes have also been proposed [8,9,10]. They all rely on the inability of the probed node to either distinguish probes from plain data traffic or identify the originator of a probe.

A whole set of more elaborate attacks against routing protocols, such as advertisement of false routing information, tampering with others' control and data packets, misrouting, wormhole attacks, etc, have been addressed in various solutions which usually aim to provide Byzantine robustness to a reactive, on-demand routing protocol as DSR or AODV [9,11,12].

As for proactive, table-driven routing protocols, the problem of Byzantine robustness is twofold: how to secure the control messages and the information they contain and how to secure the correct forwarding of data packets. The OLSR protocol has received some attention lately regarding its security. In [13], Raffo et al. propose a way to secure the content of control messages and thus prevent nodes from advertising false or expired information. In [14], another such protection is proposed, based on threshold cryptography and the requirement that a node cannot sign a TC message by itself and must ask its neighbors to do it, by the same time validating its contents.

The idea proposed in the present paper has already been put forward in the case of fixed, wired networks by Bradley et al. in [15]. It has been later argued in [16] that the assumptions on the network model are too strong and that strict checking of nodes is practically impossible. Thus in this paper, a relaxed way of checking is proposed which does not rely on these assumptions and which allows nodes to drop little traffic without being noticed.

2   Theoretical Background

This section introduces the general reasoning from the flow conservation principle up to checking it in a network using packet counters. A very similar technique was proposed by Bradley et al. in [15] for static wired networks, but it relied on assumptions that do not hold in the case of MANETs.

2.1   Single and Multiple Flows Conservation

Given a flow network in the form of a directed graph $G = (V, E)$ with vertices V and edges E, a source vertex s and a sink vertex t, a function of directed flow $f : V \times V \to \mathbb{R}^+$, the principle of flow conservation states that the net flow to a vertex is zero, except for the source s and the sink t.

$$\forall i \in V \backslash \{s,t\}, \quad \sum_{j \in V} (f(j,i) - f(i,j)) = 0 \tag{1}$$

Suppose that instead of having one (s, t, f) triplet, a collection $\mathcal{F}$ of triplets is given. The principle of flow conservation for all the triplets in $\mathcal{F}$ at once can be stated as follows.

$$\forall i \in V, \quad \sum_{\substack{j \in V}} \sum_{\substack{(s,t,f) \in \mathcal{F} \\ i \notin \{s,t\}}} (f(j,i) - f(i,j)) = 0 \tag{2}$$

2.2   Flow Conservation in a Network

A network is a set of nodes connected with links that can be symmetric or asymmetric. Thus it can be modelled by a directed graph which vertices are the nodes and which arcs are the links (a symmetric link between nodes i and j being represented by two arcs (i, j) and (j, i)). The flow on the arc (i, j) can be considered as the total amount of data that has flowed on the link from i to j.

For the sake of simplicity, let's define a few quantities.

Definition 1 (input and output). *Let I_{ij} (resp. O_{ij}), the input (resp. output) from node i to node j, be the amount of data that flows from i to j but is not destined to j (resp. is not generated by i).*

$$I_{ij} = \sum_{\substack{(s,t,f)\in\mathcal{F} \\ j\neq t}} f(i,j) \tag{3}$$

$$O_{ij} = \sum_{\substack{(s,t,f)\in\mathcal{F} \\ i\neq s}} f(i,j) \tag{4}$$

Thus I_{ij} is the amount of data sent from i to j for retransmission and similarly O_{ij} is the amount of data retransmitted from i to j.

The multiple flow conservation is then transposed as follows.

$$\forall i \in V, \quad \sum_{j\in V}(I_{ji} - O_{ij}) = 0 \tag{5}$$

Suppose no node can forge packets (i.e. generate packets that appear as if they have been generated by another node), then the amount of outgoing forwarded data is at most equal to the amount of incoming data not destined to the current node. Therefore, any node's balance (the amount of flow non-conservation) is positive.

$$\forall i \in V, \quad \sum_{j\in V}(I_{ji} - O_{ij}) \geq 0 \tag{6}$$

Moreover, in these conditions, a node's balance is precisely the amount of data lost at that node. Hence the idea in the following is to measure how much traffic a node drops by looking at its balance.

2.3   Using Packet Counters

In a real-world scenario, the amount of data that has flowed on a link is usually implemented by using packet counters in the TCP/IP stack (OSI layer 3) or in the MAC driver (OSI layer 2). This makes it difficult to compute a node's balance directly.

Indeed, instead of having counters on links that read the absolute amount of data that has flowed so far, counters are maintained on a link's both endpoints and the transmission along a link maybe unreliable.

Definition 2 (input and output view of a node). *Let I^i_{ij} and I^j_{ij} be respectively node i's and j's view of counter I_{ij}. Similarly, let O^i_{ij} and O^j_{ij} be respectively node i's and node j's view of counter O_{ij}.*

In absence of data loss on lower layers (layers below the one that performs packet accounting), the following properties hold.

$$\forall i, \; \forall j, \quad \begin{cases} I^i_{ij} = I^j_{ij} = I_{ij} \\ O^i_{ij} = O^j_{ij} = O_{ij} \end{cases} \tag{7}$$

Unfortunately, data loss usually does occur at lower layers, so only the following properties hold.

$$\forall i, \; \forall j, \quad \begin{cases} I^j_{ij} = I_{ij} \\ O^j_{ij} = O_{ij} \end{cases} \tag{8}$$

Indeed, a packet has not surely been transmitted on a link until it has been received by the corresponding layer on the receiving side (OSI Data Link or Network layers).

Using endpoints' counters, the principle of multiple flows conservation is restated as follows.

$$\forall i \in V, \quad \sum_{j \in V} \left(I^i_{ji} - O^j_{ij} \right) = 0 \tag{9}$$

3 Detecting Cheaters

This section presents the proposed solution based on flow conservation checking based on packet counters as introduced in Sect. 2.

3.1 Network Model

Cryptographic solutions are employed to be able to authenticate every originator of data and control packets. It is assumed that no node has enough resources to break the cryptographic scheme. The routing protocol employs periodic control messages for which the maximal period of time between two successive sent messages is known. The links between nodes have known finite total capacity (bandwidth).

3.2 Isolated and Non-colluding Cheaters

A cheater is a node that is not expected to collaborate with other nodes. More specifically in this case, it is expected not to perform packet accounting properly: it can change some or all of its counters with no relation to sending or receiving packets. Therefore, the content of its counters must not be relied upon.

An isolated cheater is a cheater that is not colluding with any other cheater and which has no cheater among its neighbors. If cheaters are assumed to be isolated, it is also assumed that on any link, at least one endpoint's counters are "in good faith."

Since a cheater can falsely advertise its counters, if for some counter X_{ij}, we have $X_{ij}^i \neq X_{ij}^j$, then it may be that there was some packet loss at lower layers from i to j, or either i or j is falsely advertising its version of X_{ij}. Similarly, it may happen that $X_{ij}^i = X_{ij}^j$ and there were indeed lost packets from i to j (i could falsely not count the emitted and then lost packets, or j could falsely count as received the lost packets), but this would require a good load of chance and guesswork.

It is clear that differing counters are a sign of either lost or dropped packets or false counters or both and in the following, we will not distinguish between the three situations, we will only speak about *counter discrepancy*. This is still an acceptable approach, since that information is to be eventually used to avoid routing packets through suspected or unreliable nodes (be it because they lose or drop traffic or lie about their counters).

3.3 Split Balance

Since one node's counters cannot be relied upon, a node's balance calculation has to be performed in many ways simultaneously. First, the node's internal balance (i.e. according to its own version of the counters) has to be calculated.

Definition 3 (node balance). *For a node i, its node balance $\mathcal{B}_i$ is the difference between all input and output, as viewed by itself.*

$$\mathcal{B}_i = \sum_{j \in V} \left(I_{ji}^i - O_{ij}^i \right) \tag{10}$$

A non-zero node balance would directly indicate deliberate packet dropping (or shooting itself in the foot), whereas a zero node balance does not mean anything by itself, since counters may have been manipulated incorrectly. So all link balances with that node's neighbors have to bee calculated too.

Definition 4 (input and output link balances). *An input (resp. output) link balance on link (i, j) is the difference between views of nodes i and j of counter I_{ij} (resp. O_{ij}).*

$$\mathcal{B}^I{}_{ij} = I_{ij}^i - I_{ij}^j \tag{11}$$

$$\mathcal{B}^O{}_{ij} = O_{ij}^i - O_{ij}^j \tag{12}$$

As traffic lost due to lower layer hazard is not to be distinguished from traffic lost due to deliberate packet dropping, all lost traffic should be accounted for in link balance. Unfortunately, the I_{ij} and O_{ij} counters are not enough to account for all the traffic, as for example packets generated by i, thus not counted in O_{ij}, and destined to j, thus not counted in I_{ij}, are not counted at all.

Definition 5 (total link balance). *The total link balance on link (i, j) is the difference between T_{ij}^i and T_{ij}^j, respectively i's and j's view of T_{ij}, the total amount of traffic that flows on link (i, j).*

$$\mathcal{B}^T{}_{ij} = T_{ij}^i - T_{ij}^j \tag{13}$$

The T_{ij} counter already counts packets counted by I_{ij} and O_{ij}, so for later convenience, the following counters will be used instead of T_{ij}.

Definition 6 (source and destination view of a node). *Let S_{ij}^i (resp. D_{ij}^j) be the amount of traffic generated by i (resp. destined to j) according to i (resp. j).*

$$S_{ij}^i = T_{ij}^i - O_{ij}^i \tag{14}$$
$$D_{ij}^j = T_{ij}^j - I_{ij}^j \tag{15}$$

Note that S_{ij}^j and D_{ij}^i can be defined as follows.

$$S_{ij}^j = T_{ij}^j - O_{ij}^j = D_{ij}^j + I_{ij}^j - O_{ij}^j \tag{16}$$
$$D_{ij}^i = T_{ij}^i - I_{ij}^i = D_{ij}^i + O_{ij}^i - I_{ij}^i \tag{17}$$

The total link balance can be now expressed as

$$\mathcal{B}^T{}_{ij} = S_{ij}^i + O_{ij}^i - D_{ij}^j - I_{ij}^j \tag{18}$$

3.4   Checking Split Balance

Suppose that nodes in a network have to monitor their neighbors using the split balance scheme from the previous section. During normal network operation, each node i maintains for each neighbor j the following series of counters.

S_{ij}^i : amount of data flowed from i to j and generated by i

O_{ij}^i : amount of data flowed from i to j but not generated by i

I_{ij}^i : amount of data flowed from i to j but not destined to j

D_{ji}^i : amount of data flowed from j to i and destined to i

I_{ji}^i : amount of data flowed from j to i but not destined to i

O_{ji}^i : amount of data flowed from j to i but not generated by j

At properly chosen times, nodes advertise their counters and calculate balances on nodes and links for which they have gathered enough of them. For a particular balance calculation, let the node performing it be the *observer* and the nodes about which it is performed the *observed*. For node balance calculations, the node that advertised the counters is the only *observed*, whereas for link balance calculations, both endpoints are. Depending on the underlying network model, an *observer* can maintain a degree of distrust in some subset of nodes (the ones it has observed so far). While a non-zero node balance affects the degree of distrust of the *observer* in the *observed* directly (we can safely assume that an *observer* has no interest in observing itself and thus the *observer* and *observed* are distinct), a non-zero link balance affects the degree of distrust of the *observer* in both endpoints, unless the *observer* is also one of the *observed* (a node is checking the balance on a link between itself and one of its neighbors).

3.5   Desynchronized Counters

In order to be able to make nodes check each other strictly, in a way that allows them to detect every single lost packet, nodes should be required to advertise their counters as soon as they send or receive one packet and to forward their neighbor's counters as soon as they receive them. Needless to say that this would incur a considerable control overhead.

A more flexible way is possible if the strict requirement is relaxed. Nodes can use periodic dedicated or existing control messages to advertise their counters, as well as all their neighbors' latest counters they have received so far.

Definition 7 (timed counters). *For each counter X_{ij}^i (resp. X_{ij}^j), let $X_{ij}^i(t)$ (resp. $X_{ij}^j(t)$) be its timed version, in other words its state at instant t, with the property that $X_{ij}^i(0) = 0$ (resp. $X_{ij}^j(0) = 0$).*

Let P be the upper bound on the interval of time elapsed between two consecutive advertisements sent by one node. Every sent advertisement message contains all that is required for a node receiving it to check its originator ($\mathcal{B}_i$) and the links between it and all its neighbors ($\mathcal{B}^I{}_{ij}$, $\mathcal{B}^I{}_{ji}$, $\mathcal{B}^O{}_{ij}$, $\mathcal{B}^O{}_{ji}$, $\mathcal{B}^T{}_{ij}$ and $\mathcal{B}^T{}_{ji}$).

Each node i maintains a sequence number counter which is incremented just before sending out each advertisement.

Definition 8 (ad sequence number). *Let $S_i(t)$ be the value of i's sequence number counter at instant t and let $T_i(n)$ be the instant at which i sends the advertisement with sequence number n, such that*

$$\forall i, n, t \in [T_i(n), T_i(n+1)), \quad S_i(t) = n \tag{19}$$

Then for each instant t, the time of the latest advertisement sent by i is $T_i(S_i(t))$, the time of the second latest is $T_i(S_i(t) - 1)$ and more generally $T_i(S_i(t) - p)$ is the time of the pth latest advertisement.

For practical reasons explained later in Sect. 4, we will use differential timed counters.

Definition 9 (differential timed counter). *For each timed counter $X_{ij}^i(t)$ (resp. $X_{ij}^j(t)$), let $\dot{X}_{ij}^i(t)$ (resp. $\dot{X}_{ij}^j(t)$) be the differential counter defined by*

$$\dot{X}_{ij}^i = X_{ij}^i(t) - X_{ij}^i(T_i(S_i(t))) \tag{20}$$

and respectively

$$\dot{X}_{ij}^j = X_{ij}^j(t) - X_{ij}^j(T_j(S_j(t))) . \tag{21}$$

Definition 10 (instant before advertising). *Let* $\mathsf{T}_i^-(n)$ *be the instant just before* i *sends advertisement with sequence number* n, *so we have* $\mathsf{S}_i(\mathsf{T}_i(n)) = n$ *and* $\mathsf{S}_i(\mathsf{T}_i^-(n)) = n - 1$.

The notation T^- is only used for differential timed counters, to explicitly indicate that the value of interest is the one just before sending the advertisement containing it, because usually $\dot{X}_{ij}^i(\mathsf{T}_i^-(n)) \neq \dot{X}_{ij}^i(\mathsf{T}_i(n))$, unless there has been no traffic on the link.

Definition 11 (link differential timed counter tuple). *Let* $\mathcal{C}_j^i(t)$ *be the tuple of* i's *timed counters regarding links between itself and* j *at instant* t

$$\mathcal{C}_j^i(t) = \left(S_{ij}^i(t), O_{ij}^i(t), I_{ij}^i(t), D_{ji}^i(t), I_{ji}^i(t), O_{ji}^i(t) \right) \tag{22}$$

and let $\dot{\mathcal{C}}_j^i(t)$ *be its differential counterpart*

$$\dot{\mathcal{C}}_j^i(t) = \left(\dot{S}_{ij}^i(t), \dot{O}_{ij}^i(t), \dot{I}_{ij}^i(t), \dot{D}_{ji}^i(t), \dot{I}_{ji}^i(t), \dot{O}_{ji}^i(t) \right) . \tag{23}$$

Definition 12 (link ad). *Let* $\mathcal{A}_j^i(n)$, i's *link advertisement with sequence number* n, *be a tuple of* i's *sequence number* n *and differential counters regarding links between itself and* j *right before that advertisement is sent by* i.

$$\mathcal{A}_j^i(n) = \left(n, \dot{\mathcal{C}}_j^i \left(\mathsf{T}_i^-(n) \right) \right) \tag{24}$$

Between the transmission of two successive advertisements, for each link with one of its neighbors, node i gathers the other endpoints' advertisements regarding that link.

Definition 13 (set of gathered ads' sequence numbers). *Let* $\mathcal{S}_j^i(n)$ *be the set of sequence numbers of* j's *advertisements received by* i *after the latter sent the advertisement with sequence number* $n-1$ *and before it sent the advertisement with sequence number* n.

$$\mathcal{S}_j^i(n) = \{ m : \mathsf{T}_i(n-1) \leq \mathsf{T}_j(m) < \mathsf{T}_i(n) \} \tag{25}$$

Definition 14 (set of gathered ads). *Let* $\mathcal{A}_i^j(n)$ *be the (possibly empty) set of* j's *advertisements regarding links between itself and* i *gathered by the latter between* $\mathsf{T}_i(n-1)$ *(inclusive) and* $\mathsf{T}_i(n)$ *(exclusive).*

$$\mathcal{A}_i^j(n) = \bigcup_{m \in \mathcal{S}_j^i(n)} \left\{ \mathcal{A}_i^j(m) \right\} \tag{26}$$

Definition 15 (neighbor set). *Let* $\mathcal{N}_i$ *be the set of* i's *neighbors from which it receives advertisements.*

Definition 16 (advertisement). *For each link between i and its neighbors, i's advertisement with sequence number n contains its own link advertisement regarding it and the set of all the other endpoint's advertisements regarding that same link gathered by i since its previous advertisement:*

$$\mathcal{M}^i(n) = \left\{ \left(\mathcal{A}^i_j(n), \mathcal{A}^j_i(n) \right) : j \in \mathcal{N}_i \right\} \tag{27}$$

Definition 17 (ad-based node balance). *Let $\mathcal{B}_i(n)$ be the i's node balance based on counters from its advertisement number n.*

$$\mathcal{B}_i(n) = \sum_{j \in \mathcal{N}_i} \left(\dot{I}^i_{ji} \left(\mathsf{T}^-_i(n) \right) - \dot{O}^i_{ij} \left(\mathsf{T}^-_i(n) \right) \right) \tag{28}$$

Node i's advertisement-based node balance can be checked by any node as soon as the latter receives i's $\mathcal{M}^i(n)$ containing $\mathcal{A}^i_j(n)$ for each $j \in \mathcal{N}_i$. Unfortunately, no link balance like $\mathcal{B}^I{}_{ij}$, $\mathcal{B}^I{}_{ji}$, $\mathcal{B}^O{}_{ij}$, $\mathcal{B}^O{}_{ji}$, $\dot{\mathcal{B}}^T{}_{ij}$ or $\mathcal{B}^T{}_{ji}$ can be strictly checked based solely on i's advertisement number n, without the knowledge of both $\dot{\mathcal{C}}^i_j(\mathsf{T}^-_i(n))$ and the corresponding link differential counter tuple from j for the same interval of time.

Nevertheless, a loose check can still be performed, if one looks at desynchronized versions of these link balances. Depending of what endpoint's advertisement is available, those can be computed in two similar ways.

$$\forall i, j \in \mathcal{N}_i, (k, l) \in \{(i, j), (j, i)\},$$

$$
\begin{cases}
\widetilde{\mathcal{B}^I}^i_{kl}(n) = \dot{I}^i_{kl} \left(\mathsf{T}^-_i(n) \right) - \displaystyle\sum_{m \in \mathcal{S}^i_j(n)} \dot{I}^j_{kl} \left(\mathsf{T}^-_j(m) \right) \\[2ex]
\widetilde{\mathcal{B}^O}^i_{kl}(n) = \dot{O}^i_{kl} \left(\mathsf{T}^-_i(n) \right) - \displaystyle\sum_{m \in \mathcal{S}^i_j(n)} \dot{O}^j_{kl} \left(\mathsf{T}^-_j(m) \right) \\[2ex]
\widetilde{\mathcal{B}^T}^i_{kl}(n) = \dot{S}^i_{kl} \left(\mathsf{T}^-_i(n) \right) + \dot{O}^i_{kl} \left(\mathsf{T}^-_i(n) \right) - \displaystyle\sum_{m \in \mathcal{S}^i_j(n)} \left(\dot{D}^j_{kl} \left(\mathsf{T}^-_j(m) \right) + \dot{I}^j_{kl} \left(\mathsf{T}^-_j(m) \right) \right)
\end{cases}
$$

$$\tag{29}$$

That loose check does not mean anything by itself. Since it is based on values of counters from different intervals, the values of these balances are most probably not zero when there is some traffic on the link. Fortunately, as should be noted in the following section, there still are ways to detect problems on links based on desynchronized balances.

3.6   Desynchronization and Tolerance

To calculate the exact values of desynchronized balances, we need to define $\delta^i_j(n)$, the minimum amount of time, as of $\mathsf{T}_i(n)$, elapsed since $\mathsf{T}_i(n-1)$ or last time

j's advertisement was received. Similarly, let $\Delta_j^i(n)$ be the amount of time, as of $T_i(n)$, elapsed since last time j's advertisement was received.

$$\delta_j^i(n) = \begin{cases} T_i(n) - \max_{m \in S_j^i(n)} T_j(m) & \text{if } S_j^i(n) \neq \emptyset , \\ T_i(n) - T_i(n-1) & \text{otherwise.} \end{cases} \tag{30}$$

$$\Delta_j^i(n) = \begin{cases} \delta_j^i(n) & \text{if } S_j^i(n) \neq \emptyset , \\ \delta_j^i(n) + \Delta_j^i(n-1) & \text{otherwise.} \end{cases} \tag{31}$$

For the special case of $n = 0$, let's say that $T_i(-1) = 0$ and that $\Delta_j^i(-1) = 0$.

If there is no actual discrepancy between counters (due to lost packets or wrongly manipulated counters), then $X_{ij}^i(t) = X_{ij}^j(t)$ at all instants t, for all counters X_{ij} and the the value of the desynchronized link balances are

$\forall i, j \in \mathcal{N}_i, (k,l) \in \{(i,j),(j,i)\}$,

$$\begin{cases} \tilde{B}^{I\,i}_{kl}(n) = \quad I_{kl}^i\big(T_i(n)\big) \quad - I_{kl}^i\big(T_i(n) \quad - \Delta_j^i(n)\big) \\ \qquad - I_{kl}^j\big(T_i(n-1)\big) + I_{kl}^j\big(T_i(n-1) - \Delta_j^i(n-1)\big) \\ \tilde{B}^{O\,i}_{kl}(n) = \quad O_{kl}^i\big(T_i(n)\big) \quad - O_{kl}^i\big(T_i(n) \quad - \Delta_j^i(n)\big) \\ \qquad - O_{kl}^j\big(T_i(n-1)\big) + O_{kl}^j\big(T_i(n-1) - \Delta_j^i(n-1)\big) \\ \tilde{B}^{T\,i}_{kl}(n) = \quad S_{kl}^i\big(T_i(n)\big) \quad - S_{kl}^i\big(T_i(n) \quad - \Delta_j^i(n)\big) \\ \qquad + O_{kl}^i\big(T_i(n)\big) \quad - O_{kl}^i\big(T_i(n) \quad - \Delta_j^i(n)\big) \\ \qquad - D_{kl}^j\big(T_i(n-1)\big) + D_{kl}^j\big(T_i(n-1) - \Delta_j^i(n-1)\big) \\ \qquad - I_{kl}^j\big(T_i(n-1)\big) + I_{kl}^j\big(T_i(n-1) - \Delta_j^i(n-1)\big) . \end{cases} \tag{32}$$

Let B_{ij} be the upper bound on the amount of data that can flow on links (i,j) and (j,i) per unit of time. It is obviously a reasonable assumption that this bound exists, at least in any realistic scenario. Then since counters' values are positive by definition, we have that

$\forall i, j \in \mathcal{N}_i, (k,l) \in \{(i,j),(j,i)\}$,

$$\max\left(\left|\tilde{B}^{I\,i}_{kl}(n)\right|, \left|\tilde{B}^{O\,i}_{kl}(n)\right|, \left|\tilde{B}^{T\,i}_{kl}(n)\right|\right) \leq B_{kl} \cdot \max\left(\Delta_j^i(n-1), \Delta_j^i(n)\right) . \tag{33}$$

For nodes other than i and j, values of T_j or T_i may not be known, so an upper bound to Δ_j^i and Δ_i^j has to be used instead. Since every node sends its advertisements at least P units of time apart, it is also the upper bound to Δ_j^i or Δ_i^j. In the worst possible case, we have the following property:

$\forall i, j \in \mathcal{N}_i, (k,l) \in \{(i,j),(j,i)\}$,

$$\max\left(\left|\tilde{B}^{I\,i}_{kl}(n)\right|, \left|\tilde{B}^{O\,i}_{kl}(n)\right|, \left|\tilde{B}^{T\,i}_{kl}(n)\right|\right) \leq B_{kl} \cdot P . \tag{34}$$

The use of this scheme would allow only i and j to observe counter discrepancy on link (i, j) exactly (assuming that the transmission time of packets containing advertisements is negligible). Other nodes could observe packet loss on this link only in excess of $B_{ij} \cdot \max(\Delta_j^i(n-1), \Delta_j^i(n))$ or $B_{ij} \cdot \max(\Delta_i^j(m-1), \Delta_i^j(m))$ at best (which means they receive advertisements from both i and j) or $B_{ij} \cdot P$ at worst. This leaves quite a gap for a malicious node to exploit in order to drop traffic with most of the other nodes not noticing.

3.7   Accumulated Balances

There is a way to enable nodes to observe even smaller counter discrepancies on links, provided a bit of patience. Instead of looking at link balances directly, nodes could observe their accumulated value over all advertisements:

$$\sum_n \widetilde{B}^{I\,i}_{ij}(n) \quad , \quad \sum_n \widetilde{B}^{o\,i}_{ij}(n) \quad \text{and} \quad \sum_n \widetilde{B}^{T\,i}_{ij}(n) \quad , \text{ or}$$

$$\sum_m \widetilde{B}^{I\,j}_{ij}(m) \quad , \quad \sum_m \widetilde{B}^{o\,j}_{ij}(m) \quad \text{and} \quad \sum_m \widetilde{B}^{T\,j}_{ij}(m) \, .$$

It appears that in case there is no actual counter discrepancy, these accumulated values are bounded too.

Theorem 1. *For each node i and each of its neighbor j, the accumulated values of calculated link balances over i's advertisements with numbers from n to $n+M$, for any $M \geq 0$ are exactly*

$$\forall i, j \in \mathcal{N}_i, (k, l) \in \{(i, j), (j, i)\}, n, M \geq 0,$$

$$
\left\{
\begin{aligned}
\sum_{p=n}^{n+M} \widetilde{B}^{I\,i}_{kl}(p) = \;\; & I^i_{kl}\big(\mathsf{T}_i(n+M)\big) \; - \; I^i_{kl}\big(\mathsf{T}_i(n+M) - \Delta_j^i(n+M)\big) \\
& - I^j_{kl}\big(\mathsf{T}_i(n-1)\big) \; + \; I^j_{kl}\big(\mathsf{T}_i(n-1) \; - \Delta_j^i(n-1)\big) \\[6pt]
\sum_{p=n}^{n+M} \widetilde{B}^{o\,i}_{kl}(p) = \;\; & O^i_{kl}\big(\mathsf{T}_i(n+M)\big) \; - \; O^i_{kl}\big(\mathsf{T}_i(n+M) - \Delta_j^i(n+M)\big) \\
& - O^j_{kl}\big(\mathsf{T}_i(n-1)\big) \; + \; O^j_{kl}\big(\mathsf{T}_i(n-1) \; - \Delta_j^i(n-1)\big) \\[6pt]
\sum_{p=n}^{n+M} \widetilde{B}^{T\,i}_{kl}(p) = \;\; & S^i_{ij}\big(\mathsf{T}_i(n+M)\big) \; - \; S^i_{kl}\big(\mathsf{T}_i(n+M) - \Delta_j^i(n+M)\big) \\
& + O^i_{kl}\big(\mathsf{T}_i(n+M)\big) \; - \; O^i_{kl}\big(\mathsf{T}_i(n+M) - \Delta_j^i(n+M)\big) \\
& - D^j_{kl}\big(\mathsf{T}_i(n-1)\big) \; + \; D^j_{kl}\big(\mathsf{T}_i(n-1) \; - \Delta_j^i(n-1)\big) \\
& - I^j_{kl}\big(\mathsf{T}_i(n-1)\big) \; + \; I^j_{kl}\big(\mathsf{T}_i(n-1) \; - \Delta_j^i(n-1)\big)
\end{aligned}
\right. \tag{35}
$$

Proof. By induction on $M \geq 0$. Already shown for $m = 0$ in (32). Suppose that it holds for $m \geq 0$, then we have that

$\forall i, j \in \mathcal{N}_i, (k,l) \in \{(i,j),(j,i)\}, n, m \geq 0,$

$$
\begin{cases}
\begin{aligned}
\sum_{p=n}^{n+m+1} \widetilde{\mathcal{B}^I}_{kl}^{\,i}(p) =\ & I_{kl}^i\big(\mathsf{T}_i(n+m)\big) & - I_{kl}^i\big(\mathsf{T}_i(n+m) & - \Delta_j^i(n+m)\big) \\
& - I_{kl}^j\big(\mathsf{T}_i(n-1)\big) & + I_{kl}^j\big(\mathsf{T}_i(n-1) & - \Delta_j^i(n-1)\big) \\
& + I_{kl}^i\big(\mathsf{T}_i(n+m+1)\big) - I_{kl}^i\big(\mathsf{T}_i(n+m+1) & - \Delta_j^i(n+m+1)\big) \\
& - I_{kl}^j\big(\mathsf{T}_i(n+m)\big) & + I_{kl}^j\big(\mathsf{T}_i(n+m) & - \Delta_j^i(n+m)\big)
\end{aligned} \\[2em]
\begin{aligned}
\sum_{p=n}^{n+m+1} \widetilde{\mathcal{B}^O}_{kl}^{\,i}(p) =\ & O_{kl}^i\big(\mathsf{T}_i(n+m)\big) & - O_{kl}^i\big(\mathsf{T}_i(n+m) & - \Delta_j^i(n+m)\big) \\
& - O_{kl}^j\big(\mathsf{T}_i(n-1)\big) & + O_{kl}^j\big(\mathsf{T}_i(n-1) & - \Delta_j^i(n-1)\big) \\
& + O_{kl}^i\big(\mathsf{T}_i(n+m+1)\big) - O_{kl}^i\big(\mathsf{T}_i(n+m+1) & - \Delta_j^i(n+m+1)\big) \\
& - O_{kl}^j\big(\mathsf{T}_i(n+m)\big) & + O_{kl}^j\big(\mathsf{T}_i(n+m) & - \Delta_j^i(n+m)\big)
\end{aligned} \\[2em]
\begin{aligned}
\sum_{p=n}^{n+m+1} \widetilde{\mathcal{B}^T}_{kl}^{\,i}(p) =\ & S_{kl}^i\big(\mathsf{T}_i(n+m)\big) & - S_{kl}^i\big(\mathsf{T}_i(n+m) & - \Delta_j^i(n+m)\big) \\
& + O_{kl}^i\big(\mathsf{T}_i(n+m)\big) & - O_{kl}^i\big(\mathsf{T}_i(n+m) & - \Delta_j^i(n+m)\big) \\
& - D_{kl}^j\big(\mathsf{T}_i(n-1)\big) & + D_{kl}^j\big(\mathsf{T}_i(n-1) & - \Delta_j^i(n-1)\big) \\
& - I_{kl}^j\big(\mathsf{T}_i(n-1)\big) & + I_{kl}^j\big(\mathsf{T}_i(n-1) & - \Delta_j^i(n-1)\big) \\
& + S_{kl}^i\big(\mathsf{T}_i(n+m+1)\big) - S_{kl}^i\big(\mathsf{T}_i(n+m+1) & - \Delta_j^i(n+m+1)\big) \\
& + O_{kl}^i\big(\mathsf{T}_i(n+m+1)\big) - O_{kl}^i\big(\mathsf{T}_i(n+m+1) & - \Delta_j^i(n+m+1)\big) \\
& - D_{kl}^j\big(\mathsf{T}_i(n+m)\big) & + D_{kl}^j\big(\mathsf{T}_i(n+m) & - \Delta_j^i(n+m)\big) \\
& - I_{kl}^j\big(\mathsf{T}_i(n+m)\big) & + I_{kl}^j\big(\mathsf{T}_i(n+m) & - \Delta_j^i(n+m)\big) ,
\end{aligned}
\end{cases}
\tag{36}
$$

$\forall i, j \in \mathcal{N}_i, (k,l) \in \{(i,j),(j,i)\}, n, m \geq 0,$

$$
\begin{cases}
\begin{aligned}
\sum_{p=n}^{n+m+1} \widetilde{\mathcal{B}^I}_{kl}^{\,i}(p) =\ & I_{kl}^i\big(\mathsf{T}_i(n+m+1)\big) - I_{kl}^i\big(\mathsf{T}_i(n+m+1) - \Delta_j^i(n+m+1)\big) \\
& - I_{kl}^j\big(\mathsf{T}_i(n-1)\big) & + I_{kl}^j\big(\mathsf{T}_i(n-1) & - \Delta_j^i(n-1)\big)
\end{aligned} \\[1.5em]
\begin{aligned}
\sum_{p=n}^{n+m+1} \widetilde{\mathcal{B}^O}_{kl}^{\,i}(p) =\ & O_{kl}^i\big(\mathsf{T}_i(n+m+1)\big) - O_{kl}^i\big(\mathsf{T}_i(n+m+1) - \Delta_j^i(n+m+1)\big) \\
& - O_{kl}^j\big(\mathsf{T}_i(n-1)\big) & + O_{kl}^j\big(\mathsf{T}_i(n-1) & - \Delta_j^i(n-1)\big)
\end{aligned} \\[1.5em]
\begin{aligned}
\sum_{p=n}^{n+m+1} \widetilde{\mathcal{B}^T}_{kl}^{\,i}(p) =\ & S_{kl}^i\big(\mathsf{T}_i(n+m+1)\big) - S_{kl}^i\big(\mathsf{T}_i(n+m+1) - \Delta_j^i(n+m+1)\big) \\
& + O_{kl}^i\big(\mathsf{T}_i(n+m+1)\big) - O_{kl}^i\big(\mathsf{T}_i(n+m+1) - \Delta_j^i(n+m+1)\big) \\
& - D_{kl}^j\big(\mathsf{T}_i(n-1)\big) & + D_{kl}^j\big(\mathsf{T}_i(n-1) & - \Delta_j^i(n-1)\big) \\
& - I_{kl}^j\big(\mathsf{T}_i(n-1)\big) & + I_{kl}^j\big(\mathsf{T}_i(n-1) & - \Delta_j^i(n-1)\big) ,
\end{aligned}
\end{cases}
\tag{37}
$$

since there is no counter discrepancy, so $X^i_{ij}(t)$ and $X^j_{ij}(t)$ are interchangeable and additionally we also have that $S^i_{kl}(t) + O^i_{kl}(t) = D^i_{kl}(t) + I^i_{kl}(t)$. This last formula is the statement for $m + 1$ and completes the proof.   □

Corollary 1. *It follows from Theorem 1 that accumulated values of link balances are bounded.*

$$\forall i, j \in \mathcal{N}_i, (k,l) \in \{(i,j),(j,i)\}, n, M \geq 0$$

$$\begin{cases} \left| \sum_{p=n}^{n+M} \widetilde{B}^{Ii}_{kl}(p) \right| \leq B_{kl} \cdot \max\left(\Delta^i_j(n-1), \Delta^i_j(n+M)\right) \\[3mm] \left| \sum_{p=n}^{n+M} \widetilde{B}^{oi}_{kl}(p) \right| \leq B_{ij} \cdot \max\left(\Delta^i_j(n-1), \Delta^i_j(n+M)\right) \quad (38) \\[3mm] \left| \sum_{p=n}^{n+M} \widetilde{B}^{Ti}_{kl}(p) \right| \leq B_{ij} \cdot \max\left(\Delta^i_j(n-1), \Delta^i_j(n+M)\right) \end{cases}$$

For nodes that receive advertisements from either i or j but not both, the bound has to be loosened to

$$\forall i, j \in \mathcal{N}_i, (k,l) \in \{(i,j),(j,i)\}, n, M \geq 0$$

$$\max\left(\left| \sum_{p=n}^{n+M} \widetilde{B}^{Ii}_{kl}(p) \right|, \left| \sum_{p=n}^{n+M} \widetilde{B}^{oi}_{kl}(p) \right|, \left| \sum_{p=n}^{n+M} \widetilde{B}^{Ti}_{kl}(p) \right| \right) \leq B_{ij} \cdot \mathsf{P} \ . \quad (39)$$

The use of accumulated values enables small counter discrepancies to accumulate and eventually make accumulated values of balances exceed their predicted bound.

3.8   What About Mobility?

The introduction of mobility has two effects. First, nodes may join a neighborhood, which means they could begin tracking other nodes' advertisements at some advanced point in time, when the latter have already been sending and receiving traffic. Second, nodes may part from a neighborhood, which means that other nodes may track their advertisements up to some point in time.

Both effects imply that some observer may receive advertisements from observed node i only on some interval of time, say $[t_b, t_e]$, which means it can gather advertisements from i on an interval of sequence numbers $[n_b, n_e]$, with

$$n_b = \min\{n : \mathsf{T}_i(n) \geq t_b\} \ , \quad (40)$$

$$n_e = \max\{n : \mathsf{T}_i(n) \leq t_e\} \ . \quad (41)$$

According to that definition, if $n_b > n_e$ then the observer has not gathered any advertisement from i. With at least one gathered advertisement ($n_b \leq n_e$), an observer can check accumulated link balances according to (39).

For all links (i, j) and (j, i) for which the observer gathered advertisements from both i and j, it may be that it knows $\Delta_j^i(n-1)$ and $\Delta_j^i(n+N)$ for some n and $N \geq 0$ or $\Delta_i^j(m-1)$ and $\Delta_i^j(m+M)$ for some m and $M \geq 0$. This enables the observer to check bounds on accumulated values of link balances according to (38) which is more restrictive than (39).

For an observer receiving advertisements from both endpoints of links (i, j) and (j, i) on some interval of time, the condition for it to know $\Delta_j^i(n)$ for some n is to receive enough advertisements from i and j so that

$$\exists m, \quad \mathsf{T}_j(m) < \mathsf{T}_i(n) \leq \mathsf{T}_j(m+1) , \tag{42}$$

which means that at worst, it has to wait for 2P units of time to know both $\Delta_j^i(n)$ and $\Delta_i^j(m)$ for some n and m. Then to acquire both $\Delta_j^i(n+1)$ and $\Delta_i^j(m+1)$, it may wait at worst another P units of time.

3.9 Grading System

The various checks performed by observers on the advertisements coming from observed nodes can be used to compute a *degree of distrust* the former maintains for the latter. For each link (i, j), when the accumulated values of some link balance exceed the bound according to (39) or (38), the level of distrust is increased on both i and j and a bias is introduced in the accumulated link balance that has triggered the increase to reset it to some "reasonable" state.

The lesser the counter discrepancies, possibly coming from a node dropping little traffic, the longer the time necessary for accumulated values of link balances to exceed their bound, at worst.

Using the grading system on each node for each other node in its two-hop neighborhood causes the malicious nodes that either drop traffic or tamper with their counters to accumulate a higher level of distrust by other nodes. The level of distrust may be used as a quality of service metric in routing protocols to enable the preference of more trusted nodes when computing routes.

4   Practical Considerations

A few conclusions drawn from initial simulations led us to consider some important aspects of the solution.

There are actual settings that make it difficult to make counters visible globally: diffusion of counters may be cumbersome and requiring each node to track balances for every other node and link in the network is seldom scalable. In such situations, it is advisable to limit the diffusion of counter values to only some hops away and make only those node that are in the vicinity of a node and link measure the balances. Note however that there is a lower bound on the hop limit to make the scheme useful: if the counters are not allowed to diffuse farther than one hop away, only the observed node's balance can be checked in addition to the balance of the link between it and the observer. If the counters diffuse to at least two hops away, then the observer can check the observed node's node balance and link balances on all the links between the latter and its one-hop neighbors.

If actual (vs. differential) counters are used, this limited scheme works well as long as the topology is not allowed to change. As soon as node mobility is introduced, two problems appear. First, when a node "enters" a neighborhood, when it begins receiving counters from a node it has not heard of before (or in a near past), its balance calculations regarding that node or its adjacent links are biased: it has no way to know about the values of counters advertised by past neighbors that have since gone away. Second, when some neighbor goes away, all other nodes in the neighborhood have to keep the values of its counters in memory, which would, with time, bring back the very problem that limited scope was aimed to solve: nodes would have to keep in memory a potentially growing number of values.

The solution lies in using a differential convention for counters: instead of advertising the actual value of a counter, a node advertises only the difference between the actual counter and its value the previous time it was advertised. Thus the bias of past neighbors does not last more that a period of counter advertisement and values of that bias do not have to be kept in memory at all.

The solution presented in Sect. 3 relies on the fact that advertisements are never lost. Although this assumption is unrealistic, there are ways to make lost advertisements sent again, so that eventually, every observer is able to perform all the checks, be it retroactively. To ensure that a node's advertisements may not be lost repeatedly for too much time (and to be able to detect nodes that leave a neighborhood), it is reasonable to put a limit on the number of consecutively lost advertisements before considering the node as departed.

Advertisements from some node i may contain a series of link advertisements from some of its neighbor j. As a matter of fact, it would be enough for the checks to be possible if i summed j's counters to be sent in one advertisement, but observers would not be able to authenticate that information anymore, so all j's link advertisements have to be included separately. To ensure that the number of j's link advertisements included in one i's advertisement is limited, a lower bound p on the time separating two consecutive advertisements has to be put. Setting p to be equal to P is not desirable in practice (as nodes would not be able to desynchronize their transmissions), but setting $P/2 \le p < P$ assures that no more than two j's advertisements are sent between two consecutive i's advertisements.

5   Evaluation Results

To check the accuracy and performance of the solution based on accumulated values of link balances, a batch of simulation runs has been launched using the OPNET network simulator.

5.1   Simulation Model

We created a simplified model of an ad hoc network, to avoid all the artefacts of routing and to best evaluate the solution (Fig. 1). One dropping node has four symmetric links to four 1-hop neighbors which can in turn reach 15 other nodes. During the simulation, flows are generated (exponential interarrival with $\lambda^{-1} = 30$ s) from one of the total 20 nodes to another of the remaining 19 (chosen uniformly), necessarily passing through the dropping node. Within each flow, packets have a constant size (chosen uniformly between 64 and 1500 bytes) and a rate (of constant packet interarrival) such that the total available capacity of links is never exceeded. Mobility is modeled simply by switching one of the four 1-hop neighbors on or off (exponential interarrival): when a neighbor is switched off, its counters are reset to zero and it does not participate in any flow until it is switched on again. Advertisements of counters are simulated with uniform interarrival in $[P - J, P]$, P being the maximum period of advertisement and J being the amount of jitter in the advertisement.

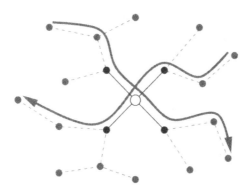

Fig. 1. Simulation model

5.2 Counter Maintenance and Advertisement

Every time a data packet gets through the links either way between the dropping node and some of its neighbors, counter maintenance is performed. Let (i, j) be the directed link on which the packet is going. First i's counters are updated as explained in Sect. 3.4 and then j's counters are updated accordingly.

Each one of the dropping node and its neighbors performs periodic counter advertisement of its own, using its own timer. On the one hand, each time a neighbor is advertising its counters, their values are added into separate secondary variables and the neighbor's counters are reset to 0. On the other hand, when the dropping node is advertising its counters, its node timed balance and all desynchronized timed balances of its links to its neighbors are calculated and logged. Balance calculations use the dropping node's counters directly, but use secondary variables into which the neighbors' counters have been accumulated (to model counter desynchronization). After balances have been calculated and logged, the dropping node's counters as well as secondary variables are reset to 0.

5.3   Influence of Mobility

To evaluate the influence of mobility on the estimation of packet loss using accumulated values of link balances, we have run two batches of simulations, varying the drop probability on the dropping node and the mean period of mobility. In the first batch, the dropping node always pretended to have retransmitted the packets it dropped, whereas in the second batch, it always pretended not to have ever received them. The simulation time of all simulations was set to one hour.

On Fig. 2, plots of the estimated total of lost packets (in fact the summed values of $\widetilde{B}^{\tau i}_{ij}(t)$ over the total packets to be transmitted (averaged on the four links) are shown, for drop rates of 1.0, 0.8, 0.6, 0.4, 0.2 and 0.0 from the first batch. Obviously, with larger mobility periods (less mobility), the estimations are more accurate, whereas with shorter periods, estimation tends to 1, since the counters are often reset and thus it may appear as though all the traffic has been dropped.

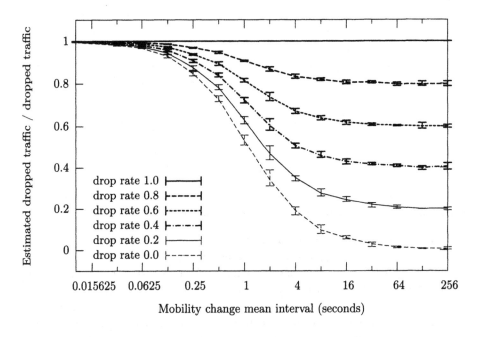

Fig. 2. Drop estimation error vs. mobility in scenario 1

On Fig. 3, the same plots are shown, but from the second batch. Here less mobility still yields better estimations, but more mobility gives negative values which modules tend to the ratio of indeed retransmitted traffic. This was to be expected, since again with high mobility, counters from the neighbors tend to zero and do not counterbalance counters of the dropping node.

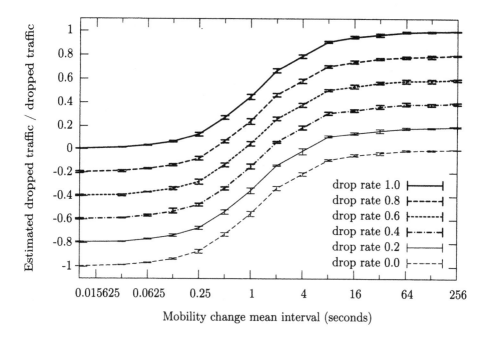

Fig. 3. Drop estimation error vs. mobility in scenario 2

6   Conclusion

The proposed solution to detect dropped traffic on nodes and links and/or counter cheating is very promising. The method integrates well into proactive protocols since it only needs packet accounting and periodic advertisement of counters.

Our current perspective is to provide even better methods of detecting counter discrepancy as well as analytical evaluations of the accuracy of the methods with respect to several parameters such as the maximum capacity of a link, node mobility, advertisement interval, etc.

References

1. Clausen, T., Jacquet, P.: Optimized link state routing (OLSR) protocol. RFC 3626, IETF (2003)
2. Perkins, C., Belding-Royer, E., Das, S.: Ad hoc on-demand distance vector (AODV) routing. RFC 3561, IETF (2003)
3. Ogier, R., Templin, F., Lewis, M.: Topology dissemination based on reverse-path forwarding (TBRPF). RFC 3684, IETF (2004)
4. Lamport, L., Shostak, R., Pease, M.: The byzantine generals problem. ACM Trans. Program. Lang. Syst. **4** (1982) 382–401
5. Marti, S., Giuli, T.J., Lai, K., Baker, M.: Mitigating routing misbehavior in mobile ad hoc networks. In: MobiCom '00: Proceedings of the 6th annual international conference on Mobile computing and networking, New York, NY, USA, ACM Press (2000) 255–265

6. Buttyán, L., Hubaux, J.P.: Stimulating cooperation in self-organizing mobile ad hoc networks. MONET **8** (2003) 579–592

7. Zhong, S., Chen, J., Yang, Y.R.: Sprite: A simple, cheat-proof, credit-based system for mobile ad-hoc networks. In: INFOCOM. (2003)

8. Just, M., Kranakis, E., Wan, T.: Resisting malicious packet dropping in wireless ad hoc networks. In Pierre, S., Barbeau, M., Kranakis, E., eds.: Ad-Hoc, Mobile, and Wireless Networks, Second International Conference, ADHOC-NOW 2003 Montreal, Canada, October 8-10, 2003, Proceedings. Volume 2865 of Lecture Notes in Computer Science., Springer (2003) 151–163

9. Awerbuch, B., Holmer, D., Nita-Rotaru, C., Rubens, H.: An on-demand secure routing protocol resilient to byzantine failures. In: WiSE '02: Proceedings of the 3rd ACM workshop on Wireless security, New York, NY, USA, ACM Press (2002) 21–30

10. Mahajan, R., Rodrig, M., Wetherall, D., Zahorjan, J.: Sustaining cooperation in multi-hop wireless networks. 2nd Symposium on Networked System Design and Implementation, Boston, MA, USA, May (2005)

11. Hu, Y.C., Perrig, A., Johnson, D.B.: Ariadne:: a secure on-demand routing protocol for ad hoc networks. In: MobiCom '02: Proceedings of the 8th annual international conference on Mobile computing and networking, New York, NY, USA, ACM Press (2002) 12–23

12. Avramopoulos, I., Kobayashi, H., Wang, R., Krishnamurthy, A.: Highly secure and efficient routing. In IEEE, ed.: INFOCOM 2004. Twenty-third AnnualJoint Conference of the IEEE Computer and Communications Societies. Volume 1., IEEE, IEEE (2004) 208–220

13. Raffo, D., Adjih, C., Clausen, T., Mühlethaler, P.: An advanced signature system for olsr. In: SASN '04: Proceedings of the 2nd ACM workshop on Security of ad hoc and sensor networks, New York, NY, USA, ACM Press (2004) 10–16

14. Fourati, A., Agha, K.A.: A shared secret-based algorithm for securing the OLSR routing protocol. Telecommunication Systems **31** (2006) 213–226

15. Bradley, K.A., Cheung, S., Puketza, N., Mukherjee, B., Olsson, R.A.: Detecting disruptive routers: a distributed network monitoring approach. Network, IEEE **12** (1998) 50–60

16. Hughes, J.R., Aura, T., Bishop, M.: Using conservation of flow as a security mechanism in network protocols. In: IEEE Symposium on Security and Privacy. (2000) 132–131

A New Hybrid Traffic Engineering Routing Algorithm for Bandwidth Guaranteed Traffic

Zhaowei Meng[1], Jinshu Su[1], and Stefano Avallone[2]

[1] School of Computer, National University of Defense Technology,
Changsha 410073, P.R. China
{zwmeng, sjs}@nudt.edu.cn
[2] COMICS Lab, Dipartimento di Informatica e Sistemistica,
Universit`a di Napoli Federico II,
Via Claudio 21, 80125 Napoli, Italy
stavallo@unina.it

Abstract. This paper presents a new hybrid traffic engineering routing algorithm for bandwidth guaranteed traffic. Former traffic engineering routing algorithms mainly optimize one of the three objectives: minimizing the hop count, balancing the load and minimizing the interference between source-destination pairs. But usually there is a tradeoff among these three factors. Single objective optimizations can't get the best performance. The main contribution of this paper is a new hybrid approach to consider the three objectives together. From the simulation results, the proposed algorithm has better performance than former algorithms.

1 Introduction

Internet's traditional shortest path first routing algorithm may lead to congestion in its nature. With the fast growth of Internet and rapid increase of end-user's bandwidth, the risk of network congestion is also increasing dramatically. Network congestion will not only degrade the performance of the network, but also break ISP's QoS guarantees to users. Traffic engineering technology can help to optimize the performance of network through efficient utilization of network resources. Multi-Protocol Label Switching (MPLS) enables the mechanism of constraint based routing (CBR) through RSVP-TE protocol. Using CBR, we can find a feasible network path based on traffic engineering objectives and QoS constraints. CBR provides a very powerful tool for traffic engineering.

Different traffic engineering optimization objectives have been researched in the literature. In RFC 2702, D.Awduche et al. pointed out that the key performance objectives associated with traffic engineering can be classified into two classes: traffic oriented objectives and resource oriented objectives. Traffic oriented objectives aim to enhance the QoS of traffic streams, such as minimization of packet loss, minimization of delay, maximization of throughput, and so on. While resource oriented objectives aim to optimize the resource utilization [1].

Samer Lahoud et al. found that three main criteria illustrate the relevant trade-offs involved in a traffic engineering scheme for MPLS: minimizing network cost, load balancing and minimizing the interference (reducing blocking probability) [2].

K. Cho and P. Jacquet (Eds.): AINTEC 2006, LNCS 4311, pp. 159–171, 2006.

Usually there is a tradeoff among these three factors. So we propose a new hybrid traffic engineering routing algorithm for routing bandwidth guaranteed label switch path, which tries to consider these objectives together. Extensive simulations were carried out to evaluate the performance of the proposed algorithm. In contrast to former algorithms, our proposed approach performs better.

The rest of this paper is structured as follows. Section 2 reviews some related works. In Section 3 we propose a new hybrid traffic engineering routing algorithm and describe it in detail. In Section 4, the efficiency of our new algorithm is evaluated and finally, Section 5 concludes our work.

2 Related Work

We have mentioned that there are three main traffic engineering objectives: minimizing network cost, load balancing and minimizing the interference.

Minimizing network cost is an important objective. In order to do this, people usually use static metrics, such as hop count or link static costs in routing algorithms. An important example is shortest path first (SPF) algorithm. Since SPF selects the shortest path from source to destination, less network resources are used by traffic flowing through the network. SPF's complexity is low, and is easy to implement and deploy. But it may potentially cause some links being bottleneck, which will leads to poor resource utilization.

In order to restrain the production of bottleneck links and hot spots, the other optimization objective - load balancing should be incorporated in. Widest-shortest-path (WSP) [3] and shortest-widest-path (SWP) [4][5] try to consider the path's capacity when choosing the route. SWP chooses the path which has the maximum bandwidth. If several such paths exist, SWP chooses the shortest one. WSP is on the contrary of the SWP. WSP chooses the shortest path. If there are several such paths, WSP chooses the one which has the maximum bandwidth. But these two algorithms lean to preserve network resources or lean to load balance. Yufei Wang et al. [6] also propose a routing algorithm which minimizes the maximum link utilization. But all these algorithms haven't considered total network resources and constraints, and also haven't considered the interference between the Source-Destination (SD) pairs.

Another important objective - minimizing interference between the source-destination pairs in the network is proposed by M. Kodialam et al. The Minimum interference routing algorithm (MIRA) [7] is the first one which attempted to reduce blocking probabilities by finding links minimizing the maximum flow reduction between other SD pairs. MIRA chooses the path which interferes the least to other SD pairs. For a given SD pair (s,d), the concept of interference on (s,d) is the decrease of maximum flow (maxflow) value between (s,d) due to route a LSP on other SD pairs. The problem of minimum interference routing is to find a path that maximizes the maxflow between all other SD pairs. This problem is shown to be NP hard. But M. Kodialam et al. give a heuristic algorithm. The core notion of MIRA is "critical link". These links have the property that when an LSP is routed over those links the maxflow values of one or more SD pairs decreases. The critical links are the arcs belonging to the mincuts of the SD pair. MIRA tries to avoid routing LSPs on such critical links of other SD pairs. So it performs better than former algorithms.

But the notion of 'critical link" defined by MIRA also has some shortcomings. For example, some links which are believed as non-critical by MIRA are shown to be indeed very important. S.Suri et al. illustrated it by three examples: parking lot topology, concentrator topology and distributor topology [8]. For solving this problem, M.S. Kodialam et al. try to model the potential critical links using the concept of $\triangle$-critical link [7]. But Ying-Xiao Xu et al. pointed out that if $\triangle$ is chosen too small, the potential critical link won't be $\triangle$-critical link; if $\triangle$ is chosen too big, too many uncritical links may be included in $\triangle$-critical link sets and cause high rejection rate [9]. So Ying-Xiao Xu et al. propose that most links use predetermined $\triangle$, but special links such as output links of concentrated nodes use different $\triangle$. But this is a temporary policy, and can't be generalized. Other authors attempted to solve this problem by new definitions of link criticality. Bin Wang et al. [10] propose an algorithm which utilizes maxflow value of SD pair and sub-flow value on the link to estimate its importance to routing possible future LSP set-up requests. In [11], the authors provide an algorithm which divides the link criticality into multiple classes. So every link has certain class of criticality. But its complexity is higher than MIRA.

Usually there is a tradeoff among these three factors. So many authors try to combine different objectives in the algorithm.

Q.Ma et al. proposed a shortest-distance path algorithm [12,13]. They try to get a compromise between preserving network resources and load balancing. The algorithm selects the path with the shortest distance. The distance of a link is defined as the inverse of the available bandwidth on the link. When the load level is high, the algorithm selects the shorter paths; and when load level is low, it selects the wider paths. Karl Hendling et al. proposed Residual Network and Link Capacity (RNLC) routing algorithm [14]. They define a constant C to control the dynamic behavior of the algorithm. If C is chosen very big, the scheme behaves like minimum-hop routing. If C is chosen very small, the scheme trends to distribute the load throughout the network. Gargi Banerjee et al. improve MIRA by first finds a candidate set of paths using the K-shortest paths algorithm [15]. So the path selected by MIRA is never longer than the K-th shortest path. By doing this, they preserve the network resources when minimizing the interference. The exponential-MIRA [16] proposed by Su-Wei Tan et al. uses an exponential weight function to translate link's utilization and criticality into cost. The scheme also tries to get balance between interference minimizing and load balancing.

Samer Lahoud[2] and Kavitha Banglore[17] proposed two different hybrid algorithms considering these three objectives together. In [2], the authors compute the tunable parameters according to total network load and total network capacity. The authors also show the relevancy of the three objectives and the benefit of their combination by the simulations. In [17], the authors give an integer linear programming formulation for the problem of achieving the balance between the three factors. The authors also proved it to be NP-hard and gave a heuristic solution. But these two solutions both based on the link criticality defined in [7] when considering the interference minimizing objective.

In next section, we will try to give a new approach of hybrid traffic engineering routing algorithm.

3 Proposed Algorithm

In the previous section we have summarized different traffic engineering routing algorithms for bandwidth guaranteed traffic. We pointed out that a routing algorithm should get appropriate tradeoff among different objectives. Therefore, in this section we will propose a new approach.

3.1 System Model

Given a network represented by a directed graph (V,E) where V is a set of nodes and E is a set of links. The number of nodes is n and the number of links is m. The LSP setup requests are between specific source nodes (ingress) and destination nodes (egress). The SD pairs are $\{S_0,D_0\},\{S_1,D_1\},...,\{S_p,D_p\}$, where p is the number of SD pairs. We denote all these SD pairs by a set P.

Each LSP set-up request arrives at ingress node, which is responsible to determine an explicit-route for the LSP. To determine the route, each ingress router should know the whole network's topology and state information of the links. In other words, this is source routing. The initial capacity of link l is denoted as $R(l)$. The current available bandwidth of link l is denoted as $r(l)$. The request for an LSP set-up r_i is defined by a triple (s_i,d_i,b_i), where $(s_i,d_i) \in P$, s_i is the ingress node, d_i is the egress node, and b_i is the amount of bandwidth required by the LSP. The requests arrive on line, one by one, and there is no prior knowledge for future demands. The objective is to find a feasible path (if exists) for LSP request r_i in the network from s_i to d_i, otherwise the request will be rejected. At the same time, the route selection must make efficient use of network resources. In this paper, we focus on the route selection of bandwidth guaranteed paths. No re-routing or request splitting is allowed.

3.2 Proposed Algorithm's Details

When selecting route for a LSP request, we consider not only the hop counts and the link residual capacity, but also the link criticality.

Given an LSP request (s,d,b) to be routed, we give a new link weight function as below.

$$w(l) = T_1 + T_2 \frac{R(l) - r(l)}{R(l)} + \frac{\sum\limits_{(a,b) \in P \backslash (s,d)} \alpha_{ab} f_{ab}(l)}{b + \alpha_{sd} f_{sd}(l)} \qquad (1)$$

T_1 and T_2 are tunable parameters which allow the operators to adjust the comprise among different objectives.

The first term T_1 represents the objective of minimizing hop counts. A shortest path will bate the consumption of network resources while routing the same bandwidth demanded. But the simple shortest path first algorithm may produce the hot spots, which will degrade the performance of operational network. So we should take link utilization and interference into consideration. When the network load is high, the algorithm will trend to hop counts minimize by setting a big value of T_1.

The second term $T_2(R(l) - r(l)) / R(l)$ represents the objective of load balancing. If the link utilization is high, our algorithm will try to avoid routing LSP on such links. If the network operators want to emphasize the objective of load balancing, they can realize this by setting a bigger value of T_2.

The third term $(\sum_{(a,b) \in P \backslash (s,d)} \alpha_{ab} f_{ab}(l)) / (b + \alpha_{sd} f_{sd}(l))$ represents the objective of minimizing interference. Where b is the bandwidth demanded, α_{sd} represents the relative importance of the SD pair (s,d), $f_{sd}(l)$ is the amount of sub-flow traveling through the link l when the maximum flow between (s,d) is achieved. $\sum_{(a,b) \in P \backslash (s,d)} \alpha_{ab} f_{ab}(l)$ represents the weighted sum of sub-flows of all other SD pairs traveling through link l. If $b + \alpha_{sd} f_{sd}(l)$ is bigger and $\sum_{(a,b) \in P \backslash (s,d)} \alpha_{ab} f_{ab}(l)$ is smaller, we believe that routing current request (s,d,b) on link l will cause less impact on other SD pairs; so the link weight will be smaller. The algorithm will trend to route LSP on such links. Otherwise the algorithm will trend to avoid such links.

The algorithm's detailed pseudo code is listed below.

The Proposed Algorithm

INPUT:
  A residual graph $G = (V, E)$ and LSP request $r(s, d, b)$, which is a request for b bandwidth units between pair (s, d).
OUTPUT:
  A path from s to d with b bandwidth units.
PROCEDURE:
1: Compute the maximum network flow for all $(a,b) \in P$.
2: Compute the weight $w(l)$ for all $l \in E$ according to equation (1).
3: Eliminate all the links whose residual bandwidth less than b and get a reduced network topology.
4: Run Dijkstra algorithm using $w(l)$ as the weights in the reduced network.
5: Create an LSP connecting s to d with b bandwidth units and update the links' available bandwidth.

3.3 Complexity Analysis

Computing maxflow for each SD pair using the highest label preflow-push algorithm needs $O(n^2 \sqrt{m})$. There are p SD pairs, so step 1 needs $O(pn^2 \sqrt{m})$. Step 2 and step 3 both need $O(m)$. Step 4 needs $O(n^2)$. So the total computation complexity is $O(pn^2 \sqrt{m})$. This is on the same level as MIRA[7] and NewMIRA's [11] complexity $O((p-1)n^2 \sqrt{m})$.

4 Performance Studies

Simulations were carried out to study the performance of our proposed routing algorithm. We extended the TOTEM (TOolbox for Traffic Engineering Methods) [18] to implement the simulations. TOTEM provides an open-source software that allows an operator to test methods coming from the academic research.

Different topologies were used. SPF and a well-known variant New-MIRA [11] were used as contrast. The simulation models and results are shown followed.

4.1 KL Topology

The network topology as well as SD pairs is shown in Figure 1. This topology was used by M.S. Kodialam et al. in [7]. It has slowly become the de-facto simulation topology in the literatures. SD pairs 1-5 are the only network input and output traffics. Lighter links have capacity of 1200 bandwidth units, while the darker ones have 4800 bandwidth units capacity, representing OC-12 and OC-48 links, respectively. Links are bi-directional, i.e., they represent two links with the same capacity in opposite directions. Requests were randomly generated using the uniform distribution in the interval [1, 4]. It is assumed that LSPs have long lives, i.e., once accepted its resources are kept until the end of the experiments. 8,000 requests were randomly generated among the five SD pairs shown in the figure. In this scene, we set T1=1, T2=10. We also assume that all SD pairs have the same importance, i.e. we set $\alpha_{sd} = 1$ for all SD pairs.

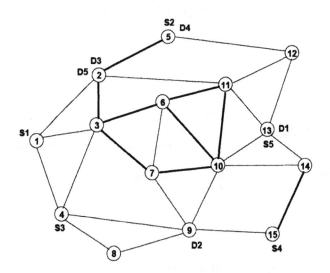

Fig. 1. The KL topology [7]

Figure 2 presents the percentage of rejected requests. From the figure we can see that both our proposed algorithm and NewMIRA rejected fewer requests than SPF and WSP all the time. And our algorithm rejected fewer requests than NewMIRA after 5000 requests.

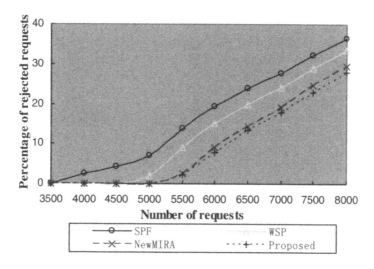

Fig. 2. Percentage of rejected requests in KL topology

Figure 3 shows the amount of accepted bandwidth till up to total 8000 requests. After 7000 requests, the network is almost saturated. From the figure we can see that our proposed algorithm also accepts more bandwidth than SPF, WSP and NewMIRA.

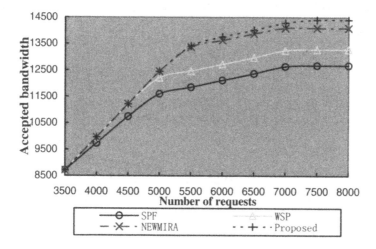

Fig. 3. Total accepted bandwidth in KL topology

Figure 4 shows the sum of maxflow for the five SD pairs up to 8000 requests. From the figure we can see that the proposed algorithm and NewMIRA can preserve more available flow than WSP and SPF in most of the time. Our proposed algorithm is lower than NewMIRA before 5000 requests, but is higher than NewMIRA after 5000 requests. (In fact, the proposed algorithm accepted more requests than NewMIRA in whole period, according to Figure.2-3).

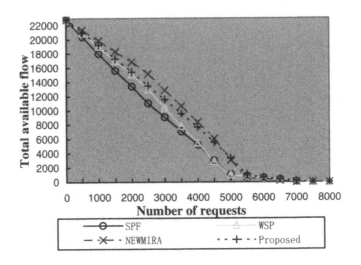

Fig. 4. Total available flow for all SD pairs in KL topology

4.2 ISPNet Topology

The network topology as well as SD pairs is shown in Figure 5. This topology is a famous realistic ISP network topology. It is widely used for studies on QoS routing by many researchers. SD pairs 1-5 are the only network input and output traffic. Lighter links have capacity of 1200 bandwidth units, while the darker ones have 4800 bandwidth units capacity, representing OC-12 and OC-48 rates, respectively. Links are bi-directional, i.e., they represent two links with the same capacity in opposite directions. Requests were randomly generated using the uniform distribution in the interval [1, 4]. It is assumed that LSPs have long lives, i.e., once accepted its resources are kept until the end of the experiments. 8,000 requests were randomly generated among the five SD pairs shown in the figure. In this scene, we set T1=1, T2=100.

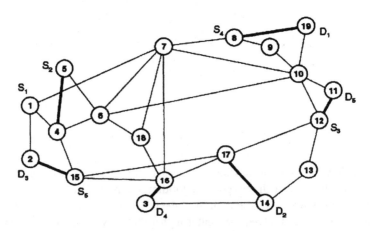

Fig. 5. The ISP network topology

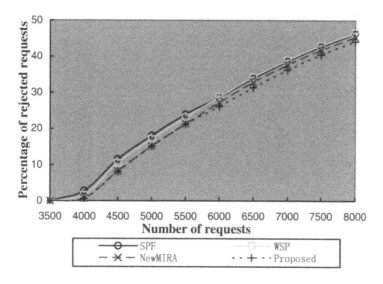

Fig. 6. Percentage of rejected requests in ISPNet topology

Figure 6 shows the percentage of requests rejected by SPF, WSP, NewMIRA and our proposed algorithm in ISP network topology. It can be seen that both the proposed and NewMIRA rejected less requests than SPF and WSP. The proposed algorithm also rejected fewer requests than NewMIRA.

Figure 7 gives similar result. The proposed algorithm accepts more bandwidth than SPF, WSP and NewMIRA, especially after 6000 requests. WSP behaves a little better than SPF.

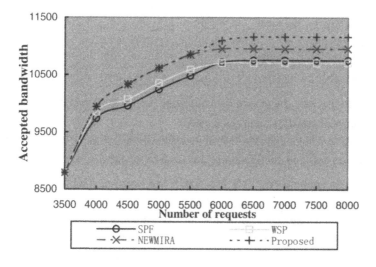

Fig. 7. Total accepted bandwidth in ISPNet topology

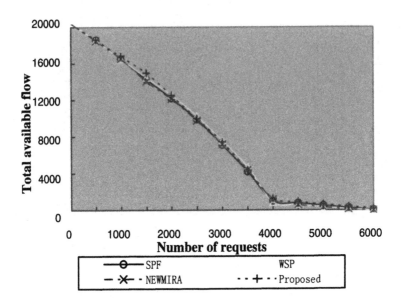

Fig. 8. Total available flow for all SD pairs in ISPNet topology

Figure 8 shows the total available flows in the network up to 6000 requests. In this figure, the four algorithms are very similar. But the proposed hybrid algorithm and NewMIRA still preserve a little more available flow than WSP and SPF. In fact, the proposed hybrid algorithm accepted more requests than NewMIRA as fore mentioned.

4.3 Tuning Parameters

In different circumstances, we may need to adjust the parameters to get better performance. In the link weight function, the parameter T_1 represents the weight of minimizing network cost, while T_2 represents the weight of load balancing. Through adjusting the parameters, the operators can adjust the algorithm's performance.

When the network load is high, the operators should increase the weight of minimizing the network cost by increasing T_1. When the network load is low or medium, the operators should decrease the weight of minimizing the network cost by decreasing T_1, so the algorithm will prefer to balance the load.

We now explain that the operators can tune the parameters to get better performance. The simulation models and configurations are same to section 4.1. The value of T_1 and T_2 can be selected among {100, 10, 1, 0.1, 0.01}. We experiment all the possible combinations and measure their performance after 8000 requests.

Table 1 shows the total accepted bandwidth when altering the values of parameters. And table 2 shows the total accepted requests when altering the values of parameters. We can find that the better performance can be achieved when $T_1, T_2 \leq 10$, especially when $T_1, T_2 \leq 1$. This indicated that the operators should give more importance to interference minimizing in KL topology.

Table 1. Total accepted bandwidth in KL topology

		T_2				
		100	10	1	0.1	0.01
	1000	13354	13414	13808	13703	13703
	100	14149	13417	13812	13703	13703
T_1	10	14291	14005	13908	13721	13697
	1	14269	14400	14399	14397	14394
	0.1	14263	14394	14394	14395	14398
	0.01	14255	14396	14400	14395	14396

Table 2. Total accepted requests in KL topology

		T_2				
		100	10	1	0.1	0.01
	1000	5356	5378	5539	5490	5491
	100	5671	5380	5540	5490	5491
T_1	10	5732	5615	5574	5496	5487
	1	5720	5775	5774	5772	5771
	0.1	5719	5770	5775	5775	5776
	0.01	5713	5771	5773	5776	5775

We do the similar simulations in ISPNet topology. The simulation models and configurations are same to section 4.2. We experiment several value combinations and measure their performance after 8000 requests.

Table 3. Total accepted bandwidth in ISPNet topology

		T_2				
		100	10	1	0.1	0.01
	100	11159	11138	11130	11130	11162
	10	11163	11123	11078	11163	11163
T_1	1	11158	11085	10840	10854	10760
	0.1	11158	11156	10917	10795	10931
	0.01	11158	11159	10916	10778	10767

Table 4. Total accepted requests in ISPNet topology

		T_2				
		100	10	1	0.1	0.01
	100	4454	4445	4443	4443	4455
	10	4452	4439	4419	4455	4455
T_1	1	4455	4423	4329	4332	4291
	0.1	4452	4453	4354	4310	4361
	0.01	4455	4454	4355	4303	4299

Table 3 and table 4 give the total accepted bandwidth and total accepted requests while altering the values of parameters. From the table, we can see the best performance is achieved in {10,100} ,{10,0.1} and {10,0.01}. When either one of the two parameters is set to a relatively big value, the algorithm's performance will be better.

5   Conclusion

In this paper, we proposed a hybrid traffic engineering routing algorithm for bandwidth guaranteed traffic. Our proposed algorithm considers three main traffic engineering objectives together: minimizing network cost, load balancing and minimizing the interference. Simulation results show that the proposed algorithm performs better than SPF, WSP and a well-known algorithm -NewMIRA. We will try to test the proposed algorithm in more scenarios, and try to consider re-routing and multi-path routing with MPLS traffic engineering in the future.

Acknowledgements

The authors would like to thank the reviewers for their valuable comments. This work is supported by the National Natural Science Foundation of China under Grant No. 90604006.

References

1. D. Awduche, J. Malcolm, J. Agogbua, et al. Requirements for Traffic Engineering Over MPLS, IETF RFC 2702; 1999.
2. Samer Lahoud, Géraldine Texier, Laurent Toutain. Classification and Evaluation of Constraint-Based Routing Algorithms for MPLS Traffic Engineering. In: 6ème rencontres francophones sur les aspects algorithmiques des télécommunications(AlgoTel 2004); Batz-sur-mer, France; 2004.
3. Gu´erin, R.A., Orda, A, Williams, D.: QoS Routing Mechanisms and OSPF Extensions. Proceedings of IEEE Global Communications Conference 1997 (GLOBECOM' 97), (1997) 1903–1908
4. Wang. Z, Crowcroft. J, Quality-of-Service Routing for Supporting Multimedia Applications. IEEE Journal on Selected Areas in Communications 14 (1996) 1228–1234
5. Ma. Q, Steenkiste. P, On Path Selection for Traffic with Bandwidth Guarantees. Proceedings of IEEE International Conference on Network Protocols 1997 (ICNP'97) (1997) 191–202
6. Yufei Wang, Zheng Wang. Explicit routing for Internet traffic engineering. In: IEEE International Conference on Computer Communications and Networks (ICCCN'99); Piscataway, NJ,USA; (1999) 582-588
7. M.S. Kodialam, T.V. Lakshman, Minimum Interference Routing with Applications to MPLS Traffic Engineering, in INFOCOM 2000, Tel Aviv, Israel, (2000) 884–893
8. Subhash Suri, Marcel Waldvogel, Priyank Ramesh Warkhede. Profilebased Routing: A new Framework for MPLS Traffic Engineering. In: Quality of future Internet Services,Volume 2516 of Lecture Notes in Computer Science; (2001) 138-157.

9. Ying-Xiao Xu, Gen-Du Zhang. Models and Algorithms of QoS-based Routing with MPLS Traffic engineering. In: IEEE 5th International Conference on High-Speed Networks and Multimedia Communications (HSNMC02); Jeju,Korea; (2002) 128-132.
10. Bin Wang, Xu Su, C. L. Philip Chen. A New Bandwidth Guaranteed Routing Algorithm for MPLS Traffic Engineering. In: IEEE International Conference on Communications 2002(ICC'02); New York, NY, USA; (2002) 1001-1005.
11. Wisitsak Sa-Ngiamsak, Ruttikorn Varakulsiripunth. A Bandwidth-Based Constraint Routing Algorithm for Multi-Protocol LabelSwitching Networks. In: The 6th International Conference on Advanced Communication Technology(IEEE ICACT2004); Phoenix Park, Korea; (2004) 933-937.
12. Qingming Ma, Peter Steenkiste. On path selection for traffic with bandwidth guarantees. In: Fifth International Conference on Network Protocols (ICNP '97); Atlanta, GA, USA; 1997. 191-202.
13. Qingming Ma, Peter Steenkiste. Supporting Dynamic Inter-Class Resource Sharing:A Multi-Class QoS Routing Algorithm. In: IEEE INFOCOM'99; New York, NY,USA; 1999. 649-660.
14. Karl Hendling, Brikena Statovci-Halimi, Gerald Franzl, et al. A New Bandwidth Guaranteed Routing Approach for Online Calculation of LSPs for MPLS Traffic Engineering. In: Management of Multimedia Networks and Services, 6th IFIP/IEEE International Conference(MMNS 2003); Belfast, Northern Ireland, UK; 2003. 220-232.
15. Gargi Banerjee, Deepinder Sidhu. Path Computation for Traffic Engineering in MPLS Networks. In: IEEE ICN 2001; Colmar, France; 2001. 302-308.
16. Su-Wei Tan, Sze-Wei Lee, Benoit Vaillaint. Non-greedy minimum interference routing algorithm for bandwidth-guaranteed flows. Computer Communications. 2002, 25(17): 1640-1652.
17. Kavitha Banglore, A Minimum Interference Hybrid Algorithm for MPLS Networks, Master thesis, Florida State University; 2002
18. G. Leduc, H. Abrahamsson, S. Balon, S. Bessler, M. D'Arienzo, O. Delcourt, J. Domingo-Pascual, S. Cerav-Erbas, I. Gojmerac, X. Masip, A. Pescaph, B. Quoitin, S.F. Romano, E. Salvatori, F. Skivée, H.T. Tran, S. Uhlig, and H. Ümit. An open source traffic engineering toolbox. Accepted to Computer Communications, 2005.

Determining the Cause and Frequency of Routing Instability with Anycast

James Hiebert[1], Peter Boothe[1], Randy Bush[2], and Lucy Lynch[3]

[1] Department of Computer and Information Science
University of Oregon, Eugene, OR 97403, USA
{jamesmh, peter}@cs.uoregon.edu
[2] Internet Initiative Japan
randy@psg.com
[3] University of Oregon
llynch@uoregon.edu

Abstract. In this article we present a methodology by which an autonomous system (AS) can estimate the stability of their BGP routes without requiring access to restricted BGP data. We demonstrate a novel measurement approach using DNS anycast as an indicator of routing instability. Using this method, even end-users may monitor their ISP's routing stability, something which was previously infeasible without the continual use of expensive ICMP traceroutes or access to generally restricted routing information. We then perform a case study from within a large ISP in order to quantify and determine the cause of the routing instability. To determine causation, we correlate external and internal BGP events with variations in the final anycast destination. We conclude that anycast is extremely sensitive to anomalous BGP events and that by monitoring anycast it may be possible for large networks to receive early warning of BGP instability.

1 Introduction

1.1 Motivation

The Internet is like a virtual community where bad behavior on one person's (or Autonomous System's (AS's)) part affects all other members of the community. The predominant inter-domain routing protocol, Border Gateway Protocol (BGP) has been shown to exhibit unstable properties which include (but are not limited to) slow convergence to a best path and the flapping of one route to another and back again [1,2,3]. Since most ASes rely on good routing information and behavior from their neighbors, bad performance by one individual becomes the community's concern.

The complex dynamics of inter-domain routing often make it difficult to discover the existence of a routing problem. The source of a routing problem is therefore even more elusive. It is difficult—bordering on impossible—for a large network to monitor all of their BGP traffic to detect a problem. What is necessary is some sort of lightweight, early warning system that detects the leading

K. Cho and P. Jacquet (Eds.): AINTEC 2006, LNCS 4311, pp. 172–185, 2006.
© Springer-Verlag Berlin Heidelberg 2006

edge of routing instability and can help identify the source. We believe that we have created the foundation of such a system and present the technique in this article.

1.2 Contributions

In this paper we present a relatively lightweight method to detect routing instability using existing IP anycast deployments. We describe how our method works and then present a case study which we performed in collaboration with a large ISP. We quantify how much route switching was detected over a twenty-six day study period and show how our method can be used to gain insight into whether the causes of switching are internal or external to the ISP.

Our contributions are as follows:

- We present a novel methodology for detecting routing instability. This technique is highly sensitive and can be an early indicator of bad routing behavior,
- we provide a case study which demonstrates good correlation between routing events that indicate likely problems and anycast route switching events,
- we show that switching events are relatively infrequent, and finally
- we show that in a well-run internal network, switching events generally occur due to external factors.

1.3 Background and Related Work

Our work aims to identify the stability of interdomain routing on the Internet through the use of anycast DNS queries. As such it is important to understand the intricacies of the Border Gateway Protocol (BGP)–the predominant interdomain routing protocol–as well as existing work related to BGP stability and IP anycast. We provide a synopsis of these concepts and related work in this section.

Overview of BGP. BGP is the predominant protocol by which AS's border routers exchange routing information. An AS's border routers maintain External BGP (*eBGP*) sessions with routers of other ASes while also maintaining Internal BGP (*eBGP*) sessions with the other border routers of their own network. Generally a router learns routes through its eBGP sessions, chooses a single best route and then advertises it to each of the internal routers.

BGP allows for some variation in how a best path is evaluated and selected. However, generally paths are evaluated based on some combination of the shortest AS path, local policy preferences, path origins and/or link dynamics [4]. In this study, we also refer to Multiple-Exit-Discriminator (MED) values which are an optional attribute value that can be manually assigned to BGP routes. Traffic engineers set MED values in order to have one path be preferred over another [5]. Because existing routes are re-announced every time a MED value changes, this can often trigger a series of BGP chatter. In these instances the routes get re-announced, yet the best paths possibly remain the same. We see some of this behavior in our results (section 3.2).

Stability of BGP. The Border Gateway Protocol (BGP) has been the predominant inter-domain routing protocol of the Internet and as such has been studied extensively. Questions about the stability of BGP, however, were first raised by Labovitz et al. [1]. Labovitz concluded at that time that pathological and redundant routing information dominated the routing traffic and that this instability resulted in traffic volumes which were significantly higher than expected. Because of these results, BGP stability has since been an area of active research. Relatively little research, however, has analyzed the dynamic interactions between internal and external BGP.

The major exception is a system developed by Wu et al. [3]. Their system seeks to provide a tool that gives network administrators insight into routing performance problems which should be immediately addressed. Their system automatically searches through a network's border router messages, identifies problems (e.g. ability to reach another network) and produces an end-of-the-day report of "actionable items" for the net admin. The system requires that an AS monitor each border router's best path to each prefix, maintain iBGP sessions with each border router, maintain prefix-level traffic statistics from each border router, etc. Our methodology of using anycast DNS queries, in contrast, is significantly more lightweight and does not even require access to generally restricted routing information; thus allowing both network administrators *and* network users to do the same. Additionally our method is able to detect the leading edge of instability (see figure 4) within seconds of a routing event.

Our methodology measures route switches between a source and the anycast DNS servers. It is, therefore, important to understand the stability of the existing infrastructure. It is noteworthy that routes to these DNS servers are extremely widely used, and therefore are required to be very stable. Rexford et al. address the question of the stability of popular routes in a 2002 study [2]. They concluded that most routes were stable, and that the majority of BGP instability stemmed from just a handful of relatively little-used routes. We can be confident that our measurements are measuring popular prefixes because the DNS infrastructure is one of the most fundamental and widely used services offered on the Internet today.

IP Anycast and DNS. Our study measures route switches between a source network and the DNS roots. Therefore, we provide a brief explanation of the DNS anycast architecture to highlight how our methods are possible.

Anycast is an IP deployment technique in which the same IP address is announced from diverse locations in the network topology. The user of the service does not care which instance of the address he or she contacts, thus anycast (hopefully) delivers the traffic to the closest anycasted instance of the service [6].

In global IP anycast, instances of the same address prefix are *replicated* throughout the Internet. For example, if an AS switches to a better path to 193.0.14.0/24 (the k root DNS servers), it may have found a shorter path or it may have found an entirely different instance of that prefix.

The root DNS servers are the most widely used service which is deployed with IP anycast. DNS roots c, f, i, j, k, and m are all anycast deployed; i.e. there are several *clusters* of each root scattered throughout the Internet. Most clusters also have some local load-balancing mechanism. Thus, any DNS query could be serviced by a different anycast cluster and a different machine within that cluster. The name of the machine answering a query can be included in a special `chaos txt` portion of a DNS response[1].

The anycast deployment strategy has been extensively used on the Internet for DNS root services and content distribution networks [7,8]. Since its deployment, it has received little research attention until a recent report by Sarat et al. [9] which evaluates the performance of DNS anycast. Additionally a recent article by Ballani and Francis [10] proposes a new IP anycast architecture. These articles evaluate anycast performance, however, to our knowledge, no studies have used our unique anycast-based methodology to detect route switching.

Recently Brownlee [11] presented a method to detect switching using the measurement of round trip times to anycasted roots. His conclusions, however, were sparse and restricted to a visible performance gain on one particular root. Unlike our conclusions, Brownlee found no clear evidence of route switching using his technique.

1.4   Caveat, This Is Not About DNS Performance

Finally, before we delve into our experiments, we provide a brief caveat. Our initial studies on network stability and anycast caused a slight stir in the network operator community, because they misunderstood the intentions of our experiments. We would like to emphasize that we are using DNS and the existing anycast infrastructure as a tool to study routing instability. We are *not* commenting on the feasibility and quality of DNS anycast or commenting on performance of the particular DNS root servers. Indeed, DNS as an application looks to be almost tailor made for anycast due to the fact that most DNS communication occurs over either single datagrams or extremely short-lived TCP flows[12].

2   Methodology

The contributions of this work required data from two primary sources. First, in order to demonstrating our methodology we performed a case study. This experiment consisted of twenty-six days of anycast route monitoring and served as our primary data set.

---

[1] This convention was agreed upon by the root operators in order to improve debugability of the anycasted DNS root servers.

Secondly, in order to validate our results and gauge the effectiveness of our methodology we compared our data to a collection of routing announcements from the same AS as our anycast monitoring. In the following sections we describe collection of these data in further detail.

2.1 Anycast Route Monitoring

Our own experiments using anycast as a tool provided the primary data set used to determine and demonstrate the presence or absence of routing stability. Because anycast routing is more sensitive to routing changes it provides an excellent early indicator of routing instability.

Our experiment consisted of obtaining one particular datum, distributed across time and space (location in the Internet). We placed a collector at various hosts across the Internet. Each collector would make a single query to each of the anycasted DNS root servers (c, f, i, j, k and m) at intervals of 2 and 20 seconds for UDP and TCP queries respectively. The query, which appeared as
$ dig @X.root-servers.net. hostname.bind chaos txt, was crafted to determine which X-root cluster received the query. By knowing which cluster received the query we were able to detect the frequency of route switches to that cluster at a frequency of half that of our query interval (4 and 40 seconds for UDP and TCP respectively).

The anycast gathering experiment would return output such as that which is shown in figure 1. Output of the script would consist of a series of 4-tuples: timestamp, DNS root (e.g. c, f, i, j, k, or m), transport, and DNS root-server. One such set of output was received from each of our collectors at regular time intervals.

```
123.456.789.123
Mon Dec 6 23:00:20 UTC 2004 c UDP jfk1b.c.root-servers.org
Mon Dec 6 23:00:20 UTC 2004 f UDP sfo2b.f.root-servers.org
Mon Dec 6 23:00:20 UTC 2004 i UDP s1.chi
Mon Dec 6 23:00:21 UTC 2004 j UDP jns1-igtld.j.root-servers.net
Mon Dec 6 23:00:21 UTC 2004 k UDP k1.ams-ix
Mon Dec 6 23:00:21 UTC 2004 m UDP M-d1
Mon Dec 6 23:00:23 UTC 2004 c UDP jfk1b.c.root-servers.org
Mon Dec 6 23:00:23 UTC 2004 f UDP sfo2b.f.root-servers.org
Mon Dec 6 23:00:23 UTC 2004 i UDP s1.chi
Mon Dec 6 23:00:23 UTC 2004 j UDP jns2-igtld.j.root-servers.net
Mon Dec 6 23:00:23 UTC 2004 k UDP k1.ams-ix
Mon Dec 6 23:00:23 UTC 2004 m UDP M-d1
Mon Dec 6 23:00:26 UTC 2004 c TCP jfk1b.c.root-servers.org
Mon Dec 6 23:00:26 UTC 2004 f TCP sfo2b.f.root-servers.org
Mon Dec 6 23:00:26 UTC 2004 i TCP s1.chi
Mon Dec 6 23:00:26 UTC 2004 j TCP jns2-igtld.j.root-servers.net
Mon Dec 6 23:00:26 UTC 2004 k TCP k1.ams-ix
Mon Dec 6 23:00:26 UTC 2004 m TCP M-d1
```

Fig. 1. Sample raw output of the anycast data gathering experiment

2.2   eBGP and iBGP Data for Validation

When a routing switch is detected using our anycast data collectors, for our analysis we require router announcement data to determine the cause of the switch. The switch is likely caused by factors outside of the particular autonomous system. However, if it is due to internal instability we (and certainly the operators of the autonomous system) would like to know.

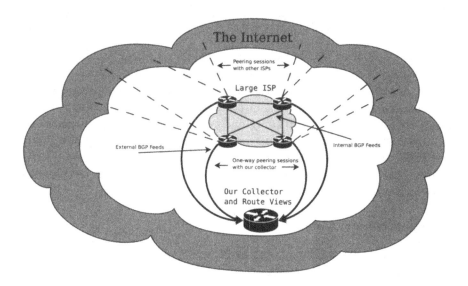

Fig. 2. Collection points of our iBGP and eBGP routing announcements

To analyze the source of the switches, we utilized existing collections of routing announcements from the Route Views project[13] and from a large ISP with whom we were cooperating to perform this study. As shown in figure 2, routing announcements were collected by setting up a router as a peer which would only receive BGP announcements (and record them) without sending announcements back. We used both external BGP (eBGP) and internal BGP (iBGP) data through two separate router sessions.

Finally we correlated the switching events discovered through our anycast experiment with routing events which were evident in the cache of routing data.

2.3   Correlation of Routing Events

We consider a time-clustered group of up to three types of measurable events to constitute a single logical event: one or more eBGP events at the ISP's peering routers, one or more iBGP announcements by the ISP's edge routers, or one or more switches in the responding anycasted cluster seen by our anycast probe (henceforth referred to as a *switching event*). The set of routing announcements considered is limited to announcements of the relevant anycast prefixes.

We correlate the three types of occurrences within a similar time frame as one routing event. We define a routing event to be any of the three aforementioned occurrences separated by no more than a time window of t seconds. In other words, each *event* is separated by a period of quiescence greater than or equal to the time window.

This windowing method was used by Wu et al. [3] in classifying BGP events. Based on BGP announcement inter-arrival times, they determined 70 seconds to be an appropriate window. Thus for all of our experiments we used a t value of 70 seconds.

With three boolean attributes—visible **iBGP** and **eBGP** traffic of the relevant prefixes, and an **anycast switch**–there are seven combinations of the presence or absence of each attribute (the eighth being where nothing happens). Our primary concern is with the four cases where an anycast switch is present (iBGP/eBGP, iBGP only, eBPG only, and neither). We also include the remaining three cases in our tables to demonstrate the relative frequency of a routing event that is *not* detected by our anycast experiment.

Given that switching events demonstrate routing instability, we use these event correlations to evaluate potential causes of such instability.

2.4   Experimental Controls

As controls for our experiment and to facilitate validation of our results, we ran a set of DNS queries to each of three control points: a unicasted DNS root server ("a"), a BGP beacon which goes through alternating two-hour cycles of announcing and withdrawing its prefix, and another DNS server (non-root).

From each of our controls we observed the expected behavior. The unicast DNS root server obviously returned the same cluster for every query. It also showed a very stable infrastructure; we received a response to every query throughout the twenty-six day study period, and only received one BGP message associated with its prefix. Our queries to the non-root DNS server exhibited similar behaviors. The queries to the BGP beacon showed the expected behavior of being reachable for only 2 hours at a time. In the alternating 2 hours we would receive no reply to our queries.

While these experimental controls are significantly more germane to a discussion regarding the performance of anycast DNS (which is not the topic of this article), they do demonstrate correct experimental setup and provide confidence in our results.

3   Results

After having performed our experiments and collected all data, we analyzed one dataset which consisted of the twenty-six day period from March 17, 2006 to April 12, 2006. We now describe the details of our analysis and the key conclusions which can be drawn from our work.

3.1 An Example Switching Event

To further clarify the switching event behavior (as defined in section 2.3) for which we are searching, we provide an illustration of an example switching event and the accompanying explanation.

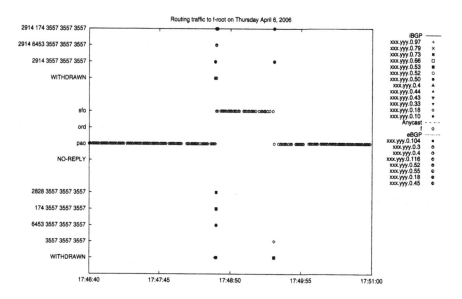

Fig. 3. A typical switching event where our sequence of anycast probes (the points in the middle rows) switches from one root cluster "pao" to another "sfo" for a brief period of time. At the same time as the initial switch and the switch back there is visible eBGP traffic (above) and iBGP traffic (below) where routers are announcing best path changes. The x-axis is time, the y-axis is separated according to AS-path announced, and each point style represents a different router.

In figure 3 is a graph which exemplifies the anycast root-cluster switching behavior. The graph shows a 5 minute slice of all three data sets: eBGP traffic on the top, our anycast probes to f-root in the middle, and iBGP traffic on the bottom. In searching for a switching event, follow the horizontal line in the middle of the graph. Notice how each of our probes to f root were responded to by the same root cluster, which in this case was paoxx.f.root-servers.org.

The route to f-root was very stable until 17:48 when our queries suddenly are routed to sfoxx.f.root-servers.org. Approximately one minute later the route switches back. Notice that corresponding exactly to the time of both switches are numerous eBGP and iBGP announcements from routers whose best path has changed. Essentially, some routing instability on the Internet has caused this very important path to change, and we have detected it through our low-cost mechanism.

In this example, both switches fall within our 70 second window. Thus, this is *one switching event*. In determining the cause of a switching event, we note that this event has both internal and external routing traffic associated with it. We therefore conclude that the cause is external since iBGP traffic is a direct result of best path changes in eBGP, and eBGP traffic is, by definition, external to the ISP.

It is important to note that most root-clusters have numerous load-balancing servers which can answer a query. For example, during the switching event above, we receive DNS responses from both sfo2a.f.root-servers.org and sfo2b.f.root-servers.or. For the purposes of detecting en-path routing changes, the name of the specific server is not important. Reaching a different cluster is the only indication of a path change. Thus we remove and ignore machine specific information.

3.2   Quantification of Switching Behavior

We searched the twenty-six day period and classified each event according to the corresponding traffic found at that time (as defined in section 2.3). The resulting counts are shown in tables 1 and 2.

Table 1. A count of switching events over the course of the 26 day study period

iBGP	Anycast	eBGP	sum of events	c	f	i	j	k	m
	X		2	0	2	0	0	0	0
	X	X	2	0	0	0	2	0	0
X	X		0	0	0	0	0	0	0
X	X	X	15	10	1	0	4	0	0
Total Switching Events			19	10	3	0	6	0	0
		X	135	4	23	24	22	31	31
X			44	37	3	1	1	1	1
X		X	3	3	0	0	0	0	0

Examining table 1, we note that there is a substantial volume of routing traffic which does not correspond to an anycast switching event. We see 135 eBGP events, 44 iBGP events, and 3 eBGP/iBGP events. At first glance this seems to indicate that there is a low correlation between routing traffic and switching events. However, in examining the data directly we notice that a significant percentage of the routing messages (98.5% eBGP, 77.3% iBGP, and 100.0% eBGP/iBGP) were reannouncements of existing paths. Presumably these reannouncements were due to MED values changing or some other relatively insignificant BGP chatter.

In the second phase of analysis we define an eBGP or iBGP event to be when a *new or different* path is announced. When the insignificant BGP chatter is eliminated, our data produce table 2 which tells a very different story. Table 2

Table 2. A count of switching events under a different definition of eBGP and iBGP traffic. In this case we only consider routing announcements which announce a new or different path.

iBGP	Anycast	eBGP	sum of events	c	f	i	j	k	m
		X	4	2	2	0	0	0	0
	X	X	2	0	0	0	2	0	0
X	X		8	8	0	0	0	0	0
X	X	X	5	0	1	0	4	0	0
Total Switching Events			19	10	3	0	6	0	0
		X	2	0	1	0	1	0	0
X			10	8	1	1	0	0	0
X		X	0	0	0	0	0	0	0

shows a total of 31 important routing events. Of these events 19 of them (61.3%) were detected by a switching event in the anycast cluster. This demonstrates that our technique is very effective at detecting routing changes and is on the leading edge of doing so.

Table 2 also show that some switching event become reclassified after the BGP chatter is eliminated. For instance table 1 shows c root as having 10 switching events which are eBGP/iBGP while table 2 shows none. This is due to the fact that 8 of the events are reclassified to be iBGP events and 2 are reclassified to be switching events with no corresponding important BGP announcements. Note that the total number of switching events is the same in both tables.

It is also important to note that during many of these switching events there was no loss of service to the anycast DNS servers, and thus even the most savvy network operators would not detect a change[2].

3.3 Ability to Detect Obscure Routing Events

In addition to detecting most routing events which would have been found by monitoring BGP messages, our technique also detects some routing events which would be otherwise impossible to discover. Both tables 1 and 2 show several switching events for which there was no corresponding eBGP or iBGP traffic. Presumably these switches were due to routing changes further down the AS path. Our method detects some such events, while directly monitoring one's own BGP feeds would fail to do so.

Another reason that most of these events are undetectable is that, even though the routes to the anycast DNS servers switch, the user continues to receive service. In only 7 of our switching events did the "dig" application register a NO-REPLY from the anycast DNS server. Throughout the entire experiment a total 68 NO-REPLY events were registered. There is no evidence of strong correlation between NO-REPLYs and anycast switches. This is consistent with

---

[2] ...unless they are directly monitoring the BGP data very closely, something which netops often do not have time to do.

research by Li et al. [14] who conclude that BGP activity has little correlation with packet loss.

Thus, a regular user and possibly a regular network administrator would have no indication that routing changes are happening. Indeed, from a user's perspective, this is the beauty of anycast and of IP level network communication! However, as researchers, we must note that our method detects these switches while casual observation would not.

3.4 Ability to Predict Behavior

In order to test whether anycast switches can be correlated with more than just BGP announcements for the anycasted DNS prefixes, we examined the volume of BGP traffic and its temporal proximity to the detected switching events.

Figure 4(a) shows the average rate of external and internal BGP messages relative to the time of all anycast switches. The overall average rate of BGP messages is also plotted (the horizontal lines at the bottom of the graphs). The big spike in the center of the graph indicates that, right around the time of the anycast switches, we also observed a tenfold increase in BGP traffic.

Figure 4(b) shows similar data, however the sum of BGP messages is restricted to those which announced a new or different path than the most recent announcement. Again, we observe a more than tenfold increase in BGP traffic around the time of each anycast switch. *This indicates that anycast switches are a good forecaster for BGP traffic, and that DNS anycast switches are not isolated events.*

This lack of isolation lends credence to the possible implications of the conclusions by Rexford et al. [2]. Their research demonstrates that routing to popular destinations is generally stable and that most Internet routing instability stems from little-used routes. Our work in monitoring these popular DNS routes is consistent with these conclusions. We see that when routing to one of these popular destinations changes–an unusual event–that the event is part of a more major routing occurrence.

3.5 Internal vs. External Sources of Instability

In initiating this study, we hypothesized that a particular internal/external BGP dynamic behavior could be possible. We suspected that in a large internal network, it may be possible for different exit routers to have best path routes to different anycast root clusters. If this were the case, then it would be possible for an unstable internal network to affect that network's view of the anycast servers. For example if an internal route switched, triggering a different exit point, then we would expect to see a switch in the root-cluster as well.

In searching for this behavior, we looked for a switching event where there was corresponding iBGP traffic, but no eBGP. As is shown in table 1 there were *no* events which matched these criteria. Because our search for this behavior only included one major network, the conclusions which we can draw are limited. However, it does deserve to be mentioned that we did not see evidence of internal stability affecting that network's paths to anycast services.

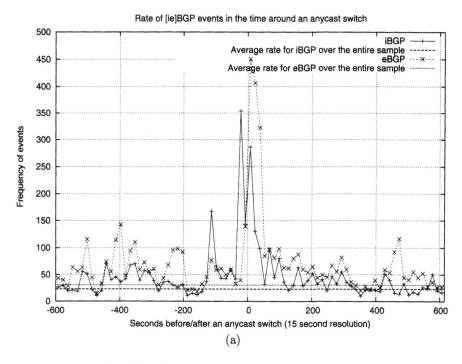

(a)

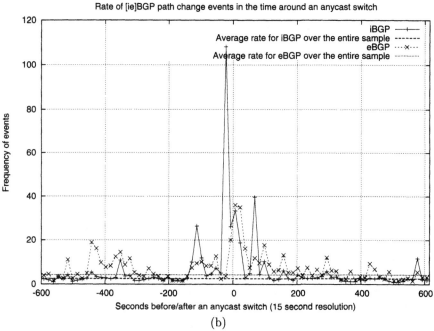

(b)

Fig. 4. Both of these graphs show the number of BGP messages (divided into internal and external) of relevant prefixes in the time surrounding switching events. Subfigure 4(a) shows the total number of BGP messages, while subfigure 4(b) is constrained to those messages announcing new or different paths.

4 Conclusions

4.1 Summary

In conclusion, we have demonstrated a novel, anycast-based approach for detecting routing instability. We have shown that our method is highly sensitive to BGP path changes, detecting routing events in real time and even slightly prior. As such, our method finds the leading edge of routing changes and serves as an effective canary for detecting important BGP events. We have also shown that our method detects a large percentage of important routing events which could—until now—only be realized by monitoring one's own BGP feeds. It also detects events which would be otherwise entirely undetectable.

In performing our case-study, we have measured the number of switching events over a twenty-six day period from the perspective of a large ISP. We note that there were only a total of 19 events between all 6 roots over the course of 26 days. Therefore, these switches are fairly uncommon.

We have shown that route switches to anycast root servers correspond to a higher volume of BGP traffic, thus indicating that they are part of a more prominent routing event. Finally, we have shown that there is little evidence in our particular case study to indicate that internal routing instability affects the stability of an AS's external routing.

Acknowledgments

In closing, we would like to thank the following individuals and projects without whose help this work would have been impossible. Thanks to John Heasley for sorting through strange routing events with us, Joel Jaeggli for technical support, the Route Views project and the anonymous "large ISP" for cooperating with us in gathering data, and the Beyond BGP Project under NSF Award #0221435.

References

1. C. Labovitz, G. R. Malan, and F. Jahanian, "Internet routing instability," *IEEE/ACM Transactions on Networking*, vol. 6, no. 5, pp. 515–528, 1998. [Online]. Available: citeseer.ist.psu.edu/labovitz97internet.html
2. J. Rexford, J. Wang, Z. Xiao, and Y. Zhang, "BGP routing stability of popular destinations," in *ACM SIGCOMM Internet Measurement Workshop*, 2002.
3. J. Wu, Z. M. Mao, J. Rexford, and J. Wang, "Finding a needle in a haystack: Pinpointing significant BGP routing changes in an IP network," *NSDI*, 2005.
4. "Application of the Border Gateway Protocol in the Internet," Internet Engineering Task Force: RFC 1772, March 1995. [Online]. Available: http://www.apps.ietf.org/rfc/rfc1772.html
5. D. McPherson and V. Gill, "BGP MULTI_EXIT_DISC (MED) considerations," Internet Engineering Task Force: RFC 4451, March 2006. [Online]. Available: http://www.apps.ietf.org/rfc/rfc4451.html

6. C. Partridge, T. Mendez, and W. Milliken, "Host anycasting service," IETF Request for Comments: 1546, November 1993. [Online]. Available: http://www.ietf.org/rfc/rfc1546.txt

7. J. Abley, "A software approach to distributing requests for DNS service using GNU Zebra, ISC BIND 9 and FreeBSD," Internet Systems Consortium, Inc., Tech. Rep. ISC-TN-2004-1, March 2004. [Online]. Available: http://www.isc.org/pubs/tn/isc-tn-2004-1.html

8. ——, "Hierarchical anycast for global service distribution," Internet Systems Consortium, Inc., Tech. Rep. ISC-TN-2003-1, 2003. [Online]. Available: http://www.isc.org/pubs/tn/isc-tn-2003-1.html

9. S. Sarat, V. Pappas, and A. Terzis, "On the use of anycast in DNS," Johns Hopkins University, Tech. Rep., December 2004.

10. H. Ballani and P. Francis, "Towards a global IP anycast service," in *SIGCOMM*, 2005.

11. N. Brownlee, "RTTs for anycast root nameservers," ISC Operations, Analysis, and Research Center 2005, July 20 2005, presentation given by KC Claffy on July 26.

12. D. Karrenberg, "DNS anycast stability: A closer look at DNSMON data," in *NANOG (presentation slides)*, March 2005.

13. University of Oregon Route Views Project, "http://routeviews.org," 1997-present. [Online]. Available: http://routeviews.org

14. J. Li, R. Bush, Z. Mao, T. Griffin, M. Roughan, D. Stutzbach, and E. Purpus, "Watching data streams toward a multi-homed sink under routing changes introduced by a BGP beacon," in *Proceedings of Passive and Active Measurement Conference 2006*, March 2006.

Modeling Mobility with Behavioral Rules: The Case of Incident and Emergency Situations

Franck Legendre, Vincent Borrel, Marcelo Dias de Amorim, and Serge Fdida

Laboratoire d'Informatique de Paris 6 (LIP6/CNRS)
Université Pierre et Marie Curie – Paris VI
{legendre, borrel, amorim, sf}@rp.lip6.fr

Abstract. Mobility models must scale accordingly to the application and reflect real scenarios in which wireless devices are deployed. Typical examples of scenarios requiring precise mobility models are critical situations (*e.g.*, vehicular traffic incident, escaping pedestrians in emergency situations) – for which the ad hoc paradigm was first designed for. In these particular situations, autonomous agents of communicating devices will assist mobile users in their displacements either to avoid traffic jam due to incidents or find the closest emergency exit. But, since the environment conditions (*i.e.*, flow of pedestrians or vehicles and incidents) may change during time in part due to mobility itself, autonomous agents assisting mobile users in their displacements must constantly exchange information and dynamically adapt to the perceived situations. This requires to precisely modeling both mobility (vehicular and pedestrian traffic) and communications systems between agents. Unfortunately, these two areas have been treated separately, although mobility and network simulators should be tightly bound. In this paper, we propose a new modeling approach to mobility, namely Behavioral Mobility models (BM), which decomposes mobility into simple atomic individual behaviors. Combined, these behaviors yield realistic displacement patterns by reproducing the mobility observed at small scales in every day life, in both space and time. We also propose to bind mobility and network simulators to run joint simulations in order to push simulations to more realness. This approach combined to BM models is particularly suited to simulate critical situations where mobility is influenced by the changing environment conditions. We demonstrate the feasibility of our approach with two cases studies.

1 Introduction

Mobility models are an essential tool for both the conception and the analysis of communication systems. In fact, real experiments are difficult to deploy at large scale and real mobility traces are still limited in their number and precision. With the widespread use of small-size communication devices, there is an increasing need for mobility models that represent mobility patterns in a precise and realistic fashion. The reasons are twofold. First, these devices operate with limited communication and sensing ranges, and are subject to link instability caused by

K. Cho and P. Jacquet (Eds.): AINTEC 2006, LNCS 4311, pp. 186–205, 2006.
© Springer-Verlag Berlin Heidelberg 2006

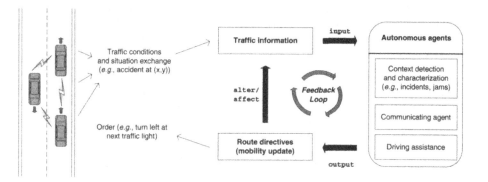

Fig. 1. Embedded autonomous agents for dynamic route re-planning and its inherent feedback loop

mobility. In this way, mobility models must reflect precise displacement patterns according to the environments these devices operate in. Second, mobility models must reflect realistic scenarios, which is necessary to ensure accurate simulation results.

The need of realistic models is all the more true to simulate mobility in critical situations when faced to incidents (*e.g.*, car wreckage) and emergency situations due to natural disasters (*e.g.*, fire, earthquake, and tsunami). With the widespread use of communicating devices embedded with mobile users (*i.e.*, pedestrians, vehicles), intelligent autonomous agents will have major importance in assisting individuals in their navigation, especially in these critical situations. For example, pedestrians exiting a building on fire should be directed toward the closest emergency exit according to the perceived incident location and flow of current escaping individuals. In the case of vehicular traffic, agents will allow drivers re-planning dynamically their route according to the perceived traffic conditions in order to avoid an incident (traffic jam). These conditions about incidents or emergency situations will be collected by sensors near these unexpected events and then sent from communicating devices to communicating devices using either infrastructure-based or infrastructure-less communications (*i.e.*, self-organizing networks or ad hoc). Autonomous agents will process data and indicate the best way to mobile individuals. The main issue with such situations is (for autonomous agents) to optimize the flow of escaping pedestrians or redirected vehicles.

Solutions of network-centric assisted navigation introduce a different approach to mobility. In fact, mobility directly affects the environment conditions (flow of pedestrians or vehicles) that in turn influence autonomous agents, which dynamically react to the received information on these conditions. This interaction between the current conditions and mobility creates a feedback loop. Figure 1 illustrates this concept in the case of vehicular traffic where interactions between autonomous agents exchanging traffic information affects mobility.

Evaluating such situations by simulation requires a precise modeling of each constituent part of the system: the incident (*e.g.*, car wreckage, fire), the communication system composed of sensors and communicating devices (with their respective protocol stack) the agents processing collected data received from ad hoc communications and sensor nodes, and the mobility of mobile users. The feedback loop compels to completely revisit the way to integrate all these constituents of the simulation and more specifically the interactions between them.

In this paper, we propose a new approach to mobility modeling, namely Behavioral Mobility modeling (BM), which aims at representing realistic mobility patterns based on the paradigm of behavioral rules. Behavioral rules, which have found great success in other domains such as physics and artificial intelligence, express atomic behaviors governing mobility. The main advantage brought by this paradigm is that simulated mobile entities are autonomous and react dynamically to their environment according to the atomic behaviors that simultaneously compose their overall mobility behavior. The environment is composed of nearby peers and obstacles but also of exterior events that can be triggered by the mobility designer or received by a network simulator. This latter component allows simulating the interaction between a mobile entity and its communicating devices. This approach has the advantage to allow binding mobility simulators with network simulators to take into account the feedback loop. Hence, both communities related to emergency situations and intelligent transportation systems and the network self-organizing community can sum up their forces and design solutions to respond to critical situations taking each other's imperatives into account.

In the following, we first review mobility models and frameworks used by the networking community. Then, we argue in favor of using behavioral rules to cope with the requirements made out above. This is followed of the description of Ghost, our meta-modeling mobility framework aimed to easily design mobility models. We present in more details the concept of behavioral modeling followed by a demonstration that these models are particularly suited to design and evaluate critical situations where ad hoc communications are involved. A first case study, focuses on a scenario of an emergency team. In a second case study, vehicles are informed of an accident via inter-vehicular communications (IVC) and dynamically re-plan their route.

2   Related Work

2.1   Review of Mobility Models

In the following, we review mobility models proposed by the networking community. For a complete and comprehensive description of individual and group mobility models, we invite the reader to refer to Camp *et al.* [1]. Many mobility models have been proposed to evaluate self-organizing networks (*e.g.*, ad hoc, delay-tolerant, sensor, and mesh networks). So far, the networking community has much relied on an individual model, the Random Waypoint (RWP) mobility model [2], which gained success from its simplicity and mathematical tractability. In order to represent the collective behavior of mobile entities, a number of group mobility models have also been proposed. The most known are the Reference Point Group Mobility model (RPGM) [3] and more specific models such as the Column mobility model and the Pursue mobility model [4], to cite a few. Then, specific mobility models have been proposed to represent real situations, such as campus [5,6,7], city [1,8], and social mobility models [9].

2.2   Mobility Frameworks in Networking

The network community has developed many mobility frameworks. Ray *et al.* propose GEMM [10] a tool for generating mobility models. In GEMM mobile entities are assigned a distinct role (*e.g.*, student or professor, bike or foot) that specifies a set of activities randomly chosen during the simulation. An activity consists of moving to a location chosen among multiple possible destinations. Kim and Bohacek [11,12] propose a framework dedicated to urban mobility in the central core of cities. They realistically model both indoor and outdoor pedestrians as well as vehicular traffic. Their model is defined using surveys from many other fields. Choffnes and Bustamante proposed an integrated network and vehicular mobility simulator named STRAW [13] based on JIST/SWANS [14].

2.3   Mobility Models and Frameworks in Other Fields

Mobility models and framework are used in many other fields ranging from physics to artificial intelligence to animation to robotics. The aims of these models are either (*i*) to find out the rules that govern the mobility of given phenomena where interactions are known to have a great impact on mobility (*e.g.*, bacterial growth, school fish) or (*ii*) used to precisely model mobility of defined mobile entities. For example, escape panic models [15] serve to help finding the best architectural design *i.e.*, for stadiums, buildings, and public places, minimizing both injuries and the draining time. In the area of transportation research, one of the issue is to find optimal geometry for roads and paths for both vehicles and pedestrians [16]. In artificial intelligence, mobility models have been designed to reproduce animal patterns of movement. Reynolds proposed the first flock mobility model [17] that has then been applied to video games or computer animation. In robotics, mobility simulators are used to validate the behavior of robots and to test cooperative behaviors between autonomous agents [18].

3   Behavioral Mobility Modeling

We reconsider the way mobility has been addressed so far by adopting a behavioral modeling approach. We first introduce the concept of rules behind behavioral mobility modeling and their advantages compared to classical approaches. Then, we explain how rules translate into motion. Eventually, we give an example of rule and its implementation.

3.1 The Behavioral Paradigm

We model mobility using a different branch of mobility – behavioral modeling – inspired from models initially developed by biological physicists [15] and researchers in artificial intelligence [17].

In our case, behavioral rules represent expectations of how mobile individuals react and are influenced by their environment. In everyday life, humans respond to social influences, rational decisions, or actions following a stimulus-reaction process.[1] Each influence can be treated by dedicated rules that affect the motion behavior – we call them *behavioral rules*. An example of a rational decision is when a pedestrian takes the shortest path to move between locations. Likewise, when a pedestrian is too close to an obstacle, she/he just avoids bumping into it by a reflex action. Other examples of behaviors are following a path, stopping at a red light, avoiding other individuals, and taking the closest exit to escape an emergency situation. The combination of such atomic behaviors defines the overall motion of a mobile entity.

In our approach, rules – independently of their complexity – are expressed as attractive or repulsive forces. For example, a mobile entity is attracted by its destination and repulsed by walls, obstacles, and other peers on its way as illustrated by Fig. 2(a) The summation of these forces results in the individual's acceleration vector a. This approach is comparable to the paradigm of force in mechanical physics where the acceleration of an object is related to both the net force acting upon it and its mass (*i.e.*, Newton's second law). In Sections 3.2 and 3.4, we explain how rules are combined and give an example of rule implementation.

We summarize below the key difference between the behavioral and the classical modeling approaches:

- *Modeling by rules.* Rules help getting an abstract view of mobility. In fact, existing mobility models (*cf.*, Section 2) can be modeled using a behavioral approach. For example, RWP can be modeled with a two-state automaton which differentiates the behavior in the pause state from the behavior in the moving state. Moreover, an interesting feature of modeling by rules is the flexibility they bring. In our approach, simulated mobile entities are autonomous in the sense that each entity can have its own behavior independently of the others. It allows instantiating mobile entities governed by different set of rules. It also allows changing, in a dynamic way, the set of rules governing the mobility of one entity depending on the context (*e.g.*, indoor vs. outdoor, alone vs. in group).
- *Dynamic interactions.* In the classical modeling approach, mobility can be partially pre-scripted before simulation since there are no dynamic interactions among entities. Mobile entities are governed independently of each other.[2] In our case, autonomous entities continuously and dynamically react

---

[1] In this article, we restrict only to the two latter kind of behaviors. An example of a social behavior is proposed in [9] (*cf.*, Section 2).

[2] They are exceptions like the original social mobility model of Musolesi *et al.* [9], in which social ties influencing displacements may change over time.

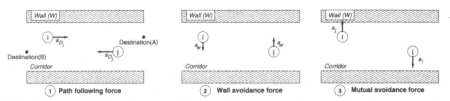

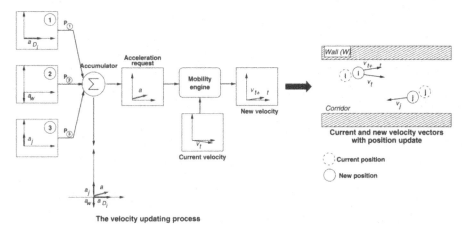

(a) Pedestrian mobility model: pedestrians follow a set of three rules that express in attractive or repulsive forces.

(b) Velocity updating of pedestrian i: independent acceleration vectors (rule forces) are combined and result in the acceleration request (net force) used to update the current velocity of i.

Fig. 2. Expression of rules and their combination

to the context in which they are placed. As previously stated, this context is defined by the surrounding environment made up by obstacles and other individuals but also by exterior events triggered by a mobility designer or by information received from a network simulator.

3.2   From Behavioral Rules to Motion

The question now is how to combine rules so that realistic motion patterns appear. In the following, we define how rules are translated into motion.

Each behavioral rule governing the motion of an entity at a given time generates an independent acceleration vector that is entered into an accumulator. The accumulator combines all inputs according to their respective weights and releases the final acceleration vector a, also called *acceleration request*. Since, in practice, some behaviors must override others, rules must be associated with a weight. For example, the behavior that prevents mobile individuals from bumping into obstacles must prevail over the one that specifies following the shortest path to a destination. Furthermore, the acceleration vector is subject itself to some constraints. For example, infinite acceleration may not be accepted. In fact, the accumulator guarantees that an entity's maximum acceleration does not go above a predefined value $a_{\max}$ (defined by the mobile entity characteristics in Section 4). Typical policies used to limit the maximum acceleration are to take all inputs into account when $|a| \leq a_{\max}$ or to consider only high-priority ones otherwise.

After the computation of the acceleration request, a *mobility engine* updates the entity's velocity according to the kinetic equation

$$v_{t+\Delta t} = v_t + a\Delta t, \tag{1}$$

where v denotes the entity's velocity, Δt the simulation time step, and a represents the entity's acceleration request computed by the accumulator. Fig. 2(b) illustrates how rules are combined and accumulated to result in the acceleration request.

3.3   Classification of Behavioral Rules

We classify behavioral rules in four categories according to the scope of the influences affecting them: internal, local, global, and omniscient. Internal feedback rules are behaviors representing an entity's *free-will* (or internal decisions). In this paper, we do not intend to model free-will; we simply resume free-will to a constant influence such as a noise factor influencing the acceleration. Local feedback rules are influenced by the proximate environment (*e.g.*, traffic lights, terrain's slope and obstacles) and correspond mostly to reflex actions such as avoiding walls and other pedestrians (*cf.* rules ② and ③ of Fig. 2(a)) or stopping at red light when conveyed. Global feedback rules represent behaviors that push an entity toward other mobile entities (*e.g.*, social ties) or defined locations (*e.g.*, attractive places). Global feedback rules represent rational decisions, for example for a pedestrian to take the shortest path to get to a given location or for a driver to decide its route when going from one location to another. Eventually, omniscient behaviors are rules that are influenced by pieces of information or directives received from communicating equipments where a feedback loop exists or by directives sent to all mobile nodes such as the emergency exit of a building.

3.4   Example of Behavioral Rule: Going Toward an Attractor

We now give an example of how to define a behavioral rule and how to compute its corresponding acceleration. We have chosen the case of the global rules of "going toward an attractor" in an open space. An attractor can be either a location or another individual that possibly be mobile. This behavior is one of the most common for a mobile entity when no obstacles exist.

Let i be the mobile entity under consideration, $z_i(t) = (x_i(t), y_i(t))$ be its coordinates at time t, and $z_p(t) = (x_p(t), y_p(t))$ be the coordinates of attractor p at the same time.

The equation that determines the acceleration of the mobile entity can be given for instance by:

$$a_{Go\_Attractor}(t) = \beta[\gamma(\frac{z_p(t) - z_i(t)}{|z_p(t) - z_i(t)|}) - v_i(t)], \qquad (2)$$

where $\gamma = C_s$ $(1/s)$, the cruising speed, β is a normalizing scalar of dimension $1/s^2$, and $v_i(t)$ is the instantaneous speed of entity i.

Observe that, by applying the example of Eq. 2, a mobile entity reproduces the real behaviors of acceleration and deceleration depending on its distance to the attractor's position. In between, a mobile entity travels at constant speed C_s.

The Go_Attractor behavioral rule (or join in common language) can be described as in the pseudo-code shown in Algorithm 1:

Algorithm 1. Go_Attractor $(v_i(t), z_i(t), z_p(t), \gamma = C_s, \beta)$

---

vector $dir(t)$, $a_{goAttractor}(t)$;
$dir(t) = z_p(t) - z_i(t)$;
if $|dir(t)| > C_s$ then
  $|dir(t)| := C_s$;
end if
$a_{goAttractor}(t) := \beta[dir(t) - v_i(t)]$;
return $a_{goAttractor}(t)$;

---

4   Ghost

In this section, we present Ghost, a mobility meta-modeling tool aimed to design mobility models. We detail the basic components on which Ghost relies including behavioral rules. We then enumerate the set of mobility primitive we have defined as the set of most common mobility behaviors representing every-day situations. These mobility primitives are an abstract view of mobility relying on a set of behavioral rules. We detail how mobility and network simulators can be bound to allow joint simulations to account for possible feedback loops. Eventually, we discuss practical issues on the functionalities offered by our framework.

4.1   Framework Components

Ghost is centered on the precise definition of mobile entities, their behaviors, and interactions. The goal is to get to the finest level-of-detail to model real mobility (if required by the application).

Since our goal is to precisely model the motion behavior of mobile entities at the microscopic scale, we have to precisely define the characteristics of a mobile entity (MEC). Each entity, geometrically represented by a disk of radius r, is associated with a desired velocity v_0, a maximum velocity $v_{\max}$, and a maximum acceleration $a_{\max}$. These characteristics are either drawn from available empirical data or deterministically set. For example, we can set the walking speed distribution of pedestrians to follow a normal distribution $\sim N(\mu = 1.34, \sigma^2 = 0.26)$ [19] or a constant speed of 1 m/s as determined by McNett and Voelker in [6].

Our mobile entities will evolve in a representation of a simulated world. A map file defines the simulation environment (SED) which contains paths, walls, and obstacles that can together model indoor and outdoor maps. One can also include meta-information such as attractive places (*e.g.*, lunchroom, cafeteria, offices) and emergency exits.

Eventually, Ghost provides a rich set of behavioral rules to deal with both local and global influences. At the local scope, we dispose of basic rules such as avoid obstacles and walls, deviate from other mobile entities, or walk in group. At the global scope, Ghost proposes rules that define indoor and outdoor displacements. Yet, rules must be precisely composed in order to lead to the desired mobility pattern. Depending on the context (we model using states in an automaton), different rules may apply. For example, walking outdoor or indoor does not involve the same set of rules (*cf.*, Section 4.2). Composition rules specify the set of rules that simultaneously apply to define a general mobility behavior we call mobility primitive. In the next section, Section 4.2, we have defined basic mobility primitives that reflect most of every-day mobility situations (*e.g.*, *walk, pause, wander, chase, gather at a place, or join someone or a group*) in different contexts (*i.e.*, indoor vs. outdoor for example).

4.2 Mobility Primitives

Here, we have abstracted mobility to the most common primitives that reflect every-day behaviors. Note there is no direct mapping between behavioral rules and mobility primitives. In fact, a mobility primitive can be defined using several behavioral rules. Table. 1 details the set of rules that govern each mobility primitive. The exact implementation of each rule is not given. Still, the denomination of each rule is self-explicit.[3]

At the internal scale (sub-micro-mobility), we have defined the following mobility primitive:

- *Noise factor.* This rule generates a noise factor that simulates Brownian motion.

At the local scale (micro-mobility), we have defined the following mobility primitives:

---

[3] Other rules can be included, like deviation from doors or preference to stay on the right side of the path. Again, our objective here is not to define a new model, but to give a basic set of usable primitives and illustrate the potentialities of behavioral modeling. Note also that here we implicitly focus on pedestrian mobility. Yet, without loss of generality, Ghost includes vehicular and animal mobility primitives. Rules related to vehicular traffic are listed in Tab. 5.

- *Individual walk.* Pedestrians decompose their displacements in successive objectives in order to reach their destination. These successive objectives can be seen as combination of successive attraction forces.
- *Wander.* This primitive defines the way pedestrian wander. We have implemented this primitive using Brownian motion combined with rules to navigate indoor and outdoor defined in the previous primitive.
- *Group walk.* Group mobility models represent the displacement of mobile individuals when they belong to a group. Battalions, student classes, or emergency teams are examples of group where mobility may be an issue. Group mobility is in general difficult to model because of the large number of parameters to be configured.

At the global scale (macro-mobility), we have defined the following mobility primitives.

- *Join or Gather.* Join is a mobility primitive that defines how pedestrian move toward an attractor either mobile or fix. This can be another individual, a group, or a place. Depending on the context different rules will apply in open space, indoor, and outdoor.
- *Chase or Pursuit.* The individual pursuit primitive with one runaway r and one chaser i is similar to the join primitive except that the destination or waypoint is fixed for the runaway and set to be the runaway for the chaser. The runaway acts then as a mobile attractive force for the chaser. The position of the waypoint is dynamically replaced by the position of the runaway. The main difference with the *Join* primitive is that the chaser travels at its maximum speed (instead of its usual walking speed).
- *Pause.* With this primitive individuals stay stationary at their current location.

At the omniscient scale, we have defined the following mobility primitive:

- *Exit-all.* This primitive requires all pedestrians in a building (*e.g.*, shopping mall, stadium) to exit in order to simulate a case of emergency.

The following table gives the set of combined behavioral rules which govern each behavioral mobility primitive.

4.3   Framework Description of Joint Traffic and Network Simulations

Interfacing a network simulator and a traffic simulator in order to interoperate requires a dedicated interface for synchronization and exchange of relevant information. We first detail the respective simulators components belonging to what we call the network plan and the mobility plan (either pedestrian plan or traffic plan depending on the kind of simulated mobility) and then describe how to make them interoperate. The overall framework including the network plan, the mobility plan, and how they communicate is described in Fig. 3 in the case of a vehicular traffic generator.

Table 1. Summary of mobility primitives to behavioral rules mapping

Scope	Primitives	Associated behavioral rule(s)
Internal	*Noise*	brownianMotion
Local	*Individual walk*	avoidWalls, avoidObstacle, mutualAvoidance
	Wander	sim. to *Individual walk* with brownianMotion
	Group walk[4]	mutualAvoidance, velocityMatching, groupCentering
Global	*Join*	Go_Attractor (open field) or Go_Attractor_Indoor (indoor) or Go_Attractor_Outdoor (outdoor)
	Chase	Go_Attractor_Chase
	Pause	Pause
Omniscient	*Exit-all*	emergencyExit

Network simulators are generally composed of basic components to simulate a protocol stack. If some components such as routing protocols or applications are not available then the designer is required to implement them. These components are then assembled using a high-level language or configuration files. When simulating self-organizing networks (ad hoc, inter-vehicular communications), the main factor influencing network simulation performances is mobility. Hence, network simulators allow loading synthetic mobility trace files from mobility generators implementing mobility models reviewed in Section 2.

In our case, mobility can not be loaded at the initialization phase of the simulator because of the feedback loop. This loop makes both simulators mutually dependent to the result of the other: the network simulator requires mobility information from the mobility simulator while this latter or more precisely behavioral rules require the current perceived conditions on the environment in order to react accordingly to the situation defined by the ad hoc behavior. This ad hoc behavior in fact models the directives given by the agent of its communicating device. For example, pedestrians escaping a building on fire will be updated by their communicating equipments for the best emergency exit to head to. This requires designing an agent which balances between the shortest-path avoiding fire and crowded areas. Hence, agents embedded in communicating equipments will require information on the exact location of the incident and the constantly updated information on the current flow of escaping pedestrians. Similarly, in the case of vehicular traffic, the traffic conditions perceived by agents will allow to update their view of the street network represented as dynamical street network database. This database serves an *en-route* route choice behavior that constantly re-computes the shortest-route avoiding traffic jams due to incidents. The simulation of both cases can be implemented with agents or application in the network plan with their communication stack.

---

[4] These rules are inspired from the way AI defines group motion.

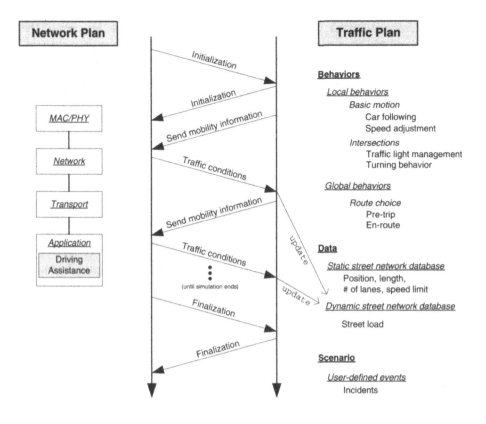

Fig. 3. Binding of network and traffic simulators

More practically in this latter case, the network and traffic simulators can work with different space and time scales. Network simulators are mostly homogeneous since a very precise simulation time step is required to simulate inter and intra-stack communications. On the other hand, microscopic traffic simulators exist at various space-time granularities with continuous versions (in fact, internally time is discretized with a very short time step period to simulate continuous time) and discretized versions such as CA. For example, a traffic simulator can have a time step of $\Delta t_{traffic}$ of $0.5s$. This indicates that the motion of vehicles is updated every half a second. But, during this time step $\Delta t_{traffic}$, a number of inter-vehicular communications can be performed. Hence, the network simulator must simulate communications occurring during this time step. Besides, the network simulator must also have a fine representation of the mobility. For a given vehicle, it must interpolate the mobility between the preceding position and the position received from the traffic simulator.

As a consequence, this requires an initialization phase where both simulators exchange their respective basic simulation parameters (*i.e.*, space and time granularity). Then, at the end of each time step of the traffic simulator, mobility information of all vehicles is sent to the network simulator which simulates the inter-vehicular communications during $\Delta t_{traffic}$. At the end of this period, the network simulator sends the newly received traffic conditions (if any) to the traffic simulator in order to update the respective dynamic street network database of the concerned vehicles. At the end of the simulation, a finalization message is sent between the two simulators to stop the all simulation. All these messages exchange are represented in Fig. 3.

4.4 Practical Issues

Ghost uses a high-level language (Object-TCL, or OTCL for short) for user inter-activity both off-line (*i.e.*, scenario definition) and on-line (*i.e.*, live interference). The simulation environment definition is loaded via a map file .sed containing the description of indoor or outdoor maps as well as the parameters of the attractors. Mobile entities are defined via .mec files that store characteristics such as the maximum speed, maximum acceleration, cruising speed, visibility range, and many more. The current version of our software already includes full classes of pedestrians, vehicles, and animals.

Designers are already provided with a rich set of rules which do not prevent them from creating new ones. In fact, the available set of rules is already representative of most behaviors at all scale (internal, local, global). Mobility primitives relying on these rules can be used as basic building blocks to design scenarios or models in a timely-fashion.

Users can interact with Ghost on the fly. For example, one can require a mobile entity to chase another mobile entity (through the "chase" primitive) or require all workers of a building to exit (through the "exit-all" primitive) to simulate a case of emergency. Eventually, Ghost offers an interface required to bind network and mobility simulators.

5 Case Study 1: Emergency Team Mobility Scenario

In this case study, we demonstrate how a simple scenario of an emergency team can be defined with our framework.

Fig. 4 gives snapshots of emergency team members evolving in a square region. Their objective is to get together at a rendezvous point and then walk up to the destination, the place of emergency. Observe that the group is formed at $t = 45$ s, when team members pause until all group members arrive. They then start walking in group formation toward a common destination (group walk primitive at the local scale and join primitive at the global scale). At $t = 65$ s, the group encounters an obstacle and separates in two halves that re-merge later at the destination at $t = 100$ s. Between $t = 0$ s and $t = 45$ s, team members apply the individual walk primitive (governed by the three rules of the pedestrian model defined in Table 1) that results in team members maintaining a certain distance between each other. This is clearly illustrated at $t = 45$ s, where team members, although having a precise RDV-point, spatially occupy the

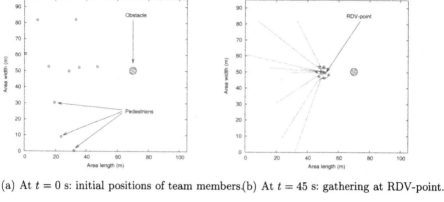

(a) At $t = 0$ s: initial positions of team members. (b) At $t = 45$ s: gathering at RDV-point.

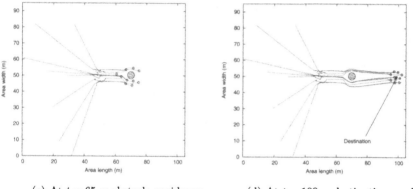

(c) At $t = 65$ s: obstacle avoidance.   (d) At $t = 100$ s: destination reached.

Fig. 4. Mixed individual and group mobility: team members meet at a RDV-point and walk in group formation toward a common destination but temporarily separate due to an obstacle

place around this point. This phenomenon is naturally obtained by the mutual avoidance rule.

Algorithm 2 presents an OTCL script used to define the scenario. Lines 1–2 of the script create a new instance of the mobility simulator with the topology display, respectively. Line 4 sets variables where N is the number of team members, $t1$ is the time at which all team members leave their initial place to gather at the rendezvous point (*cf.*, Fig. 4(b), and $t2$ is the time at which all nodes start walking in group to their common destination (*cf.*, Fig. 4(d). Line 6 sets the dimension of the simulation field to a square of 100×100 m^2. Line 8 loads the simulation environment (*i.e.*, map), which contains only one obstacle. Lines 10–11 instantiate the RDV-point with its position in the simulation field. Similarly, lines 13–14 instantiate the destination point. Line 16–22 form a loop that instantiates team members (line 17), assigns a random position to each of them from a uniform distribution (line 18–19), and schedules the different events: join the RDV-point

Algorithm 2. Scenario script of 9 team members in a 100×100 m^2 open space topology with one obstacle

```
 1: gh% set ghost_ [new Simulator]
 2: gh% set topo_ [new Topology]
 3: gh%
 4: gh% set N 9; set t1 10; set t2 45;
 5: gh%
 6: gh% $topo_ set-dimensions 100.0 100.0
 7: gh%
 8: gh% source ./map.sed
 9: gh%
10: gh% set rdv1_ [new Attractor]
11: gh% $rdv1_ set-pos 50.00 50.0
12: gh%
13: gh% set destination_ [new Attractor]
14: gh% $destination_ set-pos 100.00 50.0
15: gh%
16: gh% for {set i 0} {$i<$N } {incr i} {
17: gh%      set peds_($i) [$ghost_ peds]
18: gh%      $peds_($i) init-state-pos [$ghost_ draw-uniform 0.0 40.0] /
19:                              [$ghost_ draw-uniform 0.0 100.0]
20: gh%      $peds_ at $t1 "$ped_($i) join $rdv1_"
21: gh%      $peds_ at $t2 "$ped_($i) group-walk"
22: gh%      $peds_ at $t2.1 "$ped_($i) join $destination_"
23: gh% }
24: gh% $ghost_ run
```

at $t1$ (line 20), walk in group at $t2$ (line 21), and join the final destination at $t2 + 0.1s$ (line 22). Eventually, the simulation is launched (line 24).

6   Case Study 2: Vehicular Traffic Incident

Here, we present a case study of city traffic where vehicles detecting an incident inform other vehicles. These latter are then able to re-compute a new path to go round the concerned area. Another example of a more critical situation can be to flee an unexpected tsunami as the one that occurred in Asia on December 2004. Urban vehicular traffic is a typical scenario where drivers can benefit from route re-planning. Indeed, traffic dynamics in cities are quite different from freeways, since it is largely influenced by intersections and their traffic control elements (*e.g.*, stops, traffic lights). Hence, at the street level, route re-planning can be easily done at each intersection. At the communication level, vehicles along with their mobility allow the deployment of inter-vehicle communication networks. In the following, we study the simple case of an accident, its detection, and its diffusion to inform other vehicles. Then, vehicles receiving the information can dynamically re-plan their route (*en route*). We first detail the vehicular mobility

```
LocalBehaviors:
        Basic Motion:
             Car following: follow the preceding vehicle and keep a safety distance.
             Speed Adjustment: if no preceding vehicle, accelerate to the next intersection
                              at the speed defined for the current street portion.
        Intersection Management:
             Traffic light Management: slow down when approaching from a traffic light and
                                      stop when red and go when green.
             Turning behavior: avoid other vehicles when turning.

GlobalBehaviors:
        Pre − trip route choice: shortest-path route from one location to another
                                based on the static street network database.
        En − route route choice: shortest-path route from one location to another
                                based on the dynamic street network database.
```

Fig. 5. Vehicular motion behavioral rules

model and the simulation environment. Then we detail how the network and traffic plans were implemented, and eventually describe obtained results.

6.1   Vehicular Model

Behaviors governing the mobility of vehicles can be divided in two classes: local behaviors and global behaviors. Local behaviors are influenced by a vehicle's surrounding environment (local feedback influences) made by the front vehicle and traffic signs. The car-following rule specifies to follow the preceding vehicle while keeping a safety distance. But, if no vehicle is directly ahead, vehicles follow the street heading toward the next intersection at a speed defined by the limit on the current road portion (*i.e.*, speed adjustment). Local feedbacks also influence realistic behaviors when approaching a traffic light (*i.e.*, traffic light management rule) and when required to turn at an intersection (*i.e.*, turning behavior rule). At a global scale, vehicles have to decide their route when going from one location to another. An important factor influencing the route choice behavior in microscopic models is the formation of a consistent street network representation. We consider all vehicles to possess a static street network database. In this database, each street is considered as an edge valued proportionally to its length, its number of lanes and its speed limit. A simple implementation of the route choice behavior (*i.e.*, pre-trip rule) is to perform a shortest path computation on this database. However, intelligent transportation system designers have also propose to include a *en route* re-computation of the route plan to account for changing traffic conditions. This re-computation is based on a dynamic street network database updated with traffic conditions received through IVC. These traffic conditions are processed to compute the number of vehicles on a street or the indication that a street is being blocked by an accident. If the number of vehicles on a defined street is large compared to its length, its weight increases making it hard to be chosen as a shortest path. If an accident has occurred, the street segment is assigned an infinite value. All these rules are summarized in Figure 5.

6.2 Simulation Environment

For the purpose of this paper, we consider a continuous microscopic model part of a more general mobility framework developed at our lab. We use a single lane model with bidirectional traffic. Traffic lights and special events to simulate unexpected events such as accidents are managed via our event scheduler. Our traffic model implements the major rules defined previously (*i.e.*, the car-following and speed adjustment rules extended with rules to react appropriately to intersections with traffic lights). For the global behavior, vehicles start from a random position on the street network and choose a random destination. When arrived at destination, vehicles choose another destination and repeat this process until simulation ends.

Of course, our traffic simulator is a simplified version of simulators used in the transportation community. This choice was retained only as a prototype proof-of-concept and to show that the interoperability of our framework should still hold for other simulators from the vehicular community. For the network simulator, we use the open-source Ns-2 [20] which is one of the most achieved and used simulator by the networking community.

6.3 Scenario Implementation

We simulate a Manhattan-like grid city area of $730 \times 730 \ m^2$ with streets of $120m$ long and a maximum speed of $50km/h$. Traffic lights are placed at each intersection. Vehicles are equipped with GPS and a WiFi (802.11) radio interface with a $500m$ radio coverage range. The simulated scenario generates a car accident blocking a street. We then evaluate how traffic redirects automatically.

We adopt simple assumptions and algorithms for *(i)* event detection and characterization *(ii)* information diffusion and *(iii)* en route route re-planning. We consider the set of all vehicles around the wrecked cars to send an alert of wreckage giving the position of the incident as well as its time of detection. For these alerts to be diffused, we consider the simple algorithm where the information is propagated within a fix radius using broadcast. Hence, the information is relayed by vehicles if the distance between their current position and the reported incident's position is less than this fix radius. We could also have considered other communication paradigms such as opportunistic routing and even a hybrid approach but this is out of scope of this paper. All information about a particular incident is processed by a simulated driving assistant in Ns-2 implemented as an application agent. At the end of each time step, this agent uses our interface to send traffic conditions to the traffic simulator. In our case, this information consists in indicating the street segment where the incident occurred so that it can be valued with an infinite value in the dynamic database of the concerned vehicles. At the beginning of each time step of the traffic simulator, all vehicles get the received traffic conditions and update their dynamic street network database. Then, each simulated vehicle updates its position according to its local and global behaviors among which the en route rule can play a major role if

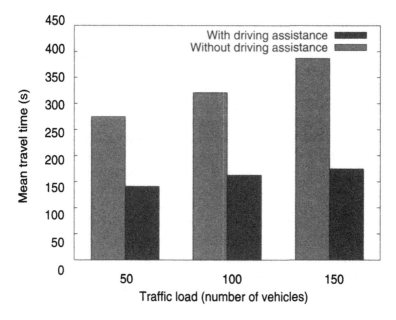

Fig. 6. Mean travel time of all vehicles with and without route re-planning for varying traffic loads

the traffic condition has been updated and that the concerned vehicle is directly affected by the changes (*i.e.*, the blocked street was in the vehicle's route path). For this rule, we also adopt the simple approach to re-compute the shortest path based on the dynamic street network database that has just been updated. We do not intend here to propose a complex incident propagation algorithm with a complex route re-computation algorithm but only a proof that our approach is feasible.

6.4   Results

We conducted several joint simulations with an increasing traffic load of 50, 100, and 150 vehicles. We compared the mean travel time of all vehicles for all their displacement with and without route re-planning. One travel time consists of the time required to go from on location to another. We can observe in Fig. 6 that when vehicles are not informed of the accident, the travel time is higher compared to the travel time when they are informed and re-plan their route. This increased travel time is due to vehicles stuck in the traffic jams on both sides of the accident. When vehicles are informed of the incident through inter-vehicular communications and are able to re-plan their route, the overall travel time can be reduced by a factor greater than 2. This even if vehicles have to take longer paths to avoid the blocked street. This clearly demonstrates the feasibility of this approach which opens a broad range of possible traffic optimizations that are not limited to the case studied here.

7   Conclusion

In this paper, we have demonstrated the power of behavioral models by their capacity to revisit the way models can be designed. Behavioral models are a different modeling approach when compared with classical mobility models currently in use by the networking community. The benefits of this approach are manifold. First, it extends network simulations with realistic patterns of mobility. Second, it allows easily defining mobility scenarios. And eventually, the dynamical property brought by the behavioral paradigm allows pushing simulation a step forward by binding mobility and network simulators. Such an approach extends the design and performance evaluation of novel solutions for dynamic intelligent navigation by considering realistic scenarios where a feedback loop exists. Behavioral mobility modeling is a potential candidate as the state-of-the- art in the design of solutions (intelligent agents and communicating solutions) aimed to respond to incidents or emergency situations. In future work, we intend to simulate an emergency scenario of escaping pedestrians assisted by their communication devices. Results will assess if the assisted navigation given by these devices can optimize the flow of pedestrians and reduce the number of injured people occurring when pedestrians panic.

References

1. T. Camp, J. Boleng, and V. Davies, "A Survey of Mobility Models for Ad Hoc Network Research," *Wireless Communications and Mobile Computing*, vol. 2, no. 5, pp. 483–502, Aug. 2002.
2. D. Johnson and D. Maltz, *Dynamic Source Routing in Ad Hoc Wireless Networks*. Kluwer Academic Publishers, 1996, vol. 353.
3. X. Hong, M. Gerla, G. Pei, and C. Chiang, "A Group Mobility Model for Ad Hoc Wireless Networks," in *Proc. ACM/IEEE MSWiM*, Seattle, WA, Aug. 1999.
4. M. Sanchez and P. Manzoni, "Anejos: A java-based simulator for ad-hoc networks," *Future Generation Computer Systems magazine - Elsevier*, Mar. 2001.
5. A. Jardosh, E. Belding-Royer, K. Almeroth, and S. Suri, "Real World Environment Models for Mobile Ad Hoc Networks," *IEEE JSAC*, vol. 23, no. 3, Mar. 2005.
6. M.McNett and G. Voelker, "Access and Mobility of Wireless PDA Users," *ACM Mobile Computing and Communications Review*, vol. 9, no. 2, pp. 40–55, Apr. 2005.
7. C. Tuduce and T. Gross, "A Mobility Model Based on Wlan Traces and its Validation," in *Proc. IEEE INFOCOM*, Miami, FL, Mar. 2005.
8. A. K. Saha and D. Johnson, "Modeling Mobility for Vehicular Ad Hoc Networks," in *Proc. ACM VANET*, Philadelphia, PA, July 2004.
9. M. Musolesi and C. Mascolo, "A Community based Mobility Model for Ad Hoc Network Research," in *Proc. ACM Realman*, Florence, Italy, May 2006.
10. S. Ray, M. Feeley, N. Hutchinson, and K. Cai, "Realistic mobility for mobile ad hoc network simulation," in *(submitted for publication)*, 2006.
11. J. Kim and S. Bohacek, "A survey-based mobility model of people for simulation of urban mesh networks," in *MeshNets'05*, Budapest, Hungary, July 2005.
12. J. Kim, A. Ilic, and S. Bohacek, "Realistic simulation of urban mesh networks - part I: Urban mobility," in *Technical Report*, University of Delaware, 2006.

13. D. Choffnes and F. Bustamante, "An integrated mobility and traffic model for vehicular wireless networks," in *Proc. ACM VANET*, Cologne, Germany, Sept. 2005.
14. R. Barr, Z. Haas, and R. V. Renesse, "JiST: An efficient approach to simulation using virtual machines," *IEEE Software Practice & Experience*, vol. 35, 6, May 2005.
15. D. Helbing, I. Farkas, and T. Vicsek, "Simulating Dynamical Features of Escape Panic," *Nature*, vol. 407, pp. 487–490, Sept. 2000.
16. Q. Yang and H. Koutsopoulos, "A microscopic traffic simulator for evaluation of dynamic traffic management systems," *Transportation Research*, vol. C, no. 4 (3), 1996.
17. C. W. Reynolds, "Flocks, Herds and Schools: A Distributed Behavioral Model," in *Proc. ACM SIGGRAPH*, Anaheim, CA, July 1987.
18. S. Balakirsky and E. Messina, "A simulation framework for evaluating mobile robots," in *PerMIS Workshop*, Gaithersburg, MD, Aug. 2002.
19. L. Henderson, "The Statistics of Crowd Fluids," *Nature*, vol. 229, pp. 381–383, Feb. 1971.
20. The VINT Project, "The Network simulator (Ns-2)." [Online]. Available: http://www.isi.edu/nsnam/ns/

Node Density Effects on Reactive Routing Protocols for Mobile Ad Hoc Wireless Networks

Hean-Loong Ong, Tat-Chee Wan, Hean-Kuan Ong, and Sureswaran Ramadass

National Advanced IPv6 Center, USM, Penang Malaysia
{hlong, tcwan, hkong, sures}@nrg.cs.usm.my
http://www.nav6.org

Abstract. The study conducted in this paper evaluates the performance of on-demand mobile ad hoc wireless network protocols under varying node densities in a large network. The focus in this study centers on the relationship between the mobility, density and connectivity of ad hoc wireless nodes. Ad hoc wireless node density is often discussed on a single group subnets of nodes. In this study a scenario is proposed to evaluate the ad hoc wireless nodes communicating between different node sub with different densities. A simulation is conducted using the two prominent on demand routing protocol for ad hoc networks namely DSR and AODV. In the simulation each protocol is given 2 different scenarios in terms of node location. The first scenario is a normal ad hoc wireless simulation scenario. The second scenario contains nodes that are partitioned into 7 areas where respective areas have their node density and connection probability. The objective of this study is to look at how on demand ad hoc wireless routing protocols react to environments with non uniform node densities and to seek and understanding for future improvement.

1 Introduction

Mobile ad hoc networks (MANETs) consists of a group of wireless nodes communicating with each other through multiple-hop wireless links and without any additional infrastructure. Each node in the network is self managed, acting as a router and host simultaneously. Nodes are also expected to forward routing information and packets to other adjacent nodes within its transmission range [18]. The network topology is very unpredictable and the number of nodes within a network could change significantly within a short period of time. However, research efforts to improve mobile ad hoc wireless network performance have intensified in recent years as portable and mobile devices becomes more commonplace.

Many MANET routing protocols and their derivatives have been developed [5]. These protocols can be classified into two major categories – Table Driven or *Proactive* vs. On Demand or *Reactive*. There are other protocols that utilize positioning [17] and other link reversal algorithms [16] as well. Comparison studies using metrics such as Packet Delivery Ratio, Throughput, Dropped Packets

K. Cho and P. Jacquet (Eds.): AINTEC 2006, LNCS 4311, pp. 206–221, 2006.
© Springer-Verlag Berlin Heidelberg 2006

and Path Optimality [5] have concluded that *reactive* MANET routing protocols perform better for networks that are more dynamic, with high node mobility.

The optimum density of MANETs was studied in [2], which discussed the tradeoffs between network density and node connectivity in the face of increasing node mobility, and proposed an optimal node density for maintaining connectivity in a stationary network. However, the results were inconclusive regarding the optimal density for maintaining connectivity in highly mobile environments. Nonetheless, [2] concluded that both transmission power and the node densities need to increase when nodes experience increasing mobility if connectivity were to be maintained.

This study analyzes the performance of reactive MANET routing protocols working under conditions of different network densities. DSR and AODV, the two most common reactive routing protocols protocols, will first be studied in an open environment with unrestricted movement, and then in a partitioned environment where there is limited node mobility. The performance of both MANET routing protocols in the two respective environments will be evaluated. Section II presents an overview of the routing mechanisms used in DSR and AODV, while Section III discusses the effect of node densities on nodes connectivity in MANETs. Section IV describes the simulation environment used for this study, while results and discussion is presented in Section V. The conclusion is found in Section VI.

2 Overview of MANET Routing Protocols

2.1 AODV

Ad Hoc On Demand Distance Vector (AODV) protocol [10] is able to support unicast, broadcast and multicast data transmission. AODV uses the next hop routing model with sequence numbers and periodic beacons to discover routes and maintain them. These features were borrowed from DSDV (Destination Sequenced Distance Vector) routing protocol [10]. AODV uses Route Discovery and Route Maintenance as basic mechanisms for establishing links among nodes.

AODV Route Discovery is required when the node has data to send. A link to the desired destination must be established before any upper layer communications could take place. Route Discovery begins with a route request (RREQ) message containing information such as the destination node's IP address, sequence number, hop count and broadcast ID. These attributes are sufficient for identifying the destination node; therefore if a non destined node receives the message it will automatically forward it until the message reaches its intended recipient. A route reply (RREP) will be sent back to the message source using the reverse route obtained from the RREQ message, otherwise a new route has to be determined using the Route Discovery mechanism if no route exists.

Route Maintenance is required by AODV to ensure that the selected or discovered routes are fresh (current), up to the point where the sender is initiating upper layer communication. The freshness of the routes is recorded in the routing table entries maintained by each node. To reduce the amount of RREQs flooding the network in the event of any failed links, an optimization technique is introduced. The technique uses the *expanding ring* search [11] to locate other alternative paths to replace a failed link.

2.2 DSR

The main feature of the Dynamic Source Routing protocol (DSR) [6] is *source routing*. By virtue of the *source routing* capability, the sender acquires the full oath information to the destination. The information is maintained by every node in the network and it is stored inside a *route cache*. The aggressive use of *route caches* is the major characteristic of DSR, it is designed to be loop free and it is effective for looking up previously known routes.

DSR shares some features with AODV where both on demand protocols have Route Discovery and Route Maintenance mechanisms. However, the manner in which DSR performs the Route Discovery and Route Maintenance is quite different from AODV. While performing Route Discovery DSR floods the network with RREQ packets. Each intermediate node will keep a copy of the Route Discovery message for future use and rebroadcast it into the network until the RREQ reaches destination node. In this instance all the routing information obtained from RREQ packets is stored in the *route cache*. Thus the RREP packet is able to traverse the network back to the source via the information acquired from the RREQ flooding phase via bi-directional links. In the case of a uni-directional link a new path from the destination to the source is discovered via piggybacking the RREP from the destination in a new RREQ packet. Route Maintenance is performed on the information that resides in the *route cache* [8]. The nodes are able to retrieve routing information in the network via *promiscuous listening* even though the routing information is not designated to it. In order to avoid a broadcast storm during link failures several approaches were suggested in [9]. One of the approaches was the use of *packet salvaging*, where intermediate nodes will try to salvage the links by aggressively searching the route cache.

2.3 Comparison Between DSR and AODV

In a study by Perkins et al. [12], DSR and AODV were compared against each other. The author highlighted the usefulness of *promiscuous listening* which allows DSR to possess a great amount of routing information compared to what AODV might have in its routing table. Therefore AODV may perform more route discoveries compared to DSR in a similar environment. On the other hand, AODV can almost always ensure that the selected route is fresher since the selection of routes is determined by the sequence number and based on the most recent routing entry. It was observed that more experiments should be conducted to examine the inter-layer coupling between the routing layer and the data link layer to provide a better insight into how both protocols work.

3   Node Density

3.1   Networks with Varying Node Density

In [5] MANETs were studied using open space models where nodes were able to move throughput the entire simulation area. However a more realistic environment should account for restricted mobility of nodes, such as in an urban city setting where there may be concentrations of nodes within specific areas (such as within buildings) and low density of nodes in other areas (such as in parks and roadways). Consequently, the simulation area should be partitioned into smaller sub-areas with varying densities to model such environments. Even in large MANETs with free space roaming, instantenous network partitioning often occur at some point due to node mobility, resulting in changing *density waves* [2]. It is important to characterize the effect of non-uniform node densities on MANET routing performance, and to determine the minimum performance threshold for these MANET routing protocols.

(a) Partitioned   (b) Normal

Fig. 1. Difference between partitioned nodes and non partitioned nodes

3.2   Effects of Node Density on Connectivity

First, the relationship between connectivity and node densities in MANETs should be defined. Bettstetter et al. [1] defined the connection probability between nodes possessing a single mutually independent path with a homogenous assigned transmission range to be almost surely (*a.s*) connected as:

$$\text{Equation 1 } P(con) \approx (1 - e^{-\mu})^n \text{ [1]}$$

and $P(con(a.s)) \geq 0.95$. A mutually independent path is uni-directional; i.e., for either send or receive only. $P(con(a.s)) \geq 0.95$ means that the nodes are in proximity to each other, suggesting that it is (*a.s*) connected. Sparse networks do not have (*a.s*) connectivity and there is no assurance that fully independent paths will be formed among all node in the network. The factor that decides the connectivity of the nodes within a homogenous assigned transmission range environment is the number of nodes located in a specific area within the larger network environment. Nonetheless, Equation 1 does not take border effects of the network into account. Thus only the connectivity of MANET nodes within a given area is taken into consideration. The factor governs the density of a given area is ρ, where $\rho = \frac{n}{A}$, used in the equation $\mu = \rho\pi r_0^2$. Hence, spatial density becomes the main determinant for node connectivity within an area.

We assume that each node belongs to a specific well-partitioned area in the simulation environment. Nodes are assumed not to straddle the border between adjacent partitions (areas) and hence such cases will not be considered in this study. Consequently, if a node in one area decide to establish connection with another node in a different area, the connection will cross a logical partition boundary separating the two. The mobility within each area is also taken into account when packets are traversing areas with different densities. Obtaining $(a.s)$ connections in sparse areas with high mobility will be difficult due to the distances involved and small number of nodes in the particular area. Nodes that are constantly moving are very susceptible to broken links, thus there can be no guarantee on the availability of any sort of connectivity.

3.3 Measuring the Efficiency of the Network

The following metrics will be used to measure the efficiency of best effort routing protocols such as AODV and source routing protocols such as DSR:

Packet Delivery Ratio: The Packet Delivery Ratio represents the successful arrival of a packet to its destination, measured using the ratio of the number of packets delivered successfully to the number of packets generated by the source. If the packet delivery ratio is low it means that the connection between the source and destination is quite often interrupted or there are no stable links available.

Average End to End Delay: Packet Delay is the total time taken for one data packet to travel successfully from the source to the destination. The average end to end delay represents how efficient the protocol manages to find the best route for data packet traversal. The best route is usually associated with the least number of hops thus providing the least delay and the shortest time taken from source to destination.

Normalized Routing Load: Normalized Routing Load measures the number of routed packets sent vs. the number of data packets received at the destination. Every transmission through a node is considered to be a packet sent, this includes forwarded packets.

Average Hop Count: Average Hop Count is the average number of hops taken for all control packet to reach its destination. This is calculated as the ratio of the number of routed data link layer control packets to the total number of network layer control packets (where each control packet transmission is added to the total at the data link layer).

4   Simulation Environment

The simulation environment is based on the NS-2 network simulator version 2.29, a widely used discrete event simulator [14] that provides detailed control over the physical and MAC layer settings, such as transmission range, topological layout and node mobility. The IEEE 802.11 DCF (Distributed Coordinated Function) MAC [15] was used as the basis for the experiments. The 802.11 DCF MAC implements unicast data transmission through the use of Request to Send (RTS) and Clear to Send (CTS) control packets. Once the destination receives the data packet an acknowledgement (ACK) packet is sent back to the source. Channel access arbitration was based on CSMA/CA. The transmission range of each node was set to 250 m using the Two-Ray Ground Propagation model.

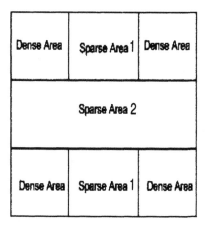

Fig. 2. Simulation Topology for Partitioned Environment

Table 1. Dense area (($a.s$) connected) grid

Area	$500 \times 500m$
Simulation duration	500 s
No. of nodes	18
Tx Range (r_0)	250 m
Speed	1, 5, 10, 20 m/s
Pause Time	0, 10, 30, 60, 120, 300 s
No. Traffic Sources	10, 20, 30, 40
Data Rate	16 kbps
$P(con)$	≥ 0.95

The simulation covers a total area of $1500 \times 1500m$. Two environments were tested–Open and Partitioned. Nodes roam throughout the entire area for the Open environment. For the Partitioned environment Figure 1(a), the topology of the network was segmented into seven different areas where the four corners of the topology grid were dense areas separated by various sparse areas; i.e., there were no adjacent areas that were both dense. Nodes roam only within their assigned areas. The Dense Areas and Sparse Area 1 have a topology of $500 \times 500m$ while Sparse Area 2 has a topology of $1500 \times 500m$. The Random Waypoint Mobility Model was used in the simulation.

Table 2. Sparse Area 1 (not $(a.s)$ connected) grid

Area (A)	$500 \times 500m$
Simulation duration	500 s
No. of nodes (n)	5
Tx Range (r_0)	250 m
Speed	1, 5, 10, 20 m/s
Pause Time	0, 10, 30, 60, 120, 300 s
No. Traffic Sources	10, 20, 30, 40
Data Rate	16 kbps
$P(con)$	≈ 0.90

Table 3. Sparse Area 2 (not $(a.s)$ connected) grid

Area (A)	$1500 \times 500m$
Simulation duration	500 s
No. of nodes (n)	18
Tx Range (r_0)	250 m
Speed	1, 5, 10, 20 m/s
Pause Time	0, 10, 30, 60, 120, 300 s
No. Traffic Sources	10, 20, 30, 40
Data Rate	16 kbps
$P(con)$	≈ 0.85

Nodes travel with fixed speeds and become stationary for fixed intervals (pause time). After each pause time a node will move towards a new destination. The pause times used in the simulations were 0, 10, 30, 60, 120 and 300 s. Stationary nodes were not considered in the experiments. The speed of the nodes were set to 1, 5, 10 and 20 m/s, while all experiments were executed for a simulation duration of 500 seconds. 20 m/s (vehicular speed) was included to test the routing protocols in a more challenging environment. Tables 1, 2 and 3 summarizes the settings for each of the different areas used in the simulations. The number of

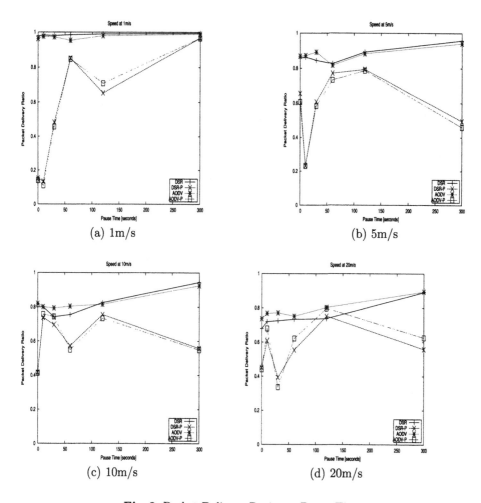

Fig. 3. Packet Delivery Ratio vs. Pause Time

unique traffic sources were set to 10, 20, 30 and 40 sources residing in a Dense Area, each transmitting to a sink located in a different Dense Area. This means that each connection will have to traverse one or more Sparse Areas. The sinks are not necessarily unique, i.e., a given destination node may receive data from more than one source. However, if a node has been designated as a source, it will not act as a sink. AODV and DSR routing protocol were evaluated using both the Open Environment as well as the Partitioned environment. The results for AODV and DSR in the Partitioned environment were denoted as AODV-P and DSR-P.

5   Analysis and Discussion

The study in [4] proposed looking into the traffic patterns on the MANET when studying the behavior of a given protocol. Each set of experiments was executed

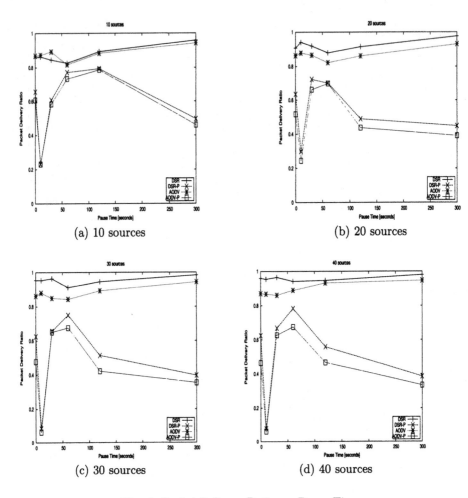

(a) 10 sources

(b) 20 sources

(c) 30 sources

(d) 40 sources

Fig. 4. Packet Delivery Ratio vs. Pause Time

as two runs, once with varying mobility for 10 sources, then repeated with varying number of sources for 5 m/s mobility. Each run consist of 10 repetitions of the same scenario but with different initial random number seeds. Therefore each point on the graphs represents an averaged value from the ten repetitions. The experiments focused on Packet Delivery Ratio, Average Delay, Average Hop Count and Normalized Routing Load vs. different pause times.

5.1   Packet Delivery Ratio

Mobility. The Packet Delivery Ratio (PDR) for both DSR-P and AODV-P are much worse compared with DSR and AODV in general. However both routing protocols have similar performance in the partitioned environment (Fig. 3a-c), except for the high mobility scenario (Fig. 3d) where AODV and AODV-P has better performance. This is most probably due to DSR having poor route selection due to 'stale' route information in its routing cache [7]. For DSR-P and AODV-P the

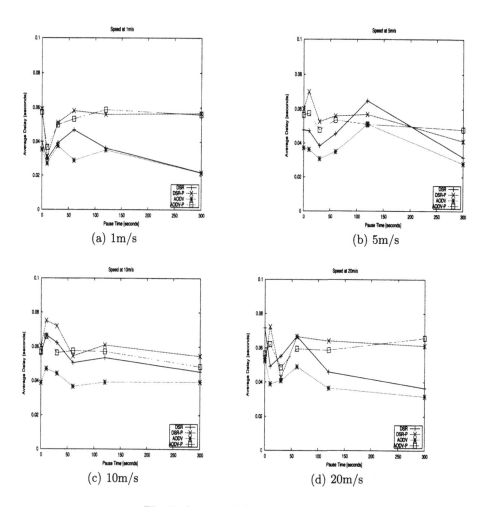

Fig. 5. Average Delay vs. Pause Time

extremely poor performance in the low mobility scenario (Fig. 3a) is due to continuous small changes of the node positions in the sparse partitioned areas, thus the chances of establishing a connection are very low. However increased pause times enable routing protocols to establish more stable routes if the node positions happen to be in a suitable location. This can be seen in the Normalized Routing Load graph (Fig. 9a). In general some degree ogf mobility with moderate pause times are needed to provide reasonably good PDR for partitioned environments.

No. Traffic Sources. AODV and AODV-P suffers from a drop in PDR under increasing traffic loads (Fig. 4a-d). Both AODV-P and DSR-P perform worse than the Open environment scenarios due to the poor recovery of routes in both protocols whereby the mechanism of route salvaging or local repair fails to provide for the loss of connection due to the unpredictable movements in the sparse areas (Fig. 10a-d). For pause times of 30 and 60, nodes are able to move

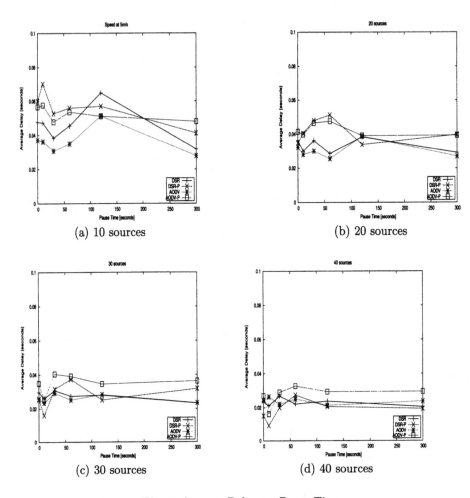

Fig. 6. Average Delay vs. Pause Time

about at moderate intervals and establish connections for a much longer period in the sparse areas. This allows the nodes to perform less Route Discovery, shown by the number of routed packets forwarded by the nodes (Fig. 10a-d).

5.2   Average Delay

Mobility. At low mobility both DSR and AODV have similar performance (Fig. 5a). AODV-P and DSR-P are not affected much by moderate mobility compared with AODV and DSR which suffers relatively worse delays (Fig. 5b,c). In general AODV performs better than DSR when mobility is present (Fig. 5b-d).

No. Traffic Sources. When the number of traffic sources are high (sources 30 and 40) DSR-P and AODV-P achieves a significant improvement in Average Delays compared with the other cases(Fig 6c-d). In this study only the delays of packets which were sent successfully were taken into consideration. Conse-

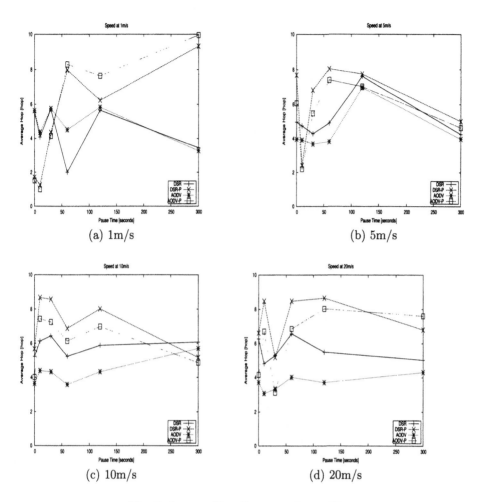

Fig. 7. Average Hop Count vs. Pause Time

quently, a lower PDR (Fig 4c-d) will decrease the Average Delay encountered by successfully sent packets.

5.3   Average Hop Count

Mobility. The Average Hop Count for open environments are lower in comparison with partitioned environments (Fig. 7a-d). In general the Average Hop Count is directly proportional to the PDR (compare Fig. 7a-d with Fig. 3a-d). This is because when the packets are dropped they do not contribute to the hop count. For the case of 1 m/s mobility with 300 second pause time, both DSR-P and AODV-P were able to establish stable routes thus ensuring high PDR at the expense of higher hop counts.

No. Traffic Sources. Average Hop Count is affected much by the traffic load (Fig.8a-b). The variation is probably due to PDR differences (Fig. 4a-d).

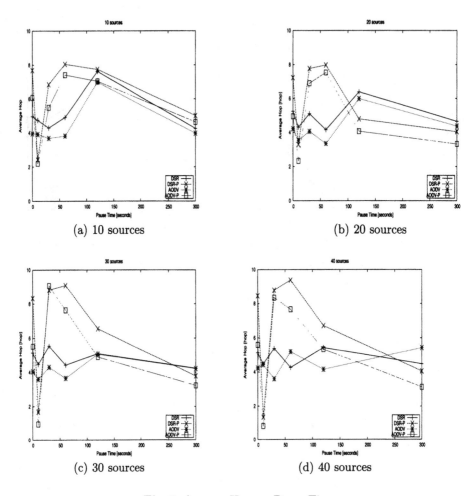

Fig. 8. Average Hop vs. Pause Time

5.4 Normalized Routing Load

Mobility The number of AODV-P packets used for routing is significantly higher for low mobility and continuous movement (pause times 0 and 10 s) due to inability to obtain suitable routes (Fig. 9a). It is evident here that AODV-P is generating a lot more routing traffic compared to DSR-P for such suboptimal topologies. However in higher mobility scenarios AODV-P performance is closer to DSR-P (Fig. 9c-d).

No. Traffic Sources The Normalized Routing Load for AODV-P increases with the number of traffic sources (Fig. 10a-d). DSR caches more routing information than AODV, therefore it can revert back to its routing cache for information everytime a link fails. Whereas AODV does not store as much information as DSR in terms of route information [12]. However the average hop count for DSR is usually higher than AODV (Fig. 8a-d).

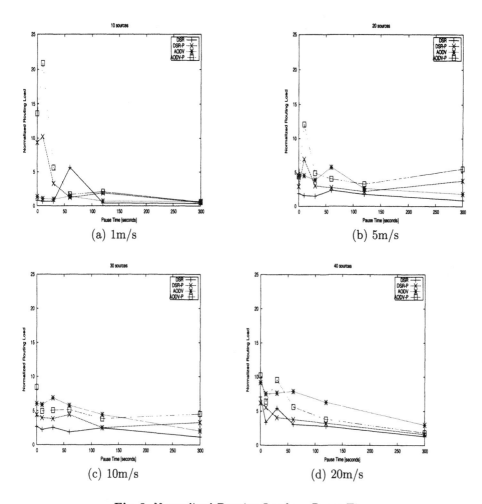

Fig. 9. Normalized Routing Load vs. Pause Time

6   Conclusion

This paper compared the performance of AODV and DSR in both Open and Partitioned environments. The experimental results for the partitioned evironments (AODV-P and DSR-P) show that both AODV and DSR routing protocols could not maintain connectivity effectively for partitioned topologies, in contrast to their respective performance in an Open environment. This can be seen in the Packet Delivery Ratio results. In general AODV-P and DSR-P perform reasonably well in moderate mobility environments with pause times between 30 to 120 seconds. In addition AODV-P has higher routing loads compared to DSR-P but achieves lower Average Hop Counts.

The Route Discovery mechanism of AODV is not good enough to make efficient choice of routes in suboptimal topologies. Ideal ad hoc wireless protocols for future applications should allow communication to be established faster and and have good selection of routes. Freshness of the *route cache* [8] for the DSR

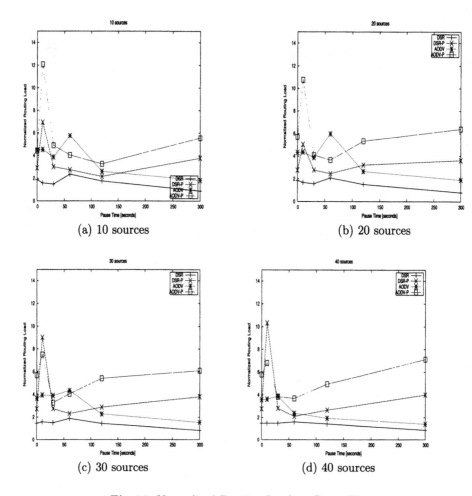

Fig. 10. Normalized Routing Load vs. Pause Time

protocol is still an issue to be resolved under the current DSR specification. By putting it in environments such as DSR-P the problem is even more evident. Future specifications for *reactive* ad hoc wireless protocols should look into improving the Route Discovery mechanisms to support partitioned environment as shown in this paper and improve on the choices of route for both protocols. Possible approaches to address this issue include AODV-UU and DSR-UU which have support for routing across multiple MANETs by making each partitioned area into a separate MANET [19].

References

1. C. Bettstetter. On the Connectivity of Wireless Multihop Networks with Homogeneous and Inhomogeneous Range Assignment. In *Proceedings. VTC 2002-Fall. 2002 IEEE 56th Volume 3*, 24-28 Sept. 2002.

2. E. Royer, P. Melliar-Smith, L. Moser. An Analysis of the Optimum Node Density for Ad Hoc Mobile Networks.In *Proceedings of the IEEE International Conference on Communications, Helsinki, Finland,* 2001.
3. C. Bettstetter, J.Zangl.How to achieve a connected ad hoc network with homogeneous range assignment: an analytical study with consideration of border effects. *Mobile and Wireless Communications Network, 2002. 4th International Workshop* on 9-11 Sept. 2002
4. A. Nilsson. Performance Analysis of Traffic Load and Node Density in Ad Hoc Networks. *Fifth European Wireless Conference on Mobile and Wireless Systems beyond 3G* Feb. 2004, Barcelona Spain.
5. J. Broch, D.A. Maltz, David.B. Johnson, Y. Hu and J. Jetcheva. A Performance Comparison of multihop wireless ad hoc networking protocols. In *Proceedings of the Fourth Annual ACM/IEEE International Conference on Mobile Networking (Mobicom'98), pp. 25-30,* March 2000.
6. D. Johnson and D. Maltz. Dynamic Source Routing in ad hoc wireless networks. *Chapter 5, pp. 153181. Kluwer Academic Publishers,* 1996.
7. Y.-C. Hu and D. Johnson. Caching strategies in on Demand routing protocols for wireless ad hoc networks. In Proc. 6th ACM MobiCom, pp. 231242, 2000.
8. Y.-C. Hu and D. Johnson. Ensuring Cache Freshness in On Demand Ad Hoc Network Routing Protocols. In *POMC'02,* October 30-31, 2002, Toulouse, France.
9. D.Maltz, Josh Broch, Jorjeta Jetcheva and David Johnson. The effects of on-demand behaviour in routing protocols for multi-hopwireless ad hoc networks. *IEEE Journal on Selected Areas in Communication 1999*
10. C. Perkins, E. Royer, S. Das. RFC 3561 Ad Hoc On Demand Distance Vector Routing. http://www.faqs.org/rfcs/rfc3561.html.
11. S.-J. Lee, E. Royer, C.E. Perkins .*Int. Journal of Network Management 13(2) pp. 97-114,* 2003.
12. S.R. Das, C.E. Perkins, and E.M. Royer. Performance comparison of two on-demand routing protocols for ad hoc networks. In *Proceedings of the IEEE Infocom, pp. 3-12,* March 2000.
13. J.Y. Li, C Blake, Douglas S.J. De Couto, H.I. Lee, R. Morris. Capacity of Ad Hoc Wireless Networks. In *Proceedings of the 7th ACM International Conference on Mobile Computing and Networking (MobiCom '01),* Rome, Italy, July 2001
14. NS2 Network Simulator 2. http://www.isi.edu/nsnam/ns/
15. C. Sweet, V. Devarapalli, D. Sidhu. IEEE 802.11 Performance in an Ad-Hoc Environment. *Technical Report, UMBC Department of Computer Science and Electrical Engineering,* 1999
16. P. Jacquet, P. Muhlethaler, T. Clausen, A Laouiti, A. Qayyum, L. Viennot. Optimized Lonk State Routing Protocol for Ad Hoc Networks. *Proceedings of the 5th IEEE Multi Topic Conference (INMIC 2001)*
17. Zygmunt J. Haas, Marc R. Pearlman, Prince Samar. The Zone Routing Protocol (ZRP) for Ad Hoc Networks. http://people.ece.cornell.edu/ haas/wnl/Publications/draft-ietf-manet-zone-zrp-04.txt. IETF Internet draft work in progress
18. J.Macker, S.Corson. Mobile ad hoc networks (MANET). http://www.ief.org/ html.charters/manet-charter.html, 1997. IETF Working Group Charter
19. AODV-UU implementation webpage. http://www.docs.uu.se/docs/research/ projects /scanet/aodv/aodvuu.shtml

Building Fault Tolerant Networks Using a Multihomed Mobile Router: A Case Study

Romain Kuntz and Jean Lorchat

The University of Tokyo and Keio University, Japan
{kuntz, lorchat}@sfc.wide.ad.jp

Abstract. In this paper, we will build a fault-tolerant network using a Multiple Care-of Addresses registration implementation on NEPL (NEMO Platform for Linux) for the GNU/Linux Operating System. As we will explain in a detailed scenario, Multiple Care-of Addresses registration is a very interesting solution for fault recovery when connecting multihomed networks to the Internet with multiple non-reliable access technologies. The feasibility of this scenario will be endorsed by an experiment using the implementation.

1 Introduction

Nowadays, more and more equipments are connected to the Internet at the same time while being mobile. To get a permanent connectivity anywhere and anytime while changing its point of attachment to the Internet, a mobile computer needs the support of mobility management protocols such as Mobile IPv6 [1] and NEMO Basic Support [2], that have been standardized at the IETF. Those protocols are based on the IPv6 protocol that solves the scalability problem raised by the actual version of the Internet Protocol (IPv4).

While Mobile IPv6 proposes a solution for host mobility, NEMO Basic Support extends the protocol to support entire networks moving in the Internet topology (fig. 1). Mobility is managed at the exit router (the Mobile Router, MR) of the moving network (also called a NEMO), and is transparent to all the nodes inside the NEMO (Mobile Network Nodes, MNNs). The MNNs and the MR are always reachable at the same address while moving, thus all IP sessions are maintained even though the network changes its point of attachment in the Internet topology. This is possible thanks to a third entity, the Home Agent (HA), located in the MR's Home Network and maintaining a binding between the MR's Home Address (HoA, the MR's identifier), the MR's Care-of Address (CoA, that represents the MR's real location), and the IPv6 prefixes advertised in the Mobile Network (Mobile Network Prefixes, MNPs) while the NEMO is moving in foreign networks. A bi-directional IPv6-over-IPv6 tunnel is maintained between the Home Agent and the Mobile Router, and all the traffic from or to the NEMO transits through this tunnel.

The Mobile Router may also be multihomed, which means having several network interfaces connected at the same time or sequentially to the Internet. As explained in [3], a node can get many benefits from multihoming, such as fault-recovery. Using multiple interfaces at the same time is the most interesting scenario, as it also allows to distribute flows amongst the available interfaces according to the user's policies. In a mobile

K. Cho and P. Jacquet (Eds.): AINTEC 2006, LNCS 4311, pp. 222–234, 2006.
© Springer-Verlag Berlin Heidelberg 2006

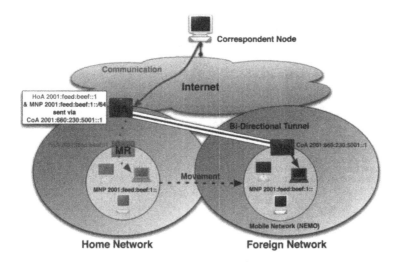

Fig. 1. NEMO Basic Support

environment, where connectivity may not be reliable all the time, Multiple Care-of Addresses registration (MCoA [4]) proposes an extension to Mobile IPv6 and NEMO Basic Support to be able to use several interfaces at the same time on the Mobile Node (being host or router). The MCoA protocol explains how the node can register several Care-of Addresses (each one identified by an unique number, the BID) at the same time, and for the same Home Address, to its Home Agent. This allows to maintain multiple IPv6-over-IPv6 tunnels between the Mobile Node and the Home Agent. The traffic destined to the Mobile Node or the HA can thus be shared amongst several tunnels (fig. 2) according to the user's policies.

NEMO Basic Support is thus a likely underlying architecture that can apply to the ITS (Intelligent Transportation System) in order to connect vehicles to the Internet [5], mountain rescue as presented in [6], or other emergency cases as discussed in the next section.

This paper is organized as follow: in section 2 we present a scenario where the use of Multiple Care-of Addresses registration will allow to deploy a fault-tolerant network for emergency cases. We explain in section 3 the basic principles of policy routing on the GNU/Linux operating system. Then we introduce in section 4 the MCoA implementation and detail its mechanisms. An evaluation is presented in section 5 to endorse the feasibility of our scenario.

2   Using IPv6 Mobility and Multihoming for Emergency Networks

When a disaster happens somewhere, there is a strong need to build a communication network, in order to be able to exchange vital information about the disaster's environment and magnitude with other sites. Such emergency network would be connected to the Internet via a router that need to be resistant to failures, and be able to send or receive traffic via different Internet access technologies according to their priority.

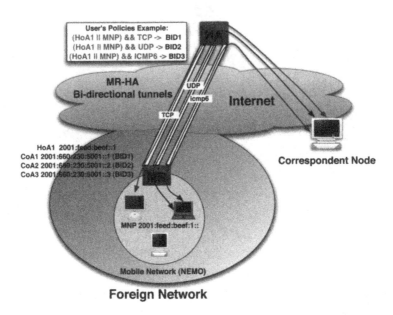

Fig. 2. MCoA registration to achieve flow distribution

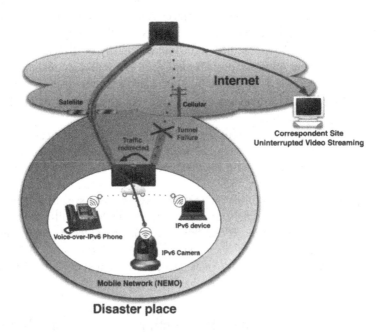

Fig. 3. The multihomed Mobile Router can survive to failures

In that case, a multihomed Mobile Router matches those requirements. The Mobile Router connects the Mobile Network to the Internet through several Internet accesses: Satellite, Cellular (3G), WiFi, Ethernet. Such a network is very easy to deploy: thanks to NEMO Basic Support, all nodes inside the NEMO (for example IPv6 sensors, cameras and videoconference tools) are directly reachable to their usual IPv6 addresses without the need to change the routing infrastructure. The Mobile Network would be geographically fixed but the Mobile Router's point of attachment to the Internet changes because it uses multiple interfaces. This endorses the need for a mobility protocol such as NEMO Basic Support.

As the MR is multihomed, the MCoA protocol allows to spread the traffic amongst several available interfaces according to the traffic type or the link characteristics. In addition, MCoA adds error resilience to existing networks as long as they are multihomed. Thanks to the multiple bindings, traffic would fall back from a broken interface to the highest priority interface still available. This way, as long as there is one interface available amongst all the egress interfaces, connection is maintained (fig. 3).

3   Policy Routing on GNU/Linux

3.1   Flow Distinction

Netfilter[1] is a packet filtering framework for the Linux 2.4 and 2.6 kernel series. It contains the **ip6tables** software used to setup rules for IPv6 packet filtering.

In the case of a multihomed node, we would like to distribute flows amongst several interfaces. We thus first have to categorize each flow according to our needs. This can be done with ip6tables by specifying a set of rules that match the flows we want to select, and give a target (an action to realize) for such flows.

The rules are usually based on fields located in the IPv6 or transport layer headers (for example the destination address, the UDP port etc.), and the target can be a packet marking, a request to drop the packets, etc.

The **mark** target which is of most interest to us in this paper, is a means of cross-layer communication for the various layers in the Linux networking stack. It is implemented as a 32 bits integer variable that is replicated within all shared structures that transport, network and datalink layers can pass to each other.

As an example, the following rules will mark with the integer value 10 (**-j MARK –set-mark 10**) all ICMPv6 packets (**-p icmpv6**) whose IPv6 source address is 2001:feed:beef::1 (**–source 2001:feed:beef::1**), and will drop (**-j DROP**) all UDP packets whose destination port is 1234 (**–dport 1234**).

```
ip6tables -A PREROUTING -t mangle
          -p icmpv6 --source 2001:feed:beef::1
          -j MARK --set-mark 10

ip6tables -A PREROUTING -t mangle
          -p udp --dport 1234
          -j DROP
```

For policy routing on a Mobile Node using MCoA, we decided to use the packet marking capability of the netfilter framework. Each rules' target will mark packets with

---

[1] http://www.netfilter.org

a number. Thus no interfaces names are ever used to define policy routing. Another part of the system will maintain a relation between the mark and the output interface used to send the matched packets. This allows the policy routing framework to be independent from the available interfaces on the node. One of the main advantage is that in case of an interface failure, ip6tables rules do not need to be changed, only the mark/interface relation has to be reorganized according to the user's preferences.

3.2 Routing Tables and Routing Policy Database

The Linux 2.6 kernel supports multiple routing tables. Beside the local (routes for local and broadcast addresses) and main (default standard routing table) ones, up to 252 additional routing tables can be used. Each routing table is independent and operates in the traditional mode. The routing policy database (RPDB) controls in which order the kernel parses the routing tables until a matching route is found.

A multihomed node can maintain in different routing tables a route via each of its interfaces connected to the Internet. Rules installed in the routing policy database will tell which routing tables to parse, and in which order, to find a matching route. For example, a rule can return the routing table where to look for a matching route according to a mark on a packet. The rules can thus make the relation between the mark on a packet and the output interface that will be used to send the packet (fig. 4).

Using ip6tables, the RPDB and multiple routing tables, IPv6 policy routing can be achieved on Linux. Section 4 explains in details how NEPL was extended to maintain the RPDB and the multiple routing tables, and how the Linux kernel was modified to support the mark selector in the RPDB.

4   Implementation Details

Multiple Care-of Addresses registration has been implemented on the GNU/Linux Operating System. The implementation has been realized within the Nautilus6 Project[2] in WIDE[3], and is freely available[4] to the public.

While the userland implementation, presented in section 4.1, takes care of the multiple MR-HA tunnels and bindings management, the kernel implementation overviewed in section 4.2 improves the IPv6 policy routing to be able to distribute different flows amongst multiple tunnels.

4.1   Userland

The implementation targets NEPL (NEMO Platform for Linux)[5], a freely available NEMO Basic Support implementation for Linux on 2.6 kernel. NEPL is based on MIPL2 (Mobile IPv6 for Linux) and has been developed and tested in cooperation between the Go-Core Project (Helsinki University of Technology) and Nautilus6.

---

[2] http://www.nautilus6.org

[3] http://www.wide.ad.jp

[4] http://software.nautilus6.org/MCoA/

[5] http://www.mobile-ipv6.org

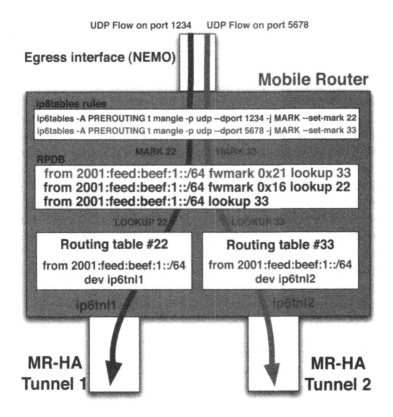

Fig. 4. The Routing Policy Database and routing decisions

We decided to implement MCoA on NEPL because NEPL is a feature-complete implementation. It currently supports Home Agent and Mobile Router, Implicit and Explicit registration modes and Dynamic Home Agent Address Discovery (DHAAD). It also supports some basic multihoming features, allowing the Mobile Router to use sequentially different Internet access technologies according to their availabilities and user's preferences. However, it does not support the use of multiple concurrent MR-HA tunnels, which is what we have brought through the MCoA implementation.

Interfaces and BID Management. The MCoA specification [4] defines a new Binding Unique Identifier number that allows to distinguish multiple bindings registered by a mobile node for the same HoA. A priority is also assigned to each binding.

When using the MCoA implementation on NEPL, the user assigns (in the NEPL configuration file) an unique BID and Binding priority to each interface he wants to use on his Mobile Node. For each interface that has a BID assigned, NEPL will try to register the CoA configured on the interface to the Home Agent, using the interface's BID as the Binding Identifier.

A user who wishes to send a flow via a specific interface will mark (with the ip6tables tool) the flow's packets using the BID of this interface as the mark target of the rule.

On the Home Agent side, the user can define restriction policies in the configuration file in order to forbid or allow MCoA registration for each HoA that can be registered on this HA.

Tunnel and Routing Table Management. When the Mobile Node boots with multiple interfaces connected to foreign networks, each interface will acquire a new CoA. Each CoA will be registered to the Home Agent, and an IPv6-over-IPv6 tunnel is setup on the Mobile Node and the Home Agent, between those two nodes, for each successful binding. NEPL has been extended to be able to maintain multiple concurrent tunnels at the same time.

On both the Mobile Node and the Home Agent, a route via the new tunnel is created for each new binding, and each route is stored in the routing table whose number matches the BID number of the binding. For example, if a tunnel is setup for a successful binding whose BID is 10, a route via this tunnel will be stored in the routing table 10.

The reader will notice that this limits the BID to be comprised between 1 and 252 (the minimum and maximum usable number for a routing table), whereas the MCoA specification allows a BID to take any value between 1 and 65535. We are working on this issue and hope to find a solution that will allow our implementation to be compliant with the specification.

Routing Policy Database Management. When a binding is successful, new rules are created by NEPL in the Routing Policy Database, on both the MR and the HA. Those rules tell that to find a matching route for the packets from or to the MR (packets whose source or destination is the MR's HoA) or from or to the Mobile Network (packets whose source or destination matches one of the NEMO's MNP) that are marked with a number equal to the binding's BID, the kernel has to lookup in the routing table whose number is the binding's BID.

Rules on the MR or the HA can be displayed with the **ip** command. The following rule, installed on the MR, tells that for all packets whose source address is 2001:feed:beef::1 (**from 2001:feed:beef::1**) and marked with the number 22 (**fwmark 0x16**, 0x16 equals 22 in hexadecimal), the kernel has to lookup the routing table number 22 (**lookup 22**).

```
from 2001:feed:beef::1 fwmark 0x16 lookup 22
```

Each time a binding is created or deleted, NEPL elects the binding whose priority is the highest, and use this binding as the default one. Thus several default rules are also setup in the RPDB, to lookup in the default binding's routing table in case a packet is not marked, or if no rules match the packet's mark. The following rule is a default rule, that all packets whose source address is 2001:feed:beef::1 will match:

```
from 2001:feed:beef::1 lookup 33
```

Rules are classified according to their priority, the kernel thus have a prioritized list of routing tables it can lookup to find a matching route for each packets. The following set of rules is typically the rules that are installed on a Mobile Router whose Home Address is 2001:feed:beef::1, owning the MNP 2001:feed:beef:1::/64, and using MCoA to register two interfaces with BID 22 and 33:

```
1000: from all to 2001:feed:beef:1::/64 lookup main
1001: from 2001:feed:beef::1 fwmark 0x21 lookup 33
1001: from 2001:feed:beef::1 fwmark 0x16 lookup 22
1002: from 2001:feed:beef::1 lookup 33
1005: from 2001:feed:beef:1::/64 fwmark 0x21 lookup 33
1005: from 2001:feed:beef:1::/64 fwmark 0x16 lookup 22
1006: from 2001:feed:beef:1::/64 lookup 33
```

NEPL can also dynamically update the rules upon some events. When an interface on the MR goes down and a binding is deleted, rules for this corresponding binding are removed. The Home Agent is notified of the failure thanks to a de-registration binding update sent by the MR that will delete the binding and rules corresponding to the failed interface. Packets marked with the deleted binding's BID will thus be routed through the default tunnel, on both the MR and the HA. This allow to easily redirect packets in case of an interface failure, without the need to change the ip6tables rules.

Handovers Verdict. NEPL was originally designed to support only one interface at the same time, and several interfaces sequentially. Thus a Mobile Node could perform either a horizontal handover (for example a handover from one access network to another using the same interface), or a vertical handover (for example moving the MN-HA tunnel from one failed interface to another available one). The current MCoA implementation restricts the handover verdicts to horizontal handovers only. If an interface goes down, no vertical handovers are performed to another interface to replace the failed one. Instead, the tunnel associated to the failed interface is destroyed, and all the traffic that was supposed to use the failed interface is redirected to another available MN-HA tunnel. MCoA simplifies the handover management.

4.2 Kernel

The actual state of the Routing Policy Database in the Linux kernel's IPv6 stack does not allow to use the packet mark as a selector for the policy routing rules. The Kernel implementation of mark-based routing is easily added to the current networking stack of the Linux Kernel using the following steps :

- Add the necessary hooks to specify the mark to be looked for in a rule of the RPDB. We need to add a new field to the RPDB entries too, and define the special case of a zero mark as the case where we ignore the mark. Otherwise, rules without mark would always fail to be recognized as default rules for marked packets. This means that the zero mark is unusable.
- Add the check for a specific mark when looking up rules, keeping in mind the special meaning of the zero mark : a *zero-marked* packet can not be matched by rules with a *non-zero mark*, but a *non-zero marked* packet can be matched by a rule with a *zero mark*.

While the hooks take care of the interface with userland, the latter point deals with the routing decision itself. A great advantage of this architecture is that we only define the route lookup table to be used, and the real routing decision is based on the alternate routing table contents.

5   Evaluation

To endorse our MCoA implementation on NEPL, we have setup a testbed that could be used in the scenario presented in section 2.

5.1   Topology

The Mobile Router is connected to the Internet via two egress interfaces (fig. 5). Both are registered to the Home Agent, the MR can thus share all the traffic coming from the NEMO amongst two tunnels. Each binding has a BID (22 and 33) and a priority (respectively 2 and 3) assigned.

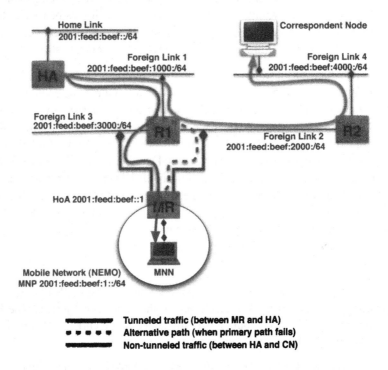

Fig. 5. The Testbed Topology

The goal of those tests is to measure the cutoff time when an interface fails while traffic is being sent over it. The test will be performed in both directions: from a MNN to a Correspondent Node (CN), and from a CN to a MNN.

5.2   Tools

VLC. A video is streamed between a CN and a MNN using the VLC media player[6]. VLC will stream the video using UDP, and allows to specify the destination port of the flow.

---

[6] http://www.videolan.org/

Tcpdump. In order to measure the cutoff time when a flow is redirected from one interface to another one, we use the tcpdump[7] software while the video streaming is ongoing.

5.3   Failure Recovery Test

From a MNN to a CN. In the first test, a MNN inside the NEMO streams some UDP traffic to a CN. The following rule at the MR allows to forward the traffic from the MNN to the interface whose BID is 22.

```
ip6tables -A PREROUTING -t mangle
          -p udp --dport 1234
          -j MARK --set-mark 22
```

The interface on the MR whose BID is 22 is then disconnected from its access network in order to simulate a failure. We calculate how long it takes for the MR to redirect the flow to the other available tunnel. After some time, we reconnect the failed interface to its access network, and calculate the handover time from the default tunnel to the recovered tunnel.

From a CN to a MNN. In the second test, the CN streams some UDP traffic to the MNN located in the NEMO. A similar ip6tables rules as for the previous test is installed on the Home Agent. The difference in this test will be the time taken by the MR to notify the failure to the HA. The interface whose BID is 22 is disconnected from its access network on the MR to simulate a failure. We calculate how long it takes to the HA to redirect the flow to another available tunnel. After some time, we reconnect the failed interface to its access network, and calculate the handover time from the default tunnel to the recovered tunnel on the HA.

5.4   Results

The results for both experiments are shown in fig. 6 and fig. 7. We plotted the latency for each packet with respect to the experiment elapsed time. According to the software environment (see section 5.2) and to the streamed file characteristics, the resulting UDP flow was made of 2 to 10 milliseconds spaced UDP packets. We thus are able to measure the impact of the access technology switching with a resolution of a few milliseconds.

Both figures are made of three parts. The first subfigures (fig. 6(a) and fig. 7(a)) show the latency for the whole experiment, whereas the next two subfigures show the latency for a very small time of the experiment around which a handover occurs. We can see in fig. 6(b) and fig. 7(b) the period immediately before and after the interface fails. Then, fig. 6(c) and fig. 7(c) show the period surrounding the interface recovery.

From a MNN to a CN. The latency of each packet is plotted in fig. 6(a) with respect to the packet arrival time. The latency for packets around the interface failure is plotted

---

[7] http://www.tcpdump.org/

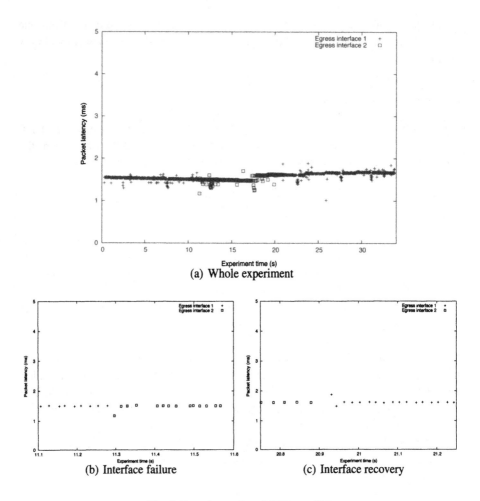

(a) Whole experiment

(b) Interface failure

(c) Interface recovery

Fig. 6. Experiment from MNN to a CN

in fig. 6(b). In this figure we can see that there is no visible impact of the interface switching consecutively to the interface failure.

In fig. 6(c) though, we can notice a 40 milliseconds gap between two packets of the flow. This gap is caused by the fact that as soon as the interface becomes ready, the Mobile Router tries to use it even though the Binding Update message has not been processed on the Home Agent yet. The high processing time of the Binding Update message comes from the architecture of the NEPL software itself, and this is currently under investigation.

From a CN to a MNN. For the second experiment, the same media file is streamed from a CN somewhere in the Internet, to a MNN attached to the Mobile Router. We can see from fig. 7(b) that when the interface fails, there is no communication disruption at all. Since the binding is already registered, there is no overhead in switching from the failed interface to the backup interface. In this communication direction, the MR sends the BU to remove the primary binding using the secondary interface as soon as

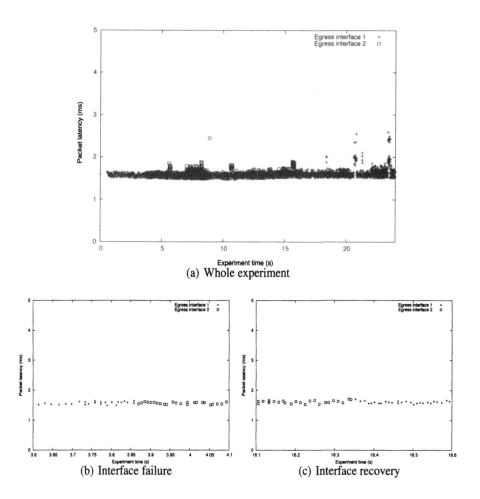

(a) Whole experiment

(b) Interface failure

(c) Interface recovery

Fig. 7. Experiment from a CN to a MNN

the primary one is known to have failed. However, according to the RTT between the HA and the MR, some packets might get lost.

When the interface recovers from failure (as seen on fig. 7(c)), there is no disruption either. The traffic is handed over to the primary interface as soon as the HA is notified of the new binding with a BU message.

6 Conclusion

In this paper, we have presented a new Multiple Care-of Addresses registration implementation on the GNU/Linux Operating System, based on the NEPL software. An use-case of this protocol has been presented in an emergency case scenario, where fault recovery and policy routing are two important requirements that can be achieved with MCoA. In order to validate this scenario, we have performed a practical experiment and showed that our implementation could match those requirements with good performance. The recovery time overhead for a failed link is just the round trip time of the signaling message plus the processing time on the Home Agent (currently forty milliseconds).

The handover time obtained in those tests can be compared to the horizontal handover time presented in [7] (section 4.7) and the vertical handover analysis presented in [8] (section 5).

Although the system presented in this paper is already useable, some improvements can be done on several aspects. We are working on a policy exchange mechanism between the Home Agent and the Mobile Router, that would allow easier deployments and allow both entities to dynamically update each other's policies. At the same time, as explained in section 5.4, we are investigating the cause for high processing times of Binding Update messages on the Home Agent side.

Acknowledgments

The authors would like to thank the Nautilus6 Project and its members for providing us all the necessary means to develop the work presented in this paper.

References

1. Johnson, D.B., Perkins, C., Arkko, J.: Mobility Support in IPv6. Request For Comments 3775, IETF (2004)
2. Devarapalli, V., Wakikawa, R., Petrescu, A., Thubert, P.: Network Mobility (NEMO) Basic Support Protocol. Request For Comments 3963, IETF (2005)
3. Ernst, T., Montavont, N., Wakikawa, R., Ng, C.W., Kuladinithi, K.: Motivations and Scenarios for Using Multiple Interfaces and Global Addresses. Internet Draft draft-ietf-monami6-multihoming-motivation-scenario-00, IETF (2006) Work in progress.
4. Wakikawa, R., Uehara, K., Ernst, T., Nagami, K.: Multiple Care-of Address Registration. Internet Draft draft-wakikawa-mobileip-multiplecoa-05.txt (2006)
5. Ernst, T., Uehara, K.: Connecting Automobiles to the Internet. In: ITST: 3rd International Workshop on ITS Telecommunications, Seoul, South Korea (2002)
6. McCarthy, B., Edwards, C., Dunmore, M.: Applying NEMO to a Mountain Rescue Domain. In: 1st International Workshop on Network Mobility (WONEMO), Sendai, Japan (2006) http://www.icoin.org/wonemo.
7. Kuntz, R., Mitsuya, K., Wakikawa, R.: Performance Evaluation of NEMO Basic Support Implementations. In: The First International Workshop on Network Mobility (WONEMO), Sendai, Japan (2006)
8. Lorchat, J., Kuntz, R.: Evaluation of NEMO Communications Using Hybrid Measurement. In: 6th International Conference on ITS Telecommunications (ITST), Chengdu, China (2006)

MANET and NEMO Converged Communication

Kouji Okada, Ryuji Wakikawa, and Jun Murai

Keio University. 5322 Endo Fujisawa Kanagawa, Japan
{okada, ryuji, jun}@sfc.wide.ad.jp

Abstract. In the near future, we expect many mobile networks (ex. vehicle in-side network, personal area network) are connected to the Internet and to the other mobile network to support rich applications for user's daliy life. There are several technology to connect these mobile networks to network and the Internet such as Mobile IP, Network Mobility (NEMO) and Mobile Ad-hoc Network (MANET). We specially investigate the use of both NEMO and MANET for efficient communication for an in-vehicle network. This paper proposes Mobile Gateway supporting policy based routing. It manages both NEMO connectivity and MANET connectivity and switches path to a destination according to application requirements and network environment. Our results shows this approach is efficient for vehicle network.

Keywords: Network Mobility, MANET, IPv6, Mobile Computing.

1 Introduction

A mobile network will be realized in the near future due to high demands from industry. We specially interested in a network inside vehicle which is the high interest area today. Vehicles will need to support several communication types such as vehicle-vehicle communication, vehicle-road communication, and vehicle-Internet communication. Vehicle-vehicle communication exchanges data between vehicles over wireless multihop networks like mobile ad-hoc networks. Some expected applications are like radio transmitters-receiver (radio communication), traffic updates, and traffic reports transmitted at the scene of the accident.

Vehicle-road communication can also be achieved through wireless multihop networks formed between the vehicle and the nodes installed at the traffic lights, and telephone poles. Some sensors and servers may be embedded at the roadside to communicate with vehicles. A roadside node can provide Internet connectivity to vehicles over the vehicle-road network, so if there is a shortage in the number of vehicles around to forward data the roadside nodes will help send the packets to enable vehicle-vehicle communications.

Vehicles can have Internet connectivity using a wide-range of communication medias such as cellular systems and wireless Metropolitan Area Network (MAN) systems. Since the connectivity is relatively stable and reliable compared to the vehicle-vehicle and vehicle-roadside communication, information such as driver safety and health conditions that requires high reliability should be achieved through vehicle-Internet communication.

K. Cho and P. Jacquet (Eds.): AINTEC 2006, LNCS 4311, pp. 235–251, 2006.

A vehicle can utilize various communication types simultaneously. For example, a vehicle can send or listen to updates on traffic accidents through vehicle-vehicle communication as well as notify driver or passengers health condition through vehicle-Internet communication. The question is how to achieve such a network environment. Though several network technologies exist, there is lack in coordination among the different technologies. The two fundamental technologies focused here are Network Mobility and Mobile Ad-hoc Networks that can support all vehicle communication types described above. The two technologies are converged by the mobile gateway system proposed in this paper.

This paper will first introduce fundamental technology for vehicles in Section 2. Then we show how to converge NEMO and MANET technology using Mobile Gateway systems, followed by related works in the area. The next section will report an experimental evaluation of vehicle-vehicle communication that takes place in a real live settings with a performance study on optimal route selection at mobile gateways. A performance evaluation on policy based routing is also conducted. Concluding observations are gathered in the final section.

2   Fundamental Technology

Various devices can be contained in the vehicles such as sensors, wearable devices carried on by passengers, and system control units such as the car engine. The number of these devices can range over a hundred. Some devices may not be extended because they only have computer resource to process sensing information.

In mobile ad-hoc networks and sensor networks, battery consumption has always been a critical issue due to limit in battery resource. Fortunately, the vehicle has a large rechargeable battery resource that can be used for devices. Compared to cell phones and other gadgets, the vehicle has larger space to install multiple devices and various network interfaces.

Taking into account about the 1500 million vehicles around the world, scalability at this level cannot be ignored, and the support for IPv6 in terms of a large available address space becomes a key issue to successfully deploy a vehicle network system. Thus, IPv6 is assumed as an IP in this paper.

2.1   Network Mobility and Mobile Ad-Hoc Network

From the view of a vehicle network, we take a position that it is necessary to apply network mobility support (i.e., the Network Mobility in IETF [4]) to an entire in-vehicle network in moving vehicles because only a representative mobile router needs to be mobility-aware; other individual nodes function without requiring mobility-aware functionality. Nevertheless, all in-vehicle nodes can be accessible from the Internet anywhere, anytime.

In addition, MANET is also key to establish wireless multihop networks among vehicles. Some recent work has focused on integrating MANET and the IPv6 Internet [6,15]. However, the emphasis has been on nodes moving between mobile ad-hoc networks and the Internet with Mobile IPv6 [5] to conceal their movements.

Network Mobility. Network Mobility (NEMO) [4] is a technology to provide movement transparency to a network. NEMO can be used to assign a permanent network prefix for in-vehicle network. NEMO is the Mobile IPv6 [5] extensions to bind a permanent prefix (called mobile network prefix) and a care-of address which a node acquires at a visiting network. Even if an automobile moves and changes its network attachment, the network in the automobile is always reachable with the same network address all the time.

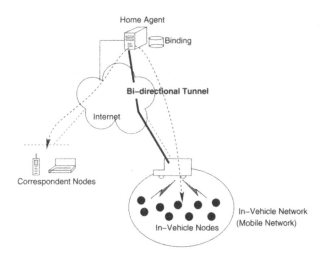

Fig. 1. The NEMO Basic Support Protocol

Figure 1 shows the configuration and operations of the NEMO basic support protocol [4]. A mobile router carries a mobile network prefix that is assigned to each vehicle. The mobile router has two network interfaces which is attached to the Internet (egress interface) and to the mobile network (ingress interface). The mobile router acquires a care-of address at the egress interface as same as Mobile IPv6. To register a binding, the mobile router needs to notify its mobile network prefixes to the home agent with a mobile network prefix sub-option defined in the NEMO basic support protocol. Once the mobile router registers its binding, it establishes a bi-directional tunnel with the home agent. The NEMO basic support protocol does not support route optimization. Thus communication with a mobile network in vehicle is always through a home agent.

Mobile Ad-Hoc Network. A Mobile Ad-hoc Network (MANET) is another key technology for vehicles. MANET is created dynamically when a set of nodes form a mesh routing state for their connectivity management, typically over a wireless multihop network. Even when a network topology is changed due to vehicle's movements, MANET routing protocols can recover connectivity by updating route information periodically Many routing protocols are proposed for MANET. These protocols aim to maintain localized routing at individual nodes despite movement of intermediate nodes that causes the routing path to change. Ad-hoc On-demand Distance Vector (AODV) [12] and Optimized Link State Routing Protocol (OLSR) [2], etc. are standardized at the MANET working group. OLSR is a link state routing protocol and exchanges route information periodically among nodes inside a mobile ad-hoc network. It has an optimized flooding mechanism called Multi Point Relay (MPR) [7]. To disseminate route information,each node needs to flood route information to a network. However this flooding causes high overhead to a wireless network. Therefore, MPR provides efficient mechanism not to flood duplicated packets.

An internet gateway [15] provides global connectivity to a mobile ad-hoc network. The internet gateway is a fixed gateway attached to both the Internet and a mobile ad-hoc network. It supplies global prefix information and IPv6 global address to a mobile ad-hoc network. The internet gateway advertises prefix information and a route to the Internet. The prefix distributed by the internet gateway can be used for configuring a (topologically global) routable IPv6 [3] address for each MANET node.

3   Convergence of NEMO and MANET

We introduce *mobile gateways* that provide enhanced routing in addition to the mobile router support specified in the NEMO basic support protocol. This enhanced routing provides efficient vehicle-vehicle and vehicle-road communication This contribution provides crucial routing necessary in connecting vehicles to the Internet.

3.1   Mobile Gateway

A mobile gateway is a nominated router from an in-vehicle nodes and is responsible for mobility and always-on Internet connectivity. The main functions of a mobile gateway are a roll of a Mobile Router of the NEMO basic support protocol and a roll of MANET Router of a MANET routing protocol.

The mobile gateway in vehicle equips with various interfaces such as wireless WAN (ex. cellular), wireless MAN (ex. 802.16e), wireless LAN (ex. 802.11b) and MANET interface (ex. 802.11b ad-hoc mode). The mobile gateway also has an interface to connect to its in-vehicle network. All these interfaces of the mobile gateway should be configured with different radio channels and radio frequency so that packets sent by each interface does not interfere with one another.

Each mobile gateway assigns a mobile network prefix to its in-vehicle network. All nodes inside the vehicle must use the permanent address generated from the mobile network prefix for all communication. All traffic sent from the in-vehicle network to a remote network are always intercepted and routed by the mobile gateway, because the mobile gateway is a default router of all nodes inside vehicle network.

The mobile gateway acquires a care-of address at an interface attached to the Internet. It then registers the care-of address to its home agent. The mobile gateway is assumed to maintain a bi-directional tunnel between the mobile gateway

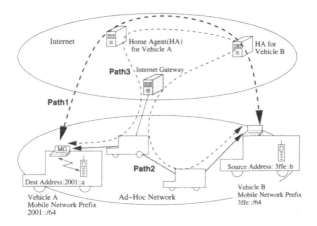

Fig. 2. Mobile Gateways

and the home agent all the time by using wireless WAN or MAN interface as shown in Figure 2 (denoted as path1). It may switch the interface for the Internet connectivity according to coverage of each wireless technology.

In addition, the mobile gateway run a MANET routing protocol at a MANET interface all the time so that it can acquire routes of adjacent vehicles (denoted as path2 in Figure 2). The mobile gateway exchanges only a route of a permanent prefix assigned to its in-vehicle network by a MANET routing protocol. These network route exchanges are preferable in terms of route aggregatation to reduce number of routes which each vehicle manages by a MANET routing protocol. If there is an internet gateway at road sides or traffic lights , the vehicle may use the internet gateway to access to the Internet (path3 in Figure 2. In this case, the mobile gateway must use the NEMO basic support protocol to reach to a destination node. Otherwise, the packets may be rejected at the internet gateway due to ingress filtering.

3.2   Multiplexed Path Toward a Destination

When an in-vehicle node starts to communicate to a destination node, there are several route paths towards the destination node. Figure 3 summarizes possible paths between an in-vehicle node and a destination. The first path is used when a mobile gateway routes packets to the Internet through its bidirectional tunnel by using one of wireless WAN, MAN, LAN interfaces. The second path has MANET paths between an internet gateway and a mobile gateway. However, the mobile gateway must encapsulates all packets to the home agent. It has to route encapsulated packets to the internet gateway first and the internet gateway routes packets to the Internet (via Home Agent). This path can be utilized when the first path is not established due to out of wireless coverage areas. The third path is directly connected between end nodes over a mobile ad-hoc network. Since a mobile gateway has a prefix route of a vehicle to which

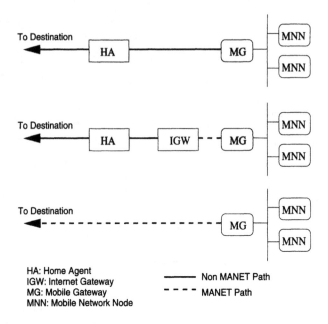

Fig. 3. Mobile Gateways

a destination node is belong, it can route packets according to the prefix route without packet encapsulation. The mobile gateway can bypass its Home Agent even if the packets' source address is generated from the mobile network prefix.

3.3   Policy Based Routing

As described in Section 3.2, a mobile gateway has various routes to deliver packets to a destination node. The mobile gateway has to determine which routes are appropriate for outgoing traffic from its in-vehicle network. The decision is made with preference information and three parameters such as bandwidth, round trip time, and hop count.

These parameters are measured during communications and route exchange of a MANET routing protocol. The bandwidth parameter is not need to be so precise, but we use estimated bandwidth value. For example, CDMA2000 1x EvDo has 2.4M-bits/sec bandwidth in specification, but actual speed is 700K-bits/sec when we measured average bandwidth with a real NEMO basic support protocol implementation. Therefore, a mobile gateway set EvDo bandwidth as 700K-bits/sec. On the other hand, the bandwidth of a MANET path is estimated according to a link distance of a MANET path between end nodes. Each vehicle is reasonably assumed to have Global Position System (GPS) and exchange link distance information by a MANET routing protocol. If there is a link which distance is very long between two vehicles, the bandwidth can be assumed to be low. Since bandwidth can not be measured in real time due to measurement overhead, we take a position that such an estimation is reasonable for the decision. The hop count parameter is acquired by a MANET routing protocol.

Most of MANET routing protocols provides the hop count for a destination to a mobile gateway.

Preference information is also introduced to prioritize the path selection depending on parameters. The information contains information of a required network of each application like delay sensitive network and stability network, etc. Preference information is sent to a destination in order to decide which path is used for vehicle-vehicle communication at the destination vehicle. It is preferable that a destination vehicle follows the same decision of the source mobile gateway.

3.4 Advantages of Mobile Gateway

A mobile gateway is a simple solution but it comes with plenty of advantages for vehicle's network listed below.

- Address assignment
  A mobile gateway employees NEMO basic support protocol and acquires a mobile network prefix for its network. By using the NEMO basic support protocol, each vehicle will have a permanent network prefix for the vehicle's network. In a mobile ad-hoc network, address assignments on a mobile ad-hoc network is complicated due to no center authority to assign address and no efficient mechanism to verify address uniqueness in a mobile ad-hoc network. Therefore, a mobile gateway solves address configuration problem of a mobile ad-hoc network in terms of permanent prefix assignment of the NEMO basic support protocol.
- Efficient communication
  When a vehicle only uses the NEMO basic support protocol, all packets are transmitted and received through a bi-directional tunnel established between a mobile router and a home agent. This becomes network bottleneck in terms of network delay and network bandwidth. On the other hand, if a vehicle only supports a MANET routing protocol, it has to transmits packets to a wireless multihop path even if the path quality become worse due to less stability and large hop counts. A mobile gateway in a vehicle always changes the path to a destination depending on the vehicle's network environment and user's preference. It can even selects an appropriate path per flow or applications and uses multiple paths at the same time.
- Fault tolerance
  Since a vehicle is moving, network environment varies quickly. Thus, communication may stop due to out of coverage area. However, a mobile gateway always maintains multiple path to the Internet and a destination. The mobile gateway detects the path break and can re-select an alternative active path for the failed path.
- Always-on Internet connectivity
  A mobile gateway is capable to handle multiple network interfaces and multiple path to the Internet. Not only wireless WAN, MAN and LAN, but also internet gateways can be used to access to the Internet. Even if one of network interface becomes out of coverage, a mobile gateway always has

alternative path to the Internet. Since many applications assume always-on Internet connectivity, this feature is necessary for vehicle's network.
– Scalability
A mobile gateway always exchanges network routes of its mobile network prefix with other vehicles by a MANET routing protocol. This route aggregation leads scalability when a number of vehicles run on a same road and exchange routes. Without a mobile gateway, all the nodes inside a vehicle needs to exchange host route with devices of other vehicles. If hundreds of devices are installed in each vehicle, the number of routes that each vehicle manages will explode. It is clearly not efficient technique for vehicle's network.

4   Related Work

There are few existing solutions to provide Internet connectivity to the MANET (e.g., [10, 14]) and to integrate Mobile IPv4 [11] and Mobile IPv6 [5] and an ad-hoc network (e.g., [9, 8, 6, 15, 1]). A DSR-based MANET is connected to the Internet with Mobile IPv6 in [9]. MIPMANET [6] integrates Mobile IPv4 and AODV utilizing *Foreign Agents* to support mobile nodes in a mobile ad-hoc network. Although Mobile IP can be integrated in our system, we focus on network mobility and not on host mobility. The approach in [15] proposes to use an Internet Gateway to connect a MANET to the Internet, by extending MANET messages for Gateway discovery and route establishment. Here, we integrate MANET routing with a mobile router for best Internet connectivity.

5   Experimental Evaluation

Three different experiments are conducted for evaluation. First is the throughput of vehicle-vehicle communication using vehicles and equipment in a real world setting. The next is the efficiency of a mobile gateway in view of scalability of a MANET routing protocols for vehicle-vehicle networks. Then the efficiency of our approach in vehicle-vehicle communication is seen in terms of bandwidth.

OLSR routing protocol is implemented with IPv6 support on GNU Zebra. Since the GNU Zebra is a multi platformed implementation, the OLSR can run on BSD and Linux. The OLSR implementation supports preference information distribution for policy based routing. The OLSR implementation and "ipfilter" program has been combined. The ipfilter is used to switch data flow between MANET and NEMO according to policy when a mobile gateway enables policy based routing.

5.1   Throughput of Vehicle-Vehicle Communication

In this experiment, a relationship between vehicle distance and network throughput is verified. This is an assumption of policy based routing to get estimated bandwidth from a link distance on mobile gateways. Three vehicles are set up in a real world with an OLSR router and 802.11b interface. OLSR can work with a single interface to relay packets, but in this experiment one of the vehicle has two 802.11b interfaces to relay packets between end vehicles. This is because the coverage area of each 802.11b interface is limited. There are no topology changes during throughput measurements. Throughput is measured with UDP stream by netperf' program every 8 seconds. The source vehicle sends 1280 bytes UDP datagram to the destination vehicle. The equipments used are listed in Table 1. All routers have FreeBSD 4.10-RELEASE with KAME IPv6 patches (kame-20041213-freebsd410-snap) installed. Our OLSR v6 implementation is running on all vehicles.

Table 1. Equipments

CPU	Memory	Wireless device
PentiumM 1.40Ghz	256MB	Melco inc. WLI-PCM-L11GP
PentiumM 1.40Ghz	256MB	Melco inc. WLI-PCM-L11GP
PentiumIII 1.06Ghz	640MB	Intersim Prism 2.5 Melco inc. WLI-PCM-L11

Figure 4 shows the test driving course used to measure throughput for vehicle-vehicle communication. Because this test course is located on the university campus, there is no traffic other than the three test vehicles.

Fig. 4. Test course for throughput measurements

The distance as well as the speed of each vehicle has been altered. The speed varies from 20km to 40km, while the distance varies from either less than 20m or over 100m. Figure 5 6 7 shows the average throughput when vehicles move in 20km/h, 30km/h and 40km/h.

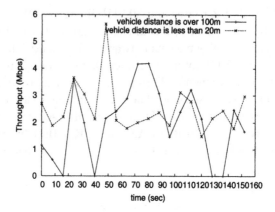

Fig. 5. Throughput when each vehicle drives in 20km/h

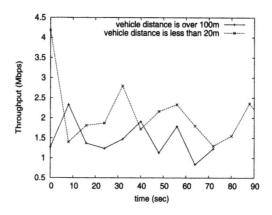

Fig. 6. Throughput when each vehicle drives in 30km/h

In all scenarios, disconnection occurs due to limits on the coverage area of 802.11b interface (about 150m). There is also interference from other 802.11b access points which are installed in buildings around campus. The disconnection also occurs when vehicles drive at blind corners. An obvious difference is seen in the throughput. The vehicle distance at 20m is better than the vehicle distance at over 100m. The average throughput for close distance is 2.35M-bits/sec and the average throughput for the farther distance is 1.41M-bits/sec.

Results from this experiment, show that there is a relationship between vehicle distance and network throughput. It is always better to create routes through nearby neighbors. Having more vehicles in the vicinity would be a preferable environment for better results in a vehicle network systems.

5.2   Efficiency of Mobile Gateway

This section evaluates whether the use of a mobile gateway is efficient for moving vehicles. Even if an in-vehicle network is also a mobile ad-hoc network,

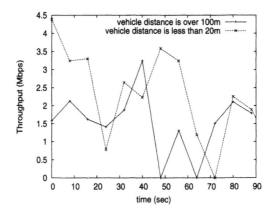

Fig. 7. Throughput when each vehicle drives in 40km/h

a mobile gateway aggregates routes of its in-vehicle mobile ad-hoc network and advertises the routes to other vehicles. In such cases it is our interest to see how performance will differ from the flat mobile ad-hoc network (i.e. all nodes inside vehicle exchange routes with nodes in other vehicles).

We implemented mobile gateways on a simulator and used AODV for local connectivity and OLSR for adjacent mobile gateways management as a case study. 30 mobile gateways were moving 10km on a rectangular flat space [10000m x 50m] for 600 seconds of simulated time (Figure 8). We tested two scenarios when all the vehicles move in same direction and half of the vehicles move in opposite direction like in Figure 8. A mobile gateway had two 802.11 compatible wireless interfaces, one as an interface for vehicle's wireless multihop network and the other as an interface for a vehicle's network. The radio propagation range was 200 meters and the channel bandwidth 2 M-bits/sec. AODV was used for the local routing management and OLSR for inter-mobile gateway connectivity. Mobile gateways are capable to route packets from local AODV MANET to the OLSR MANET. This was tested in one simulation. Constant Bit Rate (CBR) was selected as communication source to measure packet delivery ratio and routing protocol overheads. 4 randomly selected nodes sent two packets every second to a remote AODV MANET node.

The MANET carried by a mobile gateway is compared to a genuine OLSR MANET which local and inter connectivity is managed by every MANET nodes with neither mobile gateways and the NEMO basic protocol concept. Every MANET nodes exchange routes by OLSR and communicate directly to the destination not through mobile gateway. Four different experiments were simulated to compare the performance between the MANETs carrying by a mobile gateway (i.e. OLSR and AODV combination) and genuine OLSR MANETs. Figures 9 10 11 show results of this experiments. Each lines in Figures indicate 1) MANETs with mobile gateways moving in same direction , 2) genuine OLSR MANETs moving in same direction, 3) MANETs with mobile gateways driving in opposite direction, and 4) genuine OLSR MANETs moving in opposite direction.

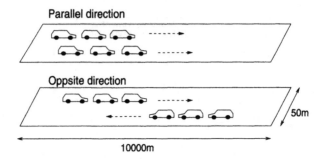

Fig. 8. Simulation Scenario

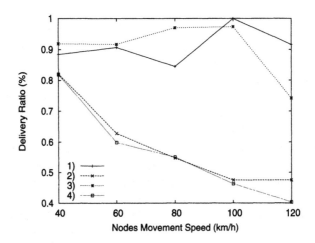

Fig. 9. Delivery Ratio versus Movement Speed

Figure 9 illustrates the performance of a mobile gateway in terms of delivery ratio depending on the speed of movement. Movement speed varies between 40km/h and 120km/h and distance between nodes is varied from 40m to 120m depending on the actual speed. Figure 9 depict two cases where vehicles are either driving in the same direction or not.

Figure 10 shows the average of hop counts of all delivered packets. The hop count when end-nodes pass over is smaller than others, because the absolute speed of each end-node becomes the total of the end-nodes' moving speed. Routing exchanges with on-coming MANET nodes requires frequent updates and causes considerable overhead to the MANET routing protocol due to topology changes.

When end-nodes are moving in the same direction, route exchanges are stable due to the small absolute speed. If the distance between nodes are long in relation to the movement speed, the average of hop count is increased. The node density within the transmission range of an ad-hoc internet is also influenced by the hop count. The density of nodes also influences the performance of the Multi Point Replay (MPR) flooding algorithm [7] used in OLSR. Our mobile gateway model

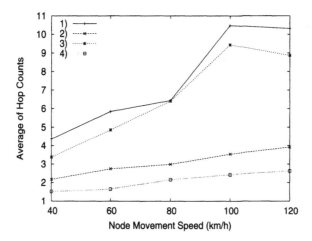

Fig. 10. Average of Hop Count versus Node Movement Speed

shows similar averages as the flat OLSR model except for about one additional hop required between an end node and a mobile gateway.

5.3 Efficiency of Policy Based Routing

In this experiment, the efficiency of policy based routing is evaluated. This experiment shows how a mobile gateway operates multiple paths for applications. Figure 12 is the network configuration of this experiment. We use vehicle traffic emulator called "Hakoniwa server". The Hakoniwa server gives driving speed, positioning information, and driving direction by emulating the driving environment

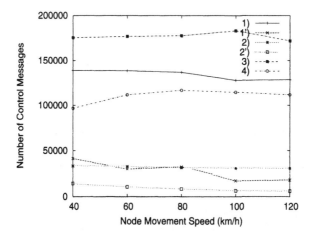

Fig. 11. Protocol Overhead versus Node Movement Speed: 1' and 2' indicate the number of AODV control messages for local connectivity management at each simulations

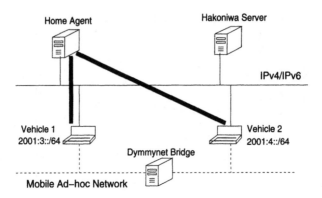

Fig. 12. Overview of Experimental Testbeds

of vehicles. The information can be accessed to the Hakoniwa server over the Internet. The Hakoniwa server is configured to emulate 100 vehicles driving around Nagoya city.

Table 2. Equipments

Type	CPU	Memory
Vehicle1	PentiumM 1.40Ghz	256MB
Vehicle2	Pentium 3 Mobile 1.20Ghz	1024MB
Home Agent	Pentium 4 Mobile 2.00Ghz	512MB
Hakoniwa Server	Xeon 3.06Ghz x 4	6.23GB

Two vehicles are randomly selected to evaluate throughput of vehicle-vehicle communication. According to the positioning information, the network environment is emulated by using "Dymmynet". Dymmynet is used to simulate network environment with various configuration of bandwidth limitations, delays and packet losses. The bandwidth is altered according to the distance of two vehicles. Buffalo's specification [13] is used to set the bandwidth transition according to the wireless distance. The NEMO basic support protocol is also emulated by using the Home Agent acting as a tunnel server. Since all traffic are sent through a bi-directional tunnel of the NEMO basic support protocol, we replaced the NEMO basic support protocol to a tunnel server and clients to eliminates binding management overheads. The path established by the NEMO basic support protocol (i.e. NEMO path) is also limited to 700 K-bits/sec at all time by a network switch. The 700K-bits/sec is the average throughput of CDMA 2000 1x EvDo. This throughput is actually measured with the NEMO basic support protocol implementation and the CDMA 2000 1x EvDo card. The throughput is almost constant to 700 K-bits/sec. Two vehicles are emulated on a laptop with an Ethernet link shaped by Dymmynet. The OLSRv6 implementation is run to establish a MANET path with ipfilter program to support policy based routing on each vehicle, however two vehicles are connected directly and bandwidth is varied by Dymmynet according to vehicle distance. The OLSR6 implementation is used to exchange preference information and three parameters for policy based routing. All vehicles have NetBSD 1.6.2-RELEASE installed and the home agent running on FreeBSD-5.3 RELEASE. The Hokoniwa server is run with Fedra Core release 2. Table 2 shows the specification of each computer.

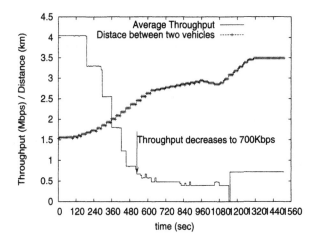

Fig. 13. Throughput transition when MANET is used

Figure 14 and 13 show the relationship between the network throughput of vehicle-vehicle communication and the distance of two vehicles. The throughput was measured with "netperf" program by sending UDP 1280 bytes every 8 seconds. Figure 13 shows when the mobile gateway does not support policy based routing, it continues to use the MANET path for vehicle-vehicle communication even if the bandwidth becomes lower than 700K-bits/sec at 528 seconds in Figure 13. This is because the mobile gateway has a network route of the destination vehicle acquired by the OLSR6 and the network route is always selected due to the long address match algorithm of the routing table lookup. Therefore, even if the link quality is worse than the path of NEMO basic support protocol, it continues to use the worse path for the vehicle-vehicle communication.

On the other hand, in Figure 14, policy based routing is enabled. The mobile gateway is configured to switch a path from the MANET path to the NEMO path when the estimated bandwidth of the MANET path is decreased to 700K-bits/sec (at 512 seconds in Figure 14). If the bandwidth is lower than 700K-bits/sec, there is no reason to continue using the MANET path. The NEMO path is stable and constant compared to the MANET path.

This experimentation shows that our OLSR6 implementation can adopt to network environment changes such as decline of bandwidth by switching a path

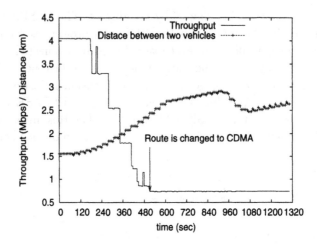

Fig. 14. Throughput transition when MANET and NEMO are used

between a MANET path and a NEMO path. Even if the path is switched, the connection can be still alive because of the use of the permanent address. In this paper, although we only uses the link distance and the bandwidth estimation as parameters of policy based routing, a mobile gateway can be easily extended to support other parameters.

6   Conclusion

We investigated the integration of the NEMO basic support protocol and MANET by the proposed mobile gateways as enhancements to mobile routers of the NEMO basic support protocol. Such an integration is key to deploying vehicle network in the real world. A mobile gateway establishes ad-hoc connectivity with other mobile gateways by a MANET routing protocol and utilizes the additional route only when it is necessary for applications to exploit an optimized route in terms of absence of a bi-directional tunnel. Policy based routing is also introduced to manage multiple paths between two vehicles. We conducted three experiments to show how a mobile gateway is efficient for vehicle communications.

References

1. M. Benzaid, P. Minet, and K. Al Agha. A framework for integrating Mobile-IP and OLSR ad-hoc networking for future wireless mobile systems. In *Proceedings of the 1st Mediterranean Ad-Hoc Networks workshop (Med-Hoc-Net)*, September 2002.
2. T. Clausen and P. Jacquet. Optimized Link State Routing Protocol OLSR. Request for Comments (Experimental) 3561, Internet Engineering Task Force, October 2003.
3. S. Deering and R. Hinden. Internet Protocol, Version 6 (ipv6) Specification. Request for Comments (Proposed Standard) 1883, Internet Engineering Task Force, December 1995.

4. V. Devaraplli, R. Wakikawa, A. Petrescu, and P. Thubert. Network Mobility (NEMO) Basic Support Protocol (proposed standard). Request for Comments 3963, Internet Engineering Task Force, January 2005.
5. D. Johnson, C. Perkins, and J. Arkko. Mobility support in IPv6. Request for Comments (Proposed Standard) 3775, Internet Engineering Task Force, June 2004.
6. U. Johnsson, F. Alriksson, T. Larsson, P. Johannson, and G. Maquire Jr. MIP-MANET - Mobile Ip for Mobile Ad hoc Networks. In *Proceedings of First Annual Workshop on Mobile Ad Hoc Networking and Computing (Mobihoc)*, August 2000.
7. A. Laouiti, A. Qayyum, and L. Viennot. Multipoint Relaying: An Efficient Technique for Flooding in Mobile Wireless Networks. In *Proceedings of the 35th Annual Hawaii International Conference on System Sciences (HICSS'2002)*, 2002.
8. H. Lei and C. E. Perkins. Ad Hoc Networking with Mobile IP. In *Proceedings of 2nd European Personal Mobile Communication Conference*, September 1997.
9. D. A. Maltz, J. Broch, and D. B. Johnson. Quantitative Lessons From a Full-Scale Multi-Hop Wireless Ad Hoc Network Testbed. In *Proceedings of the IEEE Wireless Communications and Networking Conference*, September 2000.
10. G. Cirincione M.S. Corson, J.P. Macker. Internet-based mobile ad hoc networking. In *IEEE Internet Computing, Vol.3, No. 4*, pages 63–70, Jul 1999.
11. C. Perkins. IP Mobility Support. Request for Comments (Proposed Standard) 2002, Internet Engineering Task Force, October 1996.
12. C. Perkins, E. Belding-Royer, and S. Das. Ad hoc On-Demand Distance Vector (AODV) Routing. Request for Comments (Experimental) 3561, Internet Engineering Task Force, July 2003.
13. Buffalo Specification. Web page, May 2005. http://buffalo.melcoinc.co.jp/products/new/2002/064_2.html (in Japanese), http://www.melcoinc.com/english/.
14. A. Striegel, R. Ramanujan, and J. Bonney. A protocol independent internet gateway for ad-hoc wireless networks. In *Proceedings of Local Computer Networks (LCN 2001)*, Tampa, Florida, Nov 2001.
15. R. Wakikawa, J. Malinen, C. Perkins, A. Nilsson, and A. Tuominen. Global Connectivity for IPv6 Mobile Ad Hoc Networks (work in progress, draft-wakikawa-manet-globalv6-05). Internet Draft, Internet Engineering Task Force, March 2005.

Author Index

Lecture Notes in Computer Science

For information about Vols. 1–4213

please contact your bookseller or Springer

Vol. 4256: L. Feng, G. Wang, C. Zeng, R. Huang (Eds.), Web Information Systems – WISE 2006 Workshops. XIV, 320 pages. 2006.

Vol. 4255: K. Aberer, Z. Peng, E.A. Rundensteiner, Y. Zhang, X. Li (Eds.), Web Information Systems – WISE 2006. XIV, 563 pages. 2006.

Vol. 4254: T. Grust, H. Höpfner, A. Illarramendi, S. Jablonski, M. Mesiti, S. Müller, P.-L. Patranjan, K.-U. Sattler, M. Spiliopoulou (Eds.), Current Trends in Database Technology – EDBT 2006. XXXI, 932 pages. 2006.

Vol. 4253: B. Gabrys, R.J. Howlett, L.C. Jain (Eds.), Knowledge-Based Intelligent Information and Engineering Systems, Part III. XXXII, 1301 pages. 2006. (Sublibrary LNAI).

Vol. 4252: B. Gabrys, R.J. Howlett, L.C. Jain (Eds.), Knowledge-Based Intelligent Information and Engineering Systems, Part II. XXXIII, 1335 pages. 2006. (Sublibrary LNAI).

Vol. 4251: B. Gabrys, R.J. Howlett, L.C. Jain (Eds.), Knowledge-Based Intelligent Information and Engineering Systems, Part I. LXVI, 1297 pages. 2006. (Sublibrary LNAI).

Vol. 4249: L. Goubin, M. Matsui (Eds.), Cryptographic Hardware and Embedded Systems - CHES 2006. XII, 462 pages. 2006.

Vol. 4248: S. Staab, V. Svátek (Eds.), Managing Knowledge in a World of Networks. XIV, 400 pages. 2006. (Sublibrary LNAI).

Vol. 4247: T.-D. Wang, X. Li, S.-H. Chen, X. Wang, H. Abbass, H. Iba, G. Chen, X. Yao (Eds.), Simulated Evolution and Learning. XXI, 940 pages. 2006.

Vol. 4246: M. Hermann, A. Voronkov (Eds.), Logic for Programming, Artificial Intelligence, and Reasoning. XIII, 588 pages. 2006. (Sublibrary LNAI).

Vol. 4245: A. Kuba, L.G. Nyúl, K. Palágyi (Eds.), Discrete Geometry for Computer Imagery. XIII, 688 pages. 2006.

Vol. 4244: S. Spaccapietra (Ed.), Journal on Data Semantics VII. XI, 267 pages. 2006.

Vol. 4243: T. Yakhno, E.J. Neuhold (Eds.), Advances in Information Systems. XIII, 420 pages. 2006.

Vol. 4242: A. Rashid, M. Aksit (Eds.), Transactions on Aspect-Oriented Software Development II. IX, 289 pages. 2006.

Vol. 4241: R.R. Beichel, M. Sonka (Eds.), Computer Vision Approaches to Medical Image Analysis. XI, 262 pages. 2006.

Vol. 4239: H.Y. Youn, M. Kim, H. Morikawa (Eds.), Ubiquitous Computing Systems. XVI, 548 pages. 2006.

Vol. 4238: Y.-T. Kim, M. Takano (Eds.), Management of Convergence Networks and Services. XVIII, 605 pages. 2006.

Vol. 4237: H. Leitold, E. Markatos (Eds.), Communications and Multimedia Security. XII, 253 pages. 2006.

Vol. 4236: L. Breveglieri, I. Koren, D. Naccache, J.-P. Seifert (Eds.), Fault Diagnosis and Tolerance in Cryptography. XIII, 253 pages. 2006.

Vol. 4234: I. King, J. Wang, L. Chan, D. Wang (Eds.), Neural Information Processing, Part III. XXII, 1227 pages. 2006.

Vol. 4233: I. King, J. Wang, L. Chan, D. Wang (Eds.), Neural Information Processing, Part II. XXII, 1203 pages. 2006.

Vol. 4232: I. King, J. Wang, L. Chan, D. Wang (Eds.), Neural Information Processing, Part I. XLVI, 1153 pages. 2006.

Vol. 4231: J. F. Roddick, R. Benjamins, S. Si-Saïd Cherfi, R. Chiang, C. Claramunt, R. Elmasri, F. Grandi, H. Han, M. Hepp, M. Hepp, M. Lytras, V.B. Mišić, G. Poels, I.-Y. Song, J.D. Trujillo, C. Vangenot (Eds.), Advances in Conceptual Modeling - Theory and Practice. XXII, 456 pages. 2006.

Vol. 4230: C. Priami, A. Ingólfsdóttir, B. Mishra, H.R. Nielson (Eds.), Transactions on Computational Systems Biology VII. VII, 185 pages. 2006. (Sublibrary LNBI).

Vol. 4229: E. Najm, J.F. Pradat-Peyre, V.V. Donzeau-Gouge (Eds.), Formal Techniques for Networked and Distributed Systems - FORTE 2006. X, 486 pages. 2006.

Vol. 4228: D.E. Lightfoot, C.A. Szyperski (Eds.), Modular Programming Languages. X, 415 pages. 2006.

Vol. 4227: W. Nejdl, K. Tochtermann (Eds.), Innovative Approaches for Learning and Knowledge Sharing. XVII, 721 pages. 2006.

Vol. 4226: R.T. Mittermeir (Ed.), Informatics Education – The Bridge between Using and Understanding Computers. XVII, 319 pages. 2006.

Vol. 4225: J.F. Martínez-Trinidad, J.A. Carrasco Ochoa, J. Kittler (Eds.), Progress in Pattern Recognition, Image Analysis and Applications. XIX, 995 pages. 2006.

Vol. 4224: E. Corchado, H. Yin, V. Botti, C. Fyfe (Eds.), Intelligent Data Engineering and Automated Learning – IDEAL 2006. XXVII, 1447 pages. 2006.

Vol. 4223: L. Wang, L. Jiao, G. Shi, X. Li, J. Liu (Eds.), Fuzzy Systems and Knowledge Discovery. XXVIII, 1335 pages. 2006. (Sublibrary LNAI).

Vol. 4222: L. Jiao, L. Wang, X. Gao, J. Liu, F. Wu (Eds.), Advances in Natural Computation, Part II. XLII, 998 pages. 2006.

Vol. 4221: L. Jiao, L. Wang, X. Gao, J. Liu, F. Wu (Eds.), Advances in Natural Computation, Part I. XLI, 992 pages. 2006.

Vol. 4220: C. Priami, G. Plotkin (Eds.), Transactions on Computational Systems Biology VI. VII, 247 pages. 2006. (Sublibrary LNBI).

Vol. 4219: D. Zamboni, C. Kruegel (Eds.), Recent Advances in Intrusion Detection. XII, 331 pages. 2006.

Vol. 4218: S. Graf, W. Zhang (Eds.), Automated Technology for Verification and Analysis. XIV, 540 pages. 2006.

Vol. 4217: P. Cuenca, L. Orozco-Barbosa (Eds.), Personal Wireless Communications. XV, 532 pages. 2006.

Vol. 4216: M.R. Berthold, R. Glen, I. Fischer (Eds.), Computational Life Sciences II. XIII, 269 pages. 2006. (Sublibrary LNBI).

Vol. 4215: D.W. Embley, A. Olivé, S. Ram (Eds.), Conceptual Modeling - ER 2006. XVI, 590 pages. 2006.